Henry Perry Leland

Americans in Rome

Henry Perry Leland

Americans in Rome

ISBN/EAN: 9783744783002

Printed in Europe, USA, Canada, Australia, Japan

Cover: Foto ©ninafisch / pixelio.de

More available books at **www.hansebooks.com**

BY

HENRY P. LELAND.

NEW YORK:
CHARLES T. EVANS, 448 BROADWAY.
1863.

Entered, according to act of Congress, in the year 1868, by
CHARLES T. EVANS,
In the Clerk's Office of the District Court of the United States for the District of New York.

PREFACE.

WHILE we in America, with our war and work, are fighting along stoutly in the advance guard of the world, let us not forget that there has been a past, by which we may still profit much, though it be only by measuring from it our onward course. Such a standard may be found in Rome, which is to the present day the most living specimen of a rapidly vanishing, yet cultivated age, in existence. In this great city and its territories, old times still weep and smile as they did in fairy tales and pictures, until the present age of steel came to improve the world. Rome is our direct antithesis. She is all of the past, and full of lessons, even if they be only of warning for the future.

The "antiquities" of Rome have been made to fill libraries, but of its popular and genial life, little has been recorded, though it be as interesting and instructive to the true student of history as any work of art or political chronicle. This life is itself an antique, its every peculiarity is founded on some custom centuries old, and modern invention has as yet hardly modified it in the least. But, observing that it must in a few years be utterly changed, I was led, during a residence in the City and Campagna, to note down carefully from my own observations—not from reading—many curious characteristics of popular life and humor, as well among natives as among strangers who adapted themselves to native customs; and the result of this observation will be found in the following pages. Having constantly borne in mind the variety of elements in Roman society, their relations and unity, and especially their contrast to our own American life, I have, I trust, succeeded, at least partially, in producing a work of higher aim than of mere entertainment, or even of simply faithful detail. It was the more necessary to keep this leading object of my work continually before me, owing to the light and often apparently trifling nature of the materials with which I had to deal. Humor is the current sentiment of society everywhere, and jests and small quarrels, gossiping and bargaining must be heard, as well as fierce oaths, bitter groans, and wild oratory, by him who would tell its truth. I can claim for this work that it is almost to the minutest details true in spirit, there being scarcely an incident, event, or jest in it for which I am not indebted to my own observation, or that of friends; and if the form in which it is cast has somewhat of imaginary narration, it was only done that it might be truer and nearer to the ease of every-day life, and give the latter more accuracy than can be presented by a mere journal. Were this not really the most exact method of painting mankind, novelists would long since have given us their plots in the form of diaries.

This work has been called "Americans in Rome," since the little experiences and adventures of several fellow countrymen have been made to serve as the means of developing the characteristics and peculiarities of their Roman surroundings. I am not by any means the only one who has of late described Roman popular life, and commend to the reader who is not already familiar with them, "Mademoiselle Mori," the works of Edmund About, and a series of articles entitled *Roba di Roma*, published in the *Atlantic Monthly*. Every writer has, however, his own stand-point, and his own favorite themes: such as are here given are those which struck me by their marked character, and they are portrayed faithfully as I saw them, both as regards form and spirit. In a few years these noticeable traits must vanish, and Rome, no more the prolongation of the Middle Ages will be the capital of a nation earnestly striving with the present, and rapidly assuming its characteristics.

CONTENTS.

CHAPTER I.

INTRODUCTION.—Arrival in Rome—A Short Walk—Modern Art—A Room Hunt—Maccaronical—America in Rome, ... 9

CHAPTER II.

The Voice of Rome—Sermons in Stones—A Ball in the Costa Palace, ... 26

CHAPTER III.

On the Campagna—Bacchus in Rome—Caper's Menagerie, . . 47

CHAPTER IV.

Fair at Grotto Ferrata—The Tombola, ... 72

CHAPTER V.

The Greco—Among the Wild Beasts—Roman Models—Giulia di Segni—Mr. Browne buys a Painting, ... 93

CHAPTER VI.

On the Pincio—Rome by Night—The Mysterious in Art—A Bath Hunt, ... 121

CHAPTER VII.

"A Reel Titiano for Sal"—So Long!—Roman Theatres—The Beards of Art—A Calico Painter—A Patron of Art, ... 145

CHAPTER VIII.

A Roman Vettura—Sunday in the Campagna—La Triglia—Painting a Donkey, ... 174

CHAPTER IX.

Roman Firesides—Violets of the Villa Borghese—The Carnival—The Vermilion Miracle—The Popolo Exhibition, ... 206

CHAPTER X.

A Walk around Segni—Five Fairs and Festivals, ... 232

CHAPTER XI.

The Cheap side of Roman Artist Life—Fra Volpe—Tolkoutchji, . 268

CHAPTER XII.

La Scampanacciata—Gunning around Segni—San Bruno, . . . 289

AMERICANS IN ROME.

CHAPTER I.

ROME is the cradle of art—which accounts for its sleeping there.

Nature, however, is nowhere more wide awake than it is in and around this city: therefore, Mr. James Caper, animal painter, determined to repose there for several months.

The following sketches correctly describe his Roman life.

It was on an autumn night that the travelling carriage in which sat James Caper arrived in Rome; and as he drove through that fine street, the Corso, he saw coming toward him a two-horse open carriage, filled with Roman girls of the working class (*minenti*). Dressed in their picturesque costumes, bonnetless, their black hair tressed with flowers, they stood up, waving torches, and singing in full voice one of those songs in which you can go but a few feet, metrically speaking, without meeting *amore*. And then another and another carriage, with flashing torches and sparkling-eyed girls. It was one of the turnouts of the *minenti;* they had been to Monte Testaccio, had drunk all the wine they could pay for; and, with a prudence our friend Caper could not sufficiently admire, he noticed that the women were in separate carriages from the men. It was the Feast Day of St. Crispin, and all the cobblers, or artists in leather, as they call themselves, were keeping it up bravely.

"Eight days to make a pair of shoes?" he once asked a shoemaker. "Si, Signore, there are three holidays in that time." Argument unanswerable.

As the carriages rolled by, Caper determined to observe the festivals.

The next day our artist entered his name in his banker's register, and had the horror of seeing it mangled to "Jams Scraper" in the list of arrivals published in the *Giornale di Roma*. For some time after his arrival in Rome, he was pained to receive cards, circulars, notices, letters, advertisements, &c., from divers tradesmen, all directed to the above name. In revenge, he here gives them a public airing. One firm announces:

"Manafactury of Romain Seltings, Mosaïques, Cameas, Medalls, Erasofines, &c." (Erasofines is the Roman-English for crucifixes.) And on a slip of paper, handsomely printed, is an announcement that they make "Romain Perles of all Couloueurs"—there's color for you!

A tailor, under the head of *"Ici un parle Français,"* prints: 'Merchant *and* tailor. Cloths (clothes?) Reddy maid, Mercery Roman; Scarfs, &c."

Another: "Roman Artickles Manofactorer"—hopes to be "honnoured with our Customs (American?), and flaters himsself we will find things to our likings." Everything but the English, you know; that is not exactly to our liking.

Another, from a lady, reads:

A VENTRE!

une Galérie decomposée de 300 *d'Anciens Maitres, et de l'école romaine peintres sur bois, sur cuivre et sur toit, &c.*

Ventre for *Vendre* is bad enough; but a "gallery of decomposed old masters, and of Roman school painters on wood and on the roof," when it was intended to say, "A gallery composed of 300 of the old masters—" But let us leave it untranslated; it is already *decomposée*.

Mr. Caper having indignantly rejected the services of all professors of the guiding art, or "commissionaires," slowly sauntered out of his hotel the morning after his arrival, and, map in hand, made his way to the tower on the Capitoline Hill. Threading several narrow, dirty streets, he at last went through one where in one spot there was such a heap of garbage and broccoli stumps that he raised his eyes to see how high up it reached against the walls of a palace; and there read, in black letters,

Immondezzaio;

literally translated, A Place for Dirt. On the opposite wall, which was the side of a church, he saw a number of black placards, on which were large white skulls and crossbones; and while examining these, a bareheaded, brown-bearded, stout Franciscan monk passed him. From a passing glance, Caper saw he looked good-natured, and so, hailing him, asked why the skulls and bones were pasted there.

"Who knows?" answered the monk. "I came this morning from the Campagna. This is the first time in all my life I have been in this magnificent city."

"Can you tell me what that word means, up there?" said Caper, pointing to *immondezzaio*.

"Signore, I cannot read."

"Perhaps it is the name of the street—may-be of the city?"

"It must be so," answered the priest, "unless it's a sign of a lottery office, or a caution against blasphemy up and down the pavement. Those are the only signs we have in the country, except the government salt and cigar shops." . . . He took a snuffbox from a pocket in his sleeve, and, with a bow, offered a pinch to Mr. Caper. This accepted, they bid each other profoundly farewell.

"There goes a brick!" remarked the traveller.

Arrived at the entrance door to the tower of the Capitoline Hill, James Caper first felt in one pocket for a silver piece, and in the other for a matchbox, and finding them both there, rang the bell, and then mounted to the top of the tower. Lighting a *zigarro scelto*, or papal cigar, he leaned on both elbows on the parapet, and gazed long and fixedly over the seven-hilled city.

"And this," soliloquized he, "*is* Rome. Many a day have I been kept in school without my dinner, because I was not able to parse thee idly by, *Roma*—Rome—noun of the first declension, feminine gender, that a quarter of a century ago caused me punishment, I have thee now literally under foot, and (knocking his cigar) throw ashes on thy head.

"My mission in this great city is not that of a picture peddler or art student. I come to investigate the eating, drinking, sleeping arrangements of the Eternal City—its wine more than its vinegar, its pretty girls more than its galleries, its *cafés* more than its churches. I see from here that I have a fine field to work in. Down there, clambering over the fallen ruins of the Palace of the Cæsars, is a donkey. Could one have a finer opportunity to see in this a moral and twist a tail? From those fallen stones, Memory—glorious old architect—rears a fabric wondrously beautiful; peoples it with eidolons white and purple-robed, and gleaming jewel-gemmed; or, iron armed, glistening with flashing light from polished steel—heroes and slaves, conquerors and conquered. My blood no longer flows to the slow, jerking measure of a nineteenth-century piece of mechanism, but freely, fully, and completely. Hurrah! my blood is up! Dark, liquid eyes; black, flowing locks; strange, pleasing perfumes, are around me. There is a rush as of a strong south wind through a myriad of floating banners, and I am borne onward through triumphal arches, past pillared temples, under the walls of shining palaces, into the Coliseum. . . .

"Pray, and can you tell me—if that pile of d—d old rubbish—down there, you know—is the Forum—for I do not—see it in Murray—though I'm sure—I have looked very clearly—and Murray, you know—has everything down in him—that a traveller" . . .

"A commercial traveller?" . . . interrupted Mr. Caper, speaking slowly, and looking coolly into the eyes of the blackguard Bagman. . . . "The ruins you see there, are those of the Forum. Good morning."

"Lucrezia Borgia at the Tomb of Don Giovanni! You see," said the artist, "I have chosen a good name for my painting, . . . and it's a great point gained. Forty or fifty years ago, some of those fluffy old painters would have had Venus worshipping at the shrine of Bacchus."

"Whereas, you think it would be more appropriate for her to worship Giove?" . . . asked Caper.

"No, *sir!* . . . I run dead against classic art—it's a drug. I tried my hand at it when I first came to Rome. Will you believe me, I never sold a picture. Why, that very painting"—pointing to the Borgia—"is on a canvas on which I commenced The Subjugation of Adonis."

"H'm! You find the class of Middle Age subjects most salable, then?"

"I should think I did. Something with brilliant colors, stained glass windows, armor, and all that, sells well. The only trouble is, ultramarine costs dear, although Dovizzelli's is good, and goes a great ways. I sold a picture to an Ohio man last week, for two hundred dollars; and it is a positive fact, there was twenty *scudi* (dollars) worth of blue in it. But the infernal Italians spoil trade here. Why, that fellow who paints Guido's Speranzas up there at San Pietro in Vinculo, is as smart as a Yankee. He has found out that Americans from Rhode Island take to the Speranza, because Hope is the motto of their State, and he turns out copies hand over fist. He has a stencil plate of the face, and three or four fellows to paint for him; one does the features of the face, another the hand, and another rushes in the background. Why, sir, those paintings can be sold for five *scudi*, and money made on them at that. But then, what are they? Wretched daubs, not worth house-room. Have you any thoughts of purchasing paintings?"

Caper smiled gently. . . "I had not, when I first

came to Rome; but how long I may continue to think so, is doubtful. The temptations" (glancing at the Borgia) "are very great." . . .

"Rome," . . . interrupted the artist, . . . "is the cradle of art."

Caper, on his first arrival in Rome, went to the Hotel Europe, in the Piazza di Spagna. There for two weeks he lived like a *milordo*. He formed many acquaintances among the resident colony of American artists, and was received by them with much kindness. Some of the mercenary ones of their number, having formed the opinion that he came there to buy paintings, ignorant of his profession, were excessively polite; but their offers of services were declined. When Caper finally moved to private lodgings in Babuino street, and opened a studio, hope, for a season, bade these salesmen all farewell. They groaned, and owned that they had tried, but could not sell.

Among the acquaintances formed by Caper, was a French artist named Rocjean. Born in France, he had passed eight or ten years in the United States, learned to speak English very well, and was residing in Rome "to perfect himself as an artist." He had, when Caper first met him, been there two years. In all this time he had never entered the Vatican; and having been told that Michael Angelo's Last Judgment was found to have a flaw in it, he had been waiting for repairs before passing his opinion thereon. On the other hand, he had studied the Roman *plebs*—the people—with all his might. He knew how they slept, ate, drank, loved, made their little economies, clothed themselves, and, above all, how they blackguarded each other. When Caper mentioned to him that he wished to leave his hotel, take a studio and private lodgings, then Rocjean expanded from an old owl into a spread eagle. Hurriedly taking Caper by the arm, he rushed from one end of Rome to the other, up one staircase, and down another; until, at last, finding out that Rocjean invariably presented him to fat, fair, jolly-looking landladies (*padrone*), with the remark, "Signora, the Signor is an Englishman, and very wealthy," he began to believe that something was wrong. But Rocjean assured him that it was not; that, as in Paris it was Madame who attended to renting rooms, so it was the *padrona* in Rome; and that the remark, "he is an Englishman, and very wealthy," were synonymous, and always went together. "If I were to tell them you were an American, it would do just as well—in fact, better, but for one thing, and that is, you would be swindled twice as much. The expression, 'and very wealthy,' attached to the name of an Englishman, is only a delicate piece of flattery; for the majority of the present race of travelling English are by no means lavish in their expenditures, or very wealthy. In taking you to see all these pretty women, I have undoubtedly given you pleasure; at the same time, I have gratified a little innocent curiosity of mine;—but then the chance is such a good one! We will now visit the Countess ———, for she has a very desirable apartment to let; after which we will proceed seriously to take rooms with a home-ly view."

The Countess ——— was a very lovely woman, consequently Caper was fascinated with the apartment, and told her he would reflect over it.

"Right," said Rocjean, after they had left; "better reflect

over it, than in it—as the enormous draught up chimney would in a short time compel you to."

"How so?"

"I have a German friend who has rooms there. He tells me that a cord of firewood lasts about long enough to warm one side of him; when he turns to warm the other, it is gone. He has lived there three years reflecting over this. The Countess occasionally condoles with him over the draught of that chimney."

"H'm! Let us go to the homely. Better a drawn sword, than a draught."

They found a homely landlady, with neat rooms, in the Via Babuino, and having bargained for them for twelve *scudi* a month, their labors were over.

There was, when Caper first came to Rome, an eating house, nearly opposite the fountain Trevi, called the Gabioni. It was underground—in fact, a series of cellars, popularly conjectured to have been part of the catacombs. In one of these cellars—resembling, with its arched roof, a tunnel, the ceiling so low that you could touch the apex of the round arch with your hand—every afternoon, in autumn and winter, between the hours of five and six, there assembled, by mutual consent, eight or ten artists. The table at which they sat would hold no more, and they did not want it to. Two waiters attended them—Giovanni for food, and Santi for wine and cigars. The long-stemmed Roman lamps of burnished brass, the bowl that held the oil, and wicks resembling the united prows of four vessels, shedding their light on the white cloth and white walls, made the old place cheerful. The white and red wine in the thin glass flasks gleamed brightly, and the food was well cooked, and wholesome. Here, in early winter, came the sellers of "sweet olives," as they called them, and for two or three cents (*baiocchi*) you could buy a plateful. These olives were green, and, having been soaked in lime water, the bitter taste was taken from them, and they had the flavor of almonds.

But the maccaroni was the great dish in the Gabioni. A four-cent plate of it would take the sharp edge from a fierce appetite, assisted, as it was, by a large one-cent roll of bread. There was the white pipe-stem and the dark ribbon (*fettucia*) species; and it was cooked with sauce (*al sugo*), with cheese, Neapolitan, Roman, and Milan fashion, and—otherways. Wild boar steaks came in winter, and were cheap. Veal never being sold in Rome until the calf is a two-year-old heifer, was no longer veal, but tender beef, and was eatable. Sardines fried in oil and batter were good. Game was plenty, and very reasonable in price, except venison, which was scarce. The average cost of a substantial dinner was from thirty to forty *baiocchi;* "and," said Rocjean, "I can live like a prince—like the Prince B——, who dines here occasionally—for half that sum."

The first day Caper dined in the Gabioni, what with a dog-fight under the table, cats jumping upon the table, a distressed marchioness (fact) begging him for a small sum, a beautiful girl from the Trastevere, shining like a patent-leather boot, with gold earrings, and brooch, and necklace, and coral beads, who sat at another table with a French soldier—these, and those other little *piquante* things, that the traveller learns to smile at and endure, worried him. But the dinner was good; his companions at table were companionable; and as he finished an extra *foglietta* (pint) of wine—price eight cents—with Rocjean, he concluded to give it another trial. He kept at giving it trials until the old Gabioni was closed, and from it arose the Four Nations, or Quattro Nazione, in Turkey Cock Alley (*viccolo Gallinaccio*), which, as any one knows, is near Two Murderers' street (*Via Due Macelli*).

"Now that we have finished dinner," spoke Rocjean, "we will smoke; then to the Caffe, or Café Greco.

It may be a good thing to have the conceit taken out of us —but not by the corkscrew of ignorance; the operation is too painful. Caper, proud of his country, and believing her in the front rank of nations, was destined to learn, while in Rome and the Papal States, that America was geographically unknown.

He consoled himself for this with the fact that geography is not taught in the "Elementary Schools" there;—and for the people there are no others.

The following translation of a notice advertising for a schoolmaster, copied from the walls of a palace where it was posted, shows the sum total taught in the common schools:

> The duties of the Master are to teach Reading, Writing, the First Four Rules of Arithmetic; to observe the duties prescribed in the law "*Quod divina sapientia;*" and to be subject to the biennial committee, like other salaried officers of the department; as an equivalent for which he shall enjoy (*godrá*) an annual salary of $60, payable in monthly shares.
>
> (Signed)   IL GONFALONIERE —— ——.

But what can you expect, when one of the rulers of the land asserted to Caper that he knew that "popcorn grew in America on the banks of the Nile, after the water went down —for it never rains in America."

It was a handsome man, an advocate for Prince Doria, who, once travelling in a *vettura* with Caper, asked him why he did not go to America by land, since he knew that it was in the south of England; and gently corrected a companion of his, who told Caper he had read, and thought it strange, that all Americans lived in holes in the ground, by saying to him, that if such houses were agreeable to the *Signori Americani*, they had every right to inhabit them.

The landlord of a hotel in a town about thirty miles from Rome, asked Caper if, when he returned to New York, he would not some morning call and see his cousin—in Peru!

This same landlord once drew his knife on a man, when accompanied by Caper, he went to observe a saint's day in a neighboring town. The cause of the quarrel was this: the landlord, having been asked by a man who Caper was, told him he was an American. The man asserted that Americans always wore long feathers in their hair, and that he did not see any on Caper's head. The landlord, determined to stand by Caper, swore by all the saints that they were under his hat. The man disbelieved it. Out came the "hardware," with that jarring cr-r-r-rick the blade makes when the notched knife-back catches in the spring; but Caper jumped between them, and they put off stabbing one another—until the next saint's day.

It was with pleasure that Caper, passing down the Corso one morning, saw there was a Universal Panorama, including views of America, advertised to be exhibited in the Piazza Colonna. "Here is an opportunity," thought he, "for the Romans to acquire some knowledge of a land touching which they are very much at sea. The views, undoubtedly, will do for them what the tabooed geographies are not allowed to do—give them a little education to slow music."

Accompanied by Rocjean, he went, one evening, to see it, and found it on wheels in a travelling van, drawn up at one side of the Colonna Square.

"Hawks inspected it the other evening," said Rocjean, "and he describes it as well worth seeing. The explainer of the Universal Panorama resembles the Wandering Jew exactly, with perhaps a difference about the change in his pockets; and the paintings, comical enough in themselves, considering that they are supposed to be serious likenesses of the places represented, are made still funnier by the explanations of the manager."

Securing tickets from a stout, showy ticket-seller, adorned with a stunning silk dress, crushing bracelets, and an overpowering bonnet, they subduedly entered a room twenty feet long by six or eight wide, illuminated with the mellow glow of what appeared to be about thirty moons. The first things that caught their eye were several French soldiers, who were acting as inspection guard over several moons, having stacked their muskets in one corner. Their exclamations of delight or sorrow, their criticisms of the art panoramic, in short, were full of humor and trenchant fun. But "the explanator" was before them. Where he came from, they could not see, for his footsteps were light as velvet, evidently having "gums" on his feet. His milk-white hair, parted in the middle of his forehead, hung down his back for a couple of feet; while his milk-white beard, hanging equally low in front, gave him the appearance of a venerable billy-goat. He was an Albino, and his eyes kept blinking like a white owl's at midday. He had a voice slightly tremulous, and mild as a cat's in a dairy.

"Gen-till-men, do me the play-zure to gaze within this first hole. 'Tis the be-yu-ti-fool land of Sweet-sir-land. Vi-yew from the some-mut of the Riggy Cool'm. Day break-in' in the dis-tant yeast. He has a blan-kit round him, sir; for it is cold upon the moun-tin tops at break of day. [Madame, the stupen-doss irruption of Ve-soov-yus is two holes from the corner.]

"Gen-till-men, do me the play-zure to gaze upon the second hole. 'Tis Florenz the be-yu-ti-fool, be the bangs off the flowin' Arno. 'Twas here that——"

"No matter about all that," said Caper; "show off Amer-ica to us." He slipped a couple of *pauls* into his hand, and instantly the Venerable skipped four moons.

"Gen-till-men, do me the play-zure to gaze upon this hole. 'Tis the be-yu-ti-fool city of Nuova Jorck in Ay-mer-i-kay, with the flour-ish-ing cities of Brook-lyn, Nuova Jer-sais, and Long Is-lad. The impo-sing struc-ture of rotund form is the Gr-rand Coun-cill Hall con-tain-ing the coun-cill chamber of the Amer-i-can nations. . . . [You say it is the Bat-tai-ree? It may be the Bat-tai-ree.] *What is that road in Brook-lin?* That is the ra'l-road to Nuova Or-lins di-rect. *What is that wash-tub?* 'Tis not a wash-tub—'tis a stim-boat They make the stim out of coal, which is found on the ground. *Is that the Ay-mer-i-cain eagill?* 'Tis not; 'tis a hoarse-fly, which has in-tro-doo-ced hisself behind the glass. *Are those savages in Nuova Jer-sais?* (New Jersey). Those are trees."

"Pass on, illustrious gen-till-men, to the next hole. 'Tis the be-yu-ti-fool city of Filadelfia. The houses here are all built of woo-ood. The two riv-aires that cir-cum-vent the city are the Lavar (Delaware?) and the Hud-soon. I do not know what is "a pum-king cart," but the car-riage which you see before you is a fi-ah engine, be-cause the city is all built of woo-ood. The tall stee-ple belongs to the kay-ker (Quaker) temple of San Cristo."

Rocjean now gave the Venerable a *paul*, requesting him to dwell at length upon these scenes, as he was a Frenchman in search of a little of geography.

"Excellencies, I will do my en-dea-vors. The gran-diose ship as lies in the Lavar (Delaware) riv-aire is fool of em-i-gr-rants. The signora de-scen-din' the side of the ship is in a dreadful sit-u-a-tion tru-ly. [Perhaps the artist was in a boat, and de-scri-bed the scene as he saw it.] The elephant you see de-scen-din' the street is a nay-tive of this tropical re-gion, and the cock-a-toos infest the sur-roud-in' air. The Moors you see along the wharves are the spon-ta-ne-ous born of the soil. Those are kay-kers (Quakers?) on mules with broad-brimmed hats onto their heads; the sticks in their hands are to beat the Moors who live on their su-gar plan-tay-tions. . . . *Music?* did you ask, Madame? We have none in this establish-ment. None.

"Excellencies, the next hole. 'Tis the be-yu-ti-fool city of Bal-ti-mory. You behold in the be-fore ground a gr-rand feast day of Amer-i-cain peasants; they are be-hold-ing their noble Count re-pair-ring to the chase with a serf on a white hoarse-bag (horseback?). The little joke of the cattle is a play-fool fan-cy of the jocose artiste as did the panorama. I am un-ac-count-able for veg-garies such as them. The riv-aire in the bag-ground is the Signora-pippi."

"The what?" asked Caper, shaking with laughter.

"A gen-till-man the other day told me that only the peasants in A-mer-i-kay say Missus, or Mis-triss, and that the rivaire con-se-kwen-tilly was not Missus-pippi, but, as I have had the honor of saying, the Signora-pippi riv-aire. The next hole, Excellencies!—'Tis the be-yu-ti-fool city of Vaskmenton (Washington), also on the Signora-pippi riv-aire. The white balls on the trees is cot-ton. Those are not white balls on the ground; those are ships—ships as have woollen growin' onto their sides (sheep?). 'Tis not a white bar-racks; 'tis the Palazzo di Vaskmenton, a nobil gen-e-ral woo lives there, and was for-mer-ly king of the A-mer-i-cain nations. *What does that Moor, with the white lady in his arms?*—it is a negro peas-ant taking his mis-triss out to air; 'tis the custom in those land. . . . That negress, or fe-mail Moor, with some childs, is also air-ring; and the white 'ooman tyin' up her stockings, is a sportive of the artiste. He is much for the hum-or-ous.

"Excellencies, the last hole A-mer-i-cain. 'Tis the stoo-pen-doss Signora-pippi riv-aire, in all its mag-nif-ficent booty. *What is that cock-a-too doing there?*—he is taking a fly. *You do not see the fly?* I mean a flight. *What is that bust to flin-ders?* That is a stim-boat was carryin' on too much stim; and the stim, which is made of coal, goes off like gun-pow-dair if you put lights onto it. This is a fir-ful and awe-fool sight. The other stim-boat is not bustin'; it is sailin'. What is that man behind the whil-house with the cards, while another signor kicks into him on his coat-tails, I do not know. It is steel the sportifs of the artiste."

"Excel-len-cies, the last hole. 'Tis the be-yu-ti-fool bustin'

—no, not bustin', but ex-plo-sion, of Ve-soov-yus. You can see the sublime sight, un-terrupt-ted be me ex-play-nations. I thank you for your attention auri-cu-lar and pe-coo-niar-ry. *Adio*, until I have the play-zure of seein' you oncet more."

"I tell you what, Rocjean," said Caper, as he came out from the panorama, "America has but a *poor show* in the Papal dominions."

CHAPTER II.

THE voice of Rome is baritone, always excepting that of the Roman locomotive—the donkey—which is deep bass, and comes tearing and braying along at times when it might well be spared. In the still night season, wandering among the moonlit ruins of the Coliseum, while you pause and gaze upon the rising tiers of crumbling stone above you, memory retraces all you have read of the old Roman days: the forms of the world-conquerors once more people the deserted ruin; the clash of ringing steel; hot, fiery sunlight; thin, trembling veil of dust pierced by the glaring eyes of dying gladiators; red-spouting blood; screams of the mangled martyrs torn by Numidian lions; moans of the dying; fierce shouts of exultation from the living; smiles from gold-banded girls in flowing robes, with floating hair, flower-crowned, and perfumed; the hum of thrice thirty thousand voices hushed to a whisper as the combat hangs on an uplifted sword; the—

AW-WAW-WAUN-IK! WAW-NIK! WAUN-KI-W-A-W-N! comes like blatant fish-horn over the silent air, and your dream of the Coliseum ends ignominiously with this nineteenth-century song of a jackass.

At night you will hear the shrill cry of the screech owl sounding down the silent streets in the most thickly-populated parts of the city. Or you will perhaps be aroused from sleep, as Caper often was, by the long-drawn-out cadences of some countryman singing a *rondinella* as he staggers along the street, fresh from a winehouse. Nothing can be more melancholy than the concluding part of each verse in these rondinellas, the voice being allowed to drop from one note to another, as a man falling from the roof of a very high house may catch at some projection, hold on for a time, grow weak, lose his hold, fall, catch again, hold on for a minute, and at last fall flat on the pavement, used up, and down as low as he can reach.

But the street cries of this city are countless; from the man who brings round the daily broccoli, to the one who has a wild boar for sale, not one but is determined that you shall hear all about it. Far down a narrow street you listen to a long-drawn, melancholy howl—the voice as of one hired to cry in the most mournful tones for whole generations of old pagan Romans who died unconverted—poor devils, who worshipped wine and women, and knew nothing better in this world. And who is their mourner? A great, brawny, tawny, steeple-crowned hat, blue-breeched, two-fisted fish-huckster; and he is trying to sell, by yelling as if his heart would break, a basket of fish not so long as your finger. If he cries so over anchovies, what would he do if he had a whale for sale?

Another *primo basso profundo* trolls off a wheelbarrow and a fearful cry at the same time; not in unison with his merchandise, for he has birds—quail, woodcock, and snipe—for sale, besides a string of dead nightingales, which he says he will " sell cheap for a nice stew." Think of stewed nightingales! One would as soon think of eating a boiled Cremona violin.

But out of the way! Here comes, blocking up the narrow

street, a *contadino*—a countryman from the Campagna. His square wooden cart is drawn by a donkey about the size of, and resembling, save ears, a singed Newfoundland dog. His voice, strong for a vegetarian—for he sells onions and broccoli, celery and tomatoes, *finocchio* and mushrooms—is like tearing a firm rag. How long can it last, subjected to such use?

It is in the game and meat market, near the Pantheon, that you can more fully become acquainted with the street cries of Rome; but the Piazza Navona excels even this. Passing along there one morning, Caper heard such an extraordinary piece of vocalization, sounding like a Sioux warwhoop with its back broken, that he stopped to see what it was all about. There stood a butcher, who had exposed for sale seven small stuck pigs, all one litter; and if they had been his own children, and died heretics, he could not have howled over them in a more heartrending manner.

About sunrise, and even before it—for the Romans are early risers—you will hear in spring time a sharp ringing voice under your window, "*Acqua chetosa! Acqua chetosa!*"—an abridgment of *acqua Accetosa*, or water from the fountain of Accetosa, considered a good aperient, and which is drunk before breakfast. Also a voice crying out, "*Acqua-vi-te!*" or spirits, drunk by the workmen and others at an expense of a *baiocco* or two the tablespoonful, for that is all the small glasses hold. In the early morning, too, you hear the chattering jackdaws on the roofs; and then, more distinctly than later in the day, the clocks striking their odd way. The Roman clocks ring from one to six strokes four times during the twenty-four hours, and not from one to twelve strokes, as with us. Sunset is twenty-four o'clock, and is noted by six strokes;

an hour after sunset is one o'clock, and is noted by one stroke; and so on until six hours after, when it begins striking one again. As the quarter hours are also rung by the clocks, if you happen to be near one, you will have a fine chance to get in a muddle trying to separate quarters from hours, and Roman time from your own.

Another noise comes from the game of *móra*. Caper was looking out of his window one morning, pipe in mouth, when he saw two men suddenly face each other, one of them bringing his arm down very quickly, when the other yelled, as if kicked, "*Dué!*" (two); and the first shouted at the top of his lungs, "*Tre!*" (three). Then they both went at it, pumping their hands up and down, and spreading their fingers with a quickness which was astonishing, while all the time they kept screaming, "One!" "Four!" "Three!" "Two!" "Five!" &c., &c. "Ha!" said Caper, "this is something like; 'tis an arithmetical, mathematical, etcetrical school in the open air. The dirtiest one is very quick; he will learn to count five in no time. But I don't see the necessity of saying "three," when the other brings down four fingers; or saying "five," when he shows two. But I suppose it is all right; he hasn't learned to give the right names yet." He learned later that they were gambling.

While these men were shouting, there came along an ugly old woman with a tambourine, and a one-legged man with a guitar, and seeing prey in the shape of Caper at his window, they pounced on him, as it were, and poured forth the most ear-rending discord; the old lady singing, the old gentleman backing up against a wall, and scratching at an accompaniment on a jangling old guitar. The old lady had a bandana handkerchief tied over her head, and while she watched Caper, she cast glances up and down the street, to see if some rich stranger, or *milordo*, was not coming to throw her a piece of silver.

"What are you howling about?" shouted Caper down to her.

"A new Neapolitan canzonetta, signore; all about a young man who grieves for his sweetheart, because he thinks she is not true to him, and what he says to her in a serenade." And here she screechingly sung:

> But do not rage, I beg, my dear;
> I want you for my wife;
> And morning, noon, and night likewise,
> I'll love you like my life.
>
> CHORUS.
> I only want to get a word,
> My charming girl, from thee:
> You know, Ninella, I can't breathe,
> Unless your heart's for me!

"Well," said Caper, "if this is Italian music, I don't *see* it."

The one-legged old gentleman clawed away at the strings of the guitar.

"I say, *'llustrissimo*," shouted Caper down to him, "what kind of strings are those on your instrument?"

"*Eccellénza*, catgut," he shouted, in answer.

"*Benissimo!* I prefer cats in the original packages. There's a *paolo*—travel!"

Caper had the misfortune to make the acquaintance of a professor of the mandolin, a wire-strung instrument, resembling a long-necked squash cut in two, to be played on with a quill, and which, with a guitar and violin, makes a concert that thrills you to the bones, and cuts the nerves away.

But the crowning glory of all that is ear-rending and peace-destroying, is carried around by the *pifferari* about Christmas time. It is a hogskin, filled with wind, having pipes at one end, and a jackass at the other, and is known in some lands as the bagpipe. The small shrines to the Virgin, particularly those in the streets where the wealthy English reside, are played upon assiduously by the *pifferari*, who are supposed by romantic travellers to come from the far-away Abbruzzi Mountains, and make a pilgrimage to the Eternal City to fulfil a vow to certain saints; whereas, it is sundry cents they are really after. They are for the most part artists' models, who at this season of the year get themselves up à *la pifferari*, or piper, to prey on the romantic susceptibilities and pockets of the strangers in Rome; and, with a pair of long-haired goatskin breeches, a sheepskin coat, brown rags, and sandals, or *ciocie*, with a shocking bad conical black or brown hat, in which are stuck peacocks' or cocks' feathers, they are ready equipped to attack the shrines and the strangers.

Unfortunately for Caper, there was a shrine to the Virgin in the second story front of the house next to where he lived—that is, unfortunately for his musical ear; for the lamp that burned in front of the shrine every dark night was a shining and pious light to guide him home, and thus, ordinarily, a very fortunate arrangement. In the third-story front room of the house of the shrine dwelt a Scotch artist named MacGuilp, who was a grand amateur of these pipes, and who declared that no sound in the world was so sweet to his ear as the bagpipes. They recalled the heather, haggis, and the Lothians, and the mountain dew, ye ken, and all those sorts of things.

One morning, at breakfast in the Café Greco, he discoursed at length about the pleasure the *pifferari* gave him; while Caper, taking an opposite view, said they had, during the last few days, driven him nearly crazy, and he wished the squealing hogskins well out of town.

MacGuilp told him he had a poor ear for music; that there was a charm about the bagpipes unequalled even by the unique voices of the Sistine Chapel; and there was nothing he would like better than to have all the pipers of Rome under his windows.

Caper remembered this last rash speech of Master MacGuilp, and determined at an early hour to test its truth. It happened, the very next morning at breakfast, that MacGuilp, in a triumphant manner, told him that he had received a promise of a visit from the Duchess of ———, with several other titled English; and said he had not a doubt of selling several paintings to them. MacGuilp's style was of the blood-and-thunder school: red dawns, murdered kings, blood-stained heather, and Scotch plaids—the very kind that should be shown to the sweet strainings of hogskin bagpipes.

In conversation, Caper found out the hour at which the duchess intended to make her visit. He made his preparations accordingly. Accompanied by Rocjean, he visited Gigi, who kept a costume and life school of models, found out where the pipers drank most wine, and going there, and up the Via Fratina, and down the Spanish Steps, managed to find them, and arranged it so that at the time the duchess was viewing MacGuilp's paintings, he should have the full benefit of a serenade from all the *pifferari* in Rome.

The next morning Caper, pipe in mouth, at his window,

saw the carriage of the duchess drive up, and from it the noble English dismount and ascend to the artist's studio. The carriage had hardly driven away, when up came two of the pipers, and happening to cast their eyes up, they saw Caper, who hailed them, and told them not to begin playing until the others arrived. In a few moments six of the hogskin squeezers stood ready to begin their infernal squawking.

"Go ahead!" shouted Caper, throwing a handful of *baiocchi* among them; and as soon as these were gathered, the pipers gave one awful, heart-chilling blast, and the concert was fairly commenced. Squealing, shrieking, grunting, yelling, and humming, the sounds rose higher and higher. Open flew the windows in every direction.

"*C'est foudroyante!*" said the pretty French *modiste*.

"What the devil's broke loose?" shouted an American.

"*Mein Gott im himmel! was ist das?*" roared the German baron.

"*Casaccio! cosa faceste?*" shrieked the lovely Countess Grimanny.

"*In nomine Domini!*" groaned a fat friar.

"*Caramba! vayase al infierno!*" screamed Don Santiago Gomez.

"*Bassama teremtete!*" swore the Hungarian gentleman.

Louder squealed the bagpipes; their buzz filled the air, their shrieks went ringing up to MacGuilp like the cries of Dante's condemned. The duchess found the sound barbarous. MacGuilp opened his window, upon which the pipers strained their lungs for the Signore Inglese, grand amateur of the bagpipes. He begged them to go away. "No, no, signore; we know you love our music; we won't go away."

The duchess could stand it no longer. Her servant called the carriage; the English got in, and drove off.

Still rung out the sounds of the six bagpipes. Caper threw them more *baiocchi*.

Suddenly MacGuilp burst out of the door of his house, maulstick in hand, rushing on the *pifferari* to put them to flight.

"*Iddio giusto!*" shouted two of the pipers; "it is, IT IS the *Cacciatore!* the hunter—the Great Hunter."

"He is a painter!" shouted another.

"No, he isn't; he's a hunter. *Gran Cacciatore!* Doesn't he spend all his time after quails and snipe and woodcock? Haven't I been out with him day after day at Ostia? Long live the great hunter!"

MacGulip was touched in a tender spot. The homage paid him as a great hunter more than did away with his anger at the bagpipe serenade; and the last Caper saw of him, he was leading six *pifferari* into a wine shop, where they would not come out until seven of them were unable to tell the music of bagpipes from the music of the spheres.

So ends the music, noises, and voices, of the seven-hilled city.

One bright Sunday morning in January, Rocjean called on Caper, to ask him to improve the day by taking a walk.

"I thought of going up to the English chapel outside the Popolo, to see a pretty New-Yorkeress," said the latter; "but the affair is not very pressing, and I believe a turn round the Villa Borghese will do me as much good as only looking at a pretty girl, and half hearing a poor sermon."

"As for a sermon, we need not miss that," answered Rocjean, "for we will stop in at Chapin the sculptor's studio, and if we escape one, and he there, I am mistaken. They call his studio a shop, and they call his shop the Orphan Asylum, because he manufactured an Orphan Girl some years ago, and, as it sold well, he has kept on making orphans ever since."

"The murderer!"

"Yes; but not half so atrocious as the reality. You must know, that when he first came over here, he had an order to make a small Virgin Mary for a Catholic church in Boston; but the order being countermanded after he had commenced modelling in clay, he was determined not to lose his time; and so, having somewhere read of, in a yellow-covered novel, or seen in some fashion-plate magazine, a doleful-looking female called The Orphan, he instantly determined, cruel executioner that he is, to also make an orphan. And he did. There is a dash of bogus sentiment in it that passes for coin current with many of our travelling Americans; and the thing has 'sold.' He told me, not long since, he had orders for twelve copies of different-sized Orphans; and you will see them all through his asylum. Do you remember those lines in Richard the Third:

"'Why do you look on us, and shake your head,
And call us orphans—wretched?'"

They found Chapin in his shop, alias studio, busily looking over a number of plaster casts of legs and arms. He arose quickly as they entered, and threw a cloth over the casts.

"Hah! gudmornin', Mister Caper. Glad to see you in my studyō. Hallo, Rocjan! you there? Why haven't you ben up to see my wife and daughters? She feels hurt, I tell you, 'cause you don't come near us. Do you know that Burkings of Bosting was round here to my studiyŏ yesterday?—sold *him* an Orphan. By the way, Mister Caper, air you any relation to Caper, of the great East Ingy house of Caper?"

"He is an uncle of mine, and is now in Florence; he will be in Rome next week."

A tender glow of interest beamed in Chapin's eyes. In imagination he saw another Orphan sold to the rich Caper, who might "influence" trade. His tone of voice after this was subdued. As Caper happened to brush against some plaster, coming in the studio, Chapin hastened to brush it from his coat, and he did it as if it were the down on the wing of a beautiful golden butterfly.

"I was goin' to church this mornin' 'long with Missus Chapin; but I guess I'll stay away for once in me life. I want to show you The Orphan."

"I beg that you will not let me interfere with any engagement you may have," said Caper; "I can call as well at any other time."

"Oh no; I won't lissen to that. I don't want to git to meeting before sermon, so come right stret in here now. There! there's The Orphan. You see, I've made her accordin' to the profoundest rules of art. You may take a string, or a yard measure, and go all over her—you won't find her out of the way a fraction. The figure is six times the length of the foot; this was the way Phidias worked, and I agree with him. Them were splendid old fellows, them Greeks. There was art for you—high art!"

"That in the Acropolis was of the highest order," said Rocjean.

"Yes," answered Chapin, who did not know where it was;

"far above all other. There was some sentiment in them days, but it was all of the religious stripe; they didn't come down to domestic life and feelin'; they hadn't made the strides we have toward layin' open art to the million—toward developing *hum* feelings. They worked for a precious few; but we do it up for the many. Now, there's the A-poller Belvidiary—beautiful thing; but the idea of brushin' his hair that way is ridicoolus. Did you ever see anybody with their hair fixed that way? Never! They had a way among the Greeks of fixing their drapery right well; but I've invented a plan—for which I've applied to Washington for a patent—that I think will beat anything Phidias ever did."

"You can't tell how charmed I am to hear you," spoke Rocjean.

"Well, it *is* a great invention," continued Chapin; "and as I know neither of you ain't in the 'trade' (smiling), I don't care but what I'll show it to you, if you'll promise, honor bright, you won't tell anybody. You see, I take a piece of muslin, and hang it onto a statue the way I want the folds to fall; then I take a syringe filled with starch and glue, and go all over it, so that when it dries it'll be as hard as a rock. Then I go all over it with a certain oily preparation, and lastly I run liquid plaster-paris in it; and when it hardens, I have an exact mould of the drapery. There! But I hain't explained The Orphan. You see, she's sittin' on a very light chair—*that* shows the very little support she has in this world. The hand to the head shows meditation; and the Bible on her knee shows devotion; you see, it's open to the book, chapter, and verse which refers to the young ravens."

"Excuse me," said Caper; "but may I ask why she has such a *very* low-necked dress on?"

"Well, my model has got such a fine neck and shoulders," replied Chapin, "that I re-eely couldn't help showing 'em off on the Orphan; besides, they're more in demand—the low neck and short sleeves—than the high-bodied style, which has no buyers. But there is a work I'm engaged on now, that would just soot your uncle. Mr. Caper, come this way."

Caper saw what he supposed was a safe to keep meat cool in, and approached. Chapin threw back the doors of it, like a showman about to disclose the "What Is It?" and Caper saw a dropsical-looking Cupid, with a very short shirt on, and a pair of winged shoes on his feet. The figure was starting forward as if to catch his equilibrium, which he had that moment lost, and was only prevented from tumbling forward by a bag held behind him in his left hand, while his right arm and hand, at full length, pointed a sharp arrow in front of him.

"Can you tell me what *that* figger represents?" asked Chapin. As he received no reply, he continued: "*That* is Enterprise; the two little ruts at his feet represent a railroad; the arrow, showin' he's sharp, points ahead—Go ahead! is his motto; the bag in his hand represents money, which the keen, sharp, shrewd business man knows is the reward of enterprise. The wreath round his head is laurel mixed up with lightnin', showin' he's up to the tellygraph; the pen behind his ear shows he can figger; and his short shirt shows economy—that admirable virtoo. The wings on his shoes are taken from Mercury, as I suppose you know; and——"

"I say, now, Chapin, don't you think he's got a little too much legs, and rather extra stomach on him, to make fast time?" asked Rocjean.

"Measure him! measure him!" said Chapin, indignantly;

"there's a string. Figure six times the length of his foot, everything else in proportion. No, *sir;* I have not studied the classic for nothin'. If there is any one thing I am strong on, it's anatomy. Only look at his hair! Why, sir, I spent three weeks once, dissectin'; and for more'n six months I didn't do anything, during my idle time, but dror figgers. Art is a kind of thing that's born in a man. This saying the ancients were better sculpters than we air, is no such thing; what did they know about steam engines or telegraphs? *Fiddle!* They did some fust-rate things, but they had no idee of fixin' hair as it should be fixed. No, sir; we moderns have great add-vantagiz, and we improve 'em. Rome is the cra—"

"I must bid you good day," interrupted Caper. "Your wife will miss you at the sermon; you will attribute it to me; and I would not intentionally be the cause of having her ill-will for anything."

"Well, she is a pretty hard innimy; and they do talk here in Rome, if you don't toe the mark. But ree-ly, you mustn't go off mad (smiling). You must call up with Rocjan, and see us; and I ree-ly hope that when your uncle comes, you will bring him to my studiyō. I am sure my Enterprise will soot him."

So Chapin saw them out of his studio. Not until Caper found himself seated on a stone bench under the ilexes of the Villa Borghese, watching the sunbeams darting on the little lizards, and seeing far off the Albanian Mountains, snow-capped, against the blue sky—not until then did he breathe freely.

"Rocjean," said he, "that stonecutter down there—that Chapin——"

"*Chameau!*" roared Rocjean. "He and his kind are

doing for art what the Jews did for prize-fighting—they ruin it. They make art the laughing stock of all refined and educated people. Art, applied solely to sculpture and painting, is dead; it will not rise again in these our times. But art, the fairy-fingered beautifier of all that surrounds our homes and daily walks, save paintings and statuary, never breathed so fully, clearly, nobly, as now; and her pathway amid the lowly and homely things around us is shedding beauty wherever it goes. The rough-handed artisan, who, slowly dreaming of the beautiful, at last turns out a stove that will beautify and adorn a room, instead of rendering it hideous, has done for this practical generation what he of an earlier theoretical age did for his contemporaries, when he carved the imperial Venus of Milos. Enough; *this* is the sermon *not* preached from stones."

One sunlight morning in February, while hard at work in his studio, Caper was agreeably surprised by the entrance of an elderly uncle of his, Mr. Bill Browne, of St. Louis, a gentleman of the rosy, stout, hearty school of old bachelors, who, having made a large fortune by keeping a Western country store, prudently retired from business, and finding it dull work doing nothing, wisely determined to enjoy himself with a tour over the Continent, "or any other place he might determine to visit."

"I say, Jim, did you expect to see me here?" was his first greeting.

"Why, Uncle Bill! Well, you are the last man I ever thought would turn up. They didn't write me a word of your coming over," answered Caper.

"Mistake; they wrote you all about it; and if you'll drop round at the postoffice, you'll find letters there telling you the particulars. Fact is, I am ahead of the mail. Coming over in the steamer, met a man named Orville; told me he knew you; that he was coming straight through to Rome, and offered to pilot me. So I gave up Paris, and all that, and came smack through, eighteen days from New York. But I'm dry. Got a match? Here, try one of these cigars."

Caper took a cigar from his uncle's case, lit it, and then calling the man who swept out the studios, sent him to the neighboring wine shop for a bottle of wine.

"By George, Jim, that's a pretty painting; that jackass is fairly alive, and so's the girl with a red boddice. I say, what's she got that towel on her head for? Is it put there to dry?"

"No; that's an Italian peasant girl's head-covering. Most all of them do so."

"Do they? I'm glad of that. But here comes your man with the liquor."

And, after drinking two or three tumblers full, Uncle Bill decided that it was pretty good cider. The wine finished, together with a couple of rolls that came with it, the two sallied out for a walk around the Pincian Hill, the grand promenade of Rome. Toward sunset they thought of dinner, and Uncle Bill, anxious to see life, accepted Caper's invitation to dine at the old Gabioni. Here they ordered the best dishes, and the former swore it was as good a dinner as he ever got at the Planter's House. Rocjean, who dined there, delighted the old gentleman immensely; and the two fraternized at once, and drank each other's health, old style, until Caper, fearing that neither could conveniently hold more, suggested an adjournment to the Greco for coffee and cigars.

While they were in the café, Rocjean quietly proposed something to Caper, who at once assented. The latter then said to Uncle Bill:

"You have arrived in Rome just at the right time. You may have heard at home of the great Giacinti family; well, the Prince Nicolo di Giacinti gives a grand ball to-night at the Palazzo Costa. Rocjean and I have received invitations, embracing any illustrious strangers of our acquaintance who may happen to be in Rome; so you must go with us. You have no idea, until you come to know them intimately, what a good-natured, off-hand set the best of the Roman nobility are. Compelled by circumstances to keep up for effect an appearance of great reserve and dignity before the public, they indemnify themselves for it in private, by having the highest kind of old times. They are passionately attached to their native habits and costumes; and though driven, on state occasions especially, to imitate French and English habits, yet they love nothing better than at times to enjoy themselves in their native way. The ball given by the prince to-night is what might be called a free-and-easy. It is his particular desire that no one should come in full dress; in fact, he rather likes to have his stranger guests come in their worst clothes, for this prevents the attention of the public being called to them as they enter the palace. After you have lived some time in Rome, you will see how necessary it is to keep dark; so you will see no flaring light at the palace gate; it's all quiet and commonplace as possible. The dresses, you must remember, are assumed for the occasion, because they are, or were, the national costume, which is fast disappearing; and if it were not for the noble wearers you will see to-night, you could not find them anywhere in Rome. You will perhaps think the nobility at the ball hardly realize your ideas of Italian beauty and refinement, compared with the fine specimens of men and women you may have seen among the Italian opera singers at home. Well, these same singers are picked specimens, and are chosen for their height and muscular development from the whole nation, so that strangers may think all the rest at home are like them. It is a little piece of deception we can pardon."

After this long prelude, Rocjean proposed that they should try a game of billiards in the Café Nuovo. After they had played a game or two, and drunk several *mezzo caldos*, or rum punches, they walked up the Corso to the Via San Claudio, No. 48, and entered the palace gate. It was very dark after they entered, so Rocjean, telling them to wait one moment, lit a *cerina*, or piece of waxed cord—an article indispensable to a Roman—and, crossing the broad courtyard, they entered a small door, and after climbing and twisting and turning, found a ticket-taker, and the next minute were in the ball room.

Uncle Bill was delighted with the excessively free-and-easy ball of Prince Giacinti, but was very anxious to know the names of the nobility, and Rocjean politely undertook to point out the celebrities, offering kindly to introduce him to any one he might think looked sympathetic—"what they called *simpatico* in Italian," explained Rocjean.

"That pretty girl in *Ciociara* costume, is the Condessa, or Countess Stella di Napoli."

"Introduce me," said Uncle Bill.

Rocjean went through the performance, concluding thus: "The countess expresses a wish that you should order a *bottiglia* (about two bottles) of red wine."

"Go ahead," quoth Uncle Bill; "for a nobility ball this comes as near a dance-house affair, as I ever want to approach. By the way, who is that pickpocket-looking genius, with eyes like a blacksnake?"

"Who is *that?*" said Rocjean, theatrically. "Chut! a word in your ear: that is An-to-nel-li!"

"The devil! But I heard some one only a few minutes ago call him Angeluccio."

"That was done satirically, for it means 'big angel,' which you, who read the papers, know that Antonelli is *not*. But here comes the wine, and I see the countess looks dry. Pour out a half dozen glasses for her. The Roman women, high and low, paddle in wine like ducks, and it never upsets them; for, like ducks, their feet are so large, that neither you nor wine can throw them. I wish you could speak Italian, for here comes the Princess Giacinta *con Marchese*——"

"I wish," said Uncle Bill, "you would talk English."

"Well," continued Rocjean, "with the Marchioness Nina Romana, if you like that better. Shall I introduce you?"

"Certainly," replied the old gentleman, "and order two more what-d'ye-call-'ems. It's cheap—this knowing a princess for a quart of red teaberry toothwash, for that's what this 'wine' amounts to. I am going to dance to-night, for the Princess Giacinta is a complete woman after my heart, and weighs her two hundred pound any day."

The nobility now began begging Rocjean and Caper to introduce them to his excellency *Il vecchio*, or the old man; and Uncle Bill, in his enthusiasm at finding himself surrounded with so many princes—Allegrini, Pelligrini, Sapgrini, and Dungreeny—compelled Caper to order up a barrel of wine, set it a-tap, and tell the nobility to "go in." It is needless to say that they *went* in. Many of the costumes were very rich, especially those of the female nobility; and in the rush for a glass of wine, the effect of the brilliant draperies flying here and there, struggling and pushing, was notable. The musicians, who were standing on what appeared to be barrels draped with white cloth, jumped down, and tried their luck at the wine cask, and, after satisfying their thirst, returned to their duties. There was a guitar, mandolin, violin, and flute, and the music was good for dancing. Uncle Bill was pounced on by the Princess Giacinta, and whirled off into some kind of a dance, he did not know what; round flew the room and the nobility; round flew barrels of teaberry toothwash, beautiful princesses, big devils of Antonellis. Lights, flash, hum, buzz, buzz, zzz—ooo—zoom!

Uncle Bill opened his eyes as the sunlight shed one golden bar into his sleeping room at the Hotel d'Europe, and there, by his bedside, sat his nephew, Jim Caper, reading a letter, while on a table near at hand was a goblet full of ice, a bottle of hock, and another bottle corked, with string over it.

"It's so-da wa-ter," said Uncle Bill, musing aloud.

"Hallo, uncle, you awake?" asked Caper, suddenly raising his eyes from his letter.

"I am, my son. Give thy aged father thy blessing, and open that hock and soda water quicker! I say, Jim, now, what became of the nobility, the Colonnas and Aldobrandinis, after they finished that barrel? Strikes me some of them will have an owlly appearance this morning."

"You don't know them," answered Caper.

"I am beginning to believe I don't, too," spoke Uncle Bill. "I say, now, Jim, where did we go last night?"

"Why, Uncle Bill, to tell you the plain truth, we went to a ball at the Costa Palace; and a model ball it was, too."

"I have you! Models who sit for you painters. Well, if they arn't nobility, they drink like kings, so it's all right. Give us the hock, and say no more about it."

CHAPTER III.

THERE was an indefinable charm, to a lively man like Caper, in spending a day in the open country around Rome. Whether it was passed, gun in hand, near the Solfatara, trying to shoot snipe and woodcock, or, with paintbox and stool, seated under a large white cotton umbrella, sketching in the valley of Poussin, or out on the Via Appia, that day was invariably marked down to be remembered.

On one of those golden February mornings, when the pretty English girls tramp through the long grass of the Villa Borghese, gathering the perfumed violets into those modest little bouquets, that peep out from their setting of green leaves, like faith struggling with jealousy, Caper, Rocjean, and a good-natured German, named Von Bluhmen, made an excursion out in the Campagna.

They hired a one-horse vetturo in the Piazza di Spagna, and packing in their sketching materials, and a basket well filled with luncheon and bottles of red wine, started off, soon reaching the Saint Sebastian gate. Further on, they passed the tomb of Cecilia Metella, and saw streaming over the Campagna the Roman hunt-hounds, twenty couples, making straight tails after a red fox, while a score of well-mounted horsemen—here and there a red coat and white breeches—came riding furiously after. Along the roadside were handsome open carriages, filled with wit and beauty, talent and petticoats; and bright were the blue eyes, and red the healthy cheeks of the English girls, as they saw how well their countrymen and lovers led off the chase. Englishmen *have* good legs.

Continuing along the Appian Way, either side of which was bordered by tombs crumbling to decay; some of them covered with Nature's lace, the graceful ivy, others with only a pile of turf above them, others with shattered column and mutilated statue at their base—the occupants of the vetturo were silent. They saw before them the wide plain, shut in on the horizon by high mountains, with snow-covered peaks and sides, while they were living in the warmth of an American June morning; the breeze that swept over them was gentle and exhilarating; in the long grass waving by the wayside, they heard the shrill cries of the cicalas; while the clouds, driven along the wide reach of heaven, assuming fantastic forms, and in changing light and shadow mantling the distant mountains, gave our trio a rare chance to study cloud effects to great advantage.

"I say, driver, what's your name?" asked Rocjean of the *vetturino*.

"Cæsar, *padrone mio*," answered the man.

"Are you descended from the celebrated Julius?" asked Caper, laughing.

"Yes, sir; my grandfather's name was Julius."

> "That every like is not the same, O Cæsar!
> The heart of Brutus yearns to think upon,"

soliloquized Caper; and as by this time they had reached a

place where both he and Rocjean thought a fine view of the ruined aqueduct might be taken, they ordered the driver to stop, and, taking out their sketching materials, sent him back to Rome, telling him to come out for them about four o'clock, when they would be ready to return.

While they were yet in the road, there came along a very large countryman, mounted on a very small jackass. He was sitting side-saddle fashion, one leg crossed over the other, the lower leg nearly touching the ground. One hand held a pipe to his mouth, while the other held an olive branch, by no means an emblem of peace to the jackass, who twitched one long ear, and then the other, in expectation of a momentary visit from it on either side of his head. Following, at a dutiful distance behind, came a splendid specimen of a Roman peasant-woman, a true *contadina*. Poised on her head was a very large round basket, from over the edge of which sundry chickens' heads and cocks' feathers arose; and while Caper was looking at the basket, he saw two tiny little arms stuck up suddenly above the chickens, and then heard a faint squall—it was her baby. An instantaneous desire seized Caper to make a rough sketch of the family group; and hailing the man, he asked him for a light to his cigar. The jackass was stopped by pulling his left ear—the ears answering for reins—and after giving a light, the man was going on, when Caper, taking a *scudo* from his pocket, told him that if he would let him make a sketch of himself, wife, and jackass, he would give it to him, telling him also that he would not detain them over an hour.

"If you'll give me a *buona mano* besides the *scudo*, I'll do it," he answered.

The *buona mano* is the ignis fatuus that leads on three

fourths of the Italians; it is the bright spark that wakes them up to exertion. No matter what the fixed price for doing anything may be, there must always be a something undefined ahead of it, to crown the work when accomplished. It makes labor a lottery; it makes even sawing wood a species of gambling. Caper promised a *buona mano*.

The man told his wife that the Signore was to make a *ritratto*, a picture of them all, including the jackass, at which she laughed heartily, showing a splendid set of brilliantly white teeth. A finer type of woman it would be hard to find, for she was tall, straight, with magnificent bust and broad hips. Her hair, thick and black, was drawn back from her forehead like a Chinese, and was confined behind her head with two long silver pins, the heads representing flowers; heavy, crescent-shaped gold earrings hung from her ears; around her full throat circled two strings of red coral beads. Her boddice of crimson cloth was met by the well filled out-folds of her white linen shirt, the sleeves of which fell from her shoulders below her elbows, in full, graceful folds; her skirt was of heavy white woollen stuff, while her blue apron, of the same material, had three broad stripes of golden yellow, one near the top, and the other two near each other at the bottom; the folds of the apron were few, and fell in heavy, regular lines. A full, liquid-brown pair of eyes gazed calmly on the painter, as she stood beside her husband, easily, gracefully; without a sign from the artist, taking a position that the most studied care could not have improved.

"*Benissimo!*" cried Caper, "the position couldn't be better;" and seizing his sketch book and pencils, unfolding his umbrella and planting its spiked end in the ground, and arranging his sketching stool, he was in five minutes hard at work, As soon as he could draw the basket, he told the woman she might take it from her head, and put it on the ground, for he believed the weight must incommode her. This done, she resumed her position, and Caper, working with all his might, had his sketch sufficiently finished before the hour was over to tell his group that it was finished, at the same time handing the man a *scudo* and a handsome *buona mano*.

Rocjean and Von Bluhmen, who had assiduously looked on, now and then joking with the *contadino* and his wife, proposed, after the sketch was finished, that Caper should ask his friends to help them finish their luncheon. This was joyously agreed to, and the party, having left the road, and found a pleasant spot, under a group of ilex trees, were soon busy finishing the eatables. It was refreshing to see how the handsome *contadina* emptied glass after glass of red wine. The husband did his share of drinking, but his wife eclipsed him. Having learned from Caper that his first name was Giacomo, she shouted forth a rondinella, making up the words as she went along, and in it gave a ludicrous account of Giacomo, the artist, who took a jackass's portrait, herself and husband holding him, and the baby squalling in harmony. This met with an embarrassment of success, and amid the applause of Rocjean, Caper, and Von Bluhmen, the *contadino*, wife, and baggage departed. She, however, told Caper where she lived in the Campagna, and that she had a beautiful little sister, whose *ritratta* he should take, if he would come to see her.

[It is needless to inform the reader that *he went.*]

Lighting cigars, Rocjean and Caper declared they must have a siesta, even if they had to doze on their stools, for neither of them ever could accustom himself to the Roman fashion of throwing one's self on the ground, and sleeping with their faces to the earth. Von Bluhmen, a fiery amateur of sketching, walked off to take a "near view" of the aqueduct, and the two artists were left to repose.

"I say, Caper, does it ever come into your head to people all this broad Campagna with old Romans?" asked Rocjean.

"Yes; all the time. Do you know, that when I am out here, and stumble over the doorway of an old Roman tomb, or find one of those thousand caves in the tufa rock, I often have a curious feeling, that from out that tomb or cave will stalk forth, in broad daylight, some old Roman centurion or senator, in flowing robe."

"Do you ever think," asked Rocjean, "of those seventy thousand poor devils of Jews who helped build the Coliseum and the Arch of Titus? Do you ever reflect over the millions of *slaves* who worked for these same poetical, flowing-robed old senators and centurions? *Ma foi!* for a republic, you men of the United States have a finished education for anything but republicans. The great world-long struggle of a few to crush and destroy the many, you learn profoundly; you know in all its glittering cruelty and horror the entire history, and you weave from it no godlike moral. Nothing astonished me more, during my residence in the United States, than this same lack of drawing from the experience of ages the deduction that you were the only really blessed and happy nation in the world. Your educated men know less of the history of their own country, and feel less its sublime teachings, than any other race of men in the world. The instruction your young men receive at school and college, in what way does it prepare them to become men fit for a republic?"

"You are preaching a sermon," said Caper.

"I am reciting the text; the sermon will be preached by the god of battles to the roar of cannons and the crack of rifles, and I hope you'll profit by it after you hear it."

"Well," interrupted Caper, "what do you think of the English?"

"For a practical people, they are the greatest fools on the earth. Thoroughly convinced at heart that they have no *esprit*, they rush in to show the world that they have a superabundance of it. . . . It interferes with their principles, no matter; it touches their pockets, behold! it is gone, and the cold, flat, dead reality stares you in the face."

"You are a Frenchman, Rocjean, and you do them injustice. Had Shakspeare no *esprit?*" asked Caper.

"Shakspeare was a Frenchman," replied Rocjean.

"We—ll!"

"Prove to me that he was not?"

"Prove to me that he was!"

"Certainly. The family of Jacques Pierre was as certainly French as Raimond de Rocjean's. Jacques Pierre became Shakspeare at once, on emigrating to England, and the 'Immortal Williams,' recognizing the advantages to a poor man of living in a country where only the guineas dance, took up his abode there, and made the music for the money to jump into his pockets."

"Very ingenious. But in relation to Byron, Shelley, Keats, Tennyson, and—as we are in Italy—Rogers?"

"*Mon ami*, if you seriously prefer ice cream and trifle to venison and *dindon aux truffes,* choose. If either one of the four poets—I do not include Rogers among poets—ever conceived in his mind, and then produced on paper, a work, composed from his memory, of things terrible in nature, more sublime than Dante's *Inferno*, I will grant you that he had *esprit* and imagination; otherwise, not. It is of the English as a nation, however, that I make my broad and sweeping assertion —one that was fixed in my mind yesterday, when I saw a well-dressed and well-*educated* Englishman deliberately pick up a stone, knock off the head of a figure carved on a sarcophagus, found in one of those newly-discovered tombs on the Via Latina, and put the broken head in his pocket. . . . What man, with one grain of *esprit* or imagination in his head, would mutilate a work of ancient art, solely that he might possess a piece of stone, when memory had already placed the entire work forever in his mind? *Basta!* enough. Look at the effect of the sunlight on the Albanian mountains. How proudly Mount Gennaro towers over the desolate Campagna! Hallo! Von Bluhmen, down there, is in trouble. Come along."

Throwing down his umbrella, under which he had been sitting in the shade, Rocjean grasped the iron-pointed shaft, into which the handle of the umbrella fitted, and, accompanied by Caper, rushed to the rescue of the German. It was none too soon. While sketching, a shepherd, with a very large flock of sheep, had gradually approached nearer and nearer the spot where the artist was sitting at his task. His dogs, eight or ten in number, fierce, shaggy, white and black beasts, with slouching gait and pointed ears and noses, followed near him. As Von Bluhmen paid no attention to them, the shepherd had wandered off; but one or two of his dogs hung back, and the artist, dropping a pencil, suddenly stooped to pick it up, when one of the savage creatures, thinking or "instincting" that a stone was coming at him, rushed in, with loud barking, to make mincemeat of the German noble. He seized his camp stool, and kept the dog at bay; but in a moment the whole pack were down on him. Just at this instant, in rushed Rocjean, staff in hand, beating the beasts right and left, and shouting to the shepherd, who was but a short distance off, to call off his dogs. But the *pecorajo*, evidently a cross-grained fellow, only blackguarded the artist, until Rocjean, whose blood was up, swore, if he did not call them off, he would shoot them, pulling a revolver from his pocket, and aiming at the most savage dog as he spoke. The shepherd only blackguarded him the more, and, just as the dog grabbed him by the pantaloons, Rocjean pulled the trigger, and with foaming jaws and blood pouring from his mouth, the dog fell dead at his feet. The shot scared the other dogs, who fled, tails under. The shepherd ran for the entrance of a cave, and came out in a minute with a single-barrelled gun. Coming down to within twenty feet of Rocjean, he cocked it, and taking aim, screamed out: "Give me ten *scudi* for that dog, or I fire."

"Do you see that pistol?" said Rocjean to the shepherd, while he held up his revolver. "I have five loads in it yet." And then advancing straight toward him, with death in his eyes, he told him to throw down his gun, or he was a dead man. . . . Down fell the gun. Rocjean picked it up. "To-morrow," said he, "inquire of the chief of police in Rome for this gun, and for the ten *scudi!*"

They were never called for.

"You see," said Caper, as, shortly after this little excitement, the one-horse vetturo, bearing Cæsar and his fortunes, hove in sight, and they entered, and returned to Rome; "you see how charming it is to sketch on the Campagna."

"Very," replied Von Bluhmen; "but, my dear Rocjean, how long were you in America?"

"Ten years."

"*Mein Gott!* they were not wasted."

It is not at all astonishing that a god who was born to the tune of Jove's thunderbolts, should have escaped scot free from the thunders of the Vatican, and should prove at the present time one of the strongest opponents to the latter kind of fireworks. We read, in the work of that learned Jesuit, Galtruchius, that

> "Bacchus was usually painted with a mitre upon his head, an ornament proper to Women. He never had other Priests but Satyrs and Women; because the latter had followed him in great Companies in his Journeys, crying, singing, and dancing continually. Titus Livius relates a strange story of the Festivals of Bacchus in Rome. Three times in a year, the Women of all qualities met in a Grove called Simila, and there acted all sorts of Villainies; those that appeared most reserved were sacrificed to Bacchus; and that the cries of the ravished Creatures might not be heard, they did howl, sing, and run up and down with lighted Torches."

The May and October festivals in Rome, at present, are substituted for the Bacchanalian orgies, and are, of course, not so objectionable, in many particulars, as the ancient ceremonies; still, no stranger in Rome, at these times, should neglect to attend them. Caper entered Rome at night, during the October festival, and the carriage loads of Roman women, waving torches and singing tipsily, forcibly reminded him that the Bacchante still lived, and only needed a very little encouragement to revive their ancient rites in full.

Sentimental travellers tell you that the Romans are a temperate people. They have never seen the people. They have never seen the delight that reigns in the heart of the *plebs*, when they learn that the vintage has been good, and that good wine will be sold in Rome for three or four cents *la foglietta* (about a pint, American measure). They have never visited the *spacii di vini*, the wineshops. They have never heard of the murders committed when the wine was in and the wit out. None of these things ever appear in the *Giornale di Roma* or in the *Vero Amico del Popolo*, the only newspapers published in Rome.

"Roman newspapers," said an intelligent Roman to Caper, "were invented to conceal the news."

The first thing that a foreigner does on entering Rome, is to originate a derogatory name for the juice of the grape native to the soil, the *vino nostrale*. He calls it, if red wine, red ink, pink cider, red tea; if white wine, balm of gooseberries, blood of turnips, apple juice, alum water, and slops for babes; finally, . . . if not killed off with a fever, from drinking the adulterated foreign wines, spirits, and liqueurs sold in the city, he takes kindly to the Roman wines, and does not worry his great soul about them.

The truth is, that while other nations have done everything to improve wine-making, Italy follows the same careless way she has done for centuries. Far more attention was bestowed on the grape, too, in ancient times than now; and we read that vineyards were so much cultivated, to the neglect of agriculture, that, under Domitian, an edict forbade the planting of any new vineyards in Italy.

One brilliant morning in October, Caper, who was then

living in a town perched atop of a conical mountain, descended five or six miles on foot, and passed a day in a vineyard, in order to see the vintage. The vines were trained on trees or on sticks of cane, and the peasant girls and women were busy picking the great bunches of white or purple grapes, which were thrown into copper *conche*, or jars. These *conche*, when filled, were carried on the head to a central spot, where they were emptied on fern leaves placed on the ground to receive them. And from these piles, the wooden barrels of the mules returning from the town were filled with the grapes, which were carried up there to be pressed.

The grape crop had been so affected by the *malattia*, or blight, that, the yield being small, the fruit to an extent was not pressed in the vineyards, and the juice only brought up to the town in goat-skins as usual; but the fruit itself was carried up by those having the proper places, and was pressed in tubs in the *cantine*, or rooms on the ground floor, where the wine is kept. Across the huge saddles of the mules they swung a couple of truncated, cone-shaped barrels, and filled them with grapes; these were tumbled into tubs, ranged in the *cantina*, good, bad, and indifferent fruit all together; and when enough were poured in, in jumped the *pistatore d'uve*, or grape presser, with bare legs and feet, and began pressing and stamping, until the juice ran out in a tolerable stream. This juice was then poured into a headless hogshead, and, when more than half full, they piled on the grapeskins and stones and stems that had undergone the pressure, until the hogshead was full to the top. A weight was then placed over all. In twenty days, fermentation having taken place, they drew from the hogshead the new wine, which was afterward clarified with whites of eggs.

In this rough-and-ready way, the common wine is made. Without selection, all grapes, ripe, unripe, and rotten, sweet and sour, are mashed up together, hurriedly and imperfectly pressed, and the wine is sent to market, to sell for what it will bring. Having thus seen it made, let us see it disposed of.

Of all the monuments to Bacchus, in Rome, the one near the pyramid of Caius Cestius, and still nearer the Protestant burying ground, is by far the most noticeable. Jealous of the lofty manner in which it lifts its head above the surrounding fields and walls of the city, the church has seen fit to crown its head with a cross, which it seems inclined to shake off. This small mountain of a monument is conical in shape, and is composed entirely of broken crockery; hence its name, *Testaccio*. In its crockery sides, they have found a certain coolness and evenness of temperature exactly suited to the storage of wine, and to maturing it; hence, all around the mountain are deep vaults, filled with red and white wines, working themselves up for a fit state to enter into the joy and the gullets of the Roman *minenti*.

If the reader of this sketch is at all of a philosophical frame of mind, and should ever visit Rome, it is the writer's advice that, in the first place, having learned Italian enough, and, in the second place, having his purse fairly filled—silver will do—he should, during the month of October, on a holiday, go out to Monte Testaccio alone, or at least in company with some one who knows enough to let him be alone when he wants to be with somebody else, and then and there fraternizing for a few hours with the Roman *plebs*, let him at his ease see what he shall see. Then shall he sit him down at the door of the *Antica Osteria di Cappanone*, at the rough wood table, on a rougher wooden bench; talk, right and left, with tailors, shoemakers, artists, soldiers, and God knows what, drinking the cool, amber-colored wine of Monte Rotonda, gleaming brightly in the sunlight that dashes through his glass, and so cheerfully winning the good will of them all—and of some of the young women who are with them—that he shall find himself at some future time either the sheath for a Roman knife, or the recipient of a great deal of affection, and the purchaser of indefinite *bottiglie* of *vino nostrale*.

In his ardent pursuit of natural art, Caper believed it his duty to hunt up the picturesque wherever it could be found; and it was while pursuing this duty, in company with Rocjean, that he found himself at Monte Testaccio, one October day, and there made his *début*. After a luncheon of raw ham, bread, cheese, sausage, and a *bottiglia* of wine, they ascended the mountain, and sitting down at the foot of the cross, they quietly smoked and communed with nature unreservedly.

Crumbling old walls of Rome that lay before them; wild, uncultivated Campagna; purple range of mountains, snow-tipped; thousand-legged, ruined aqueducts; distant sea, but faintly revealed through the veil of haze-bounded horizon; yellow Tiber, flowing along crumbling banks; dome of St. Peter's, rising above the hill that shuts the Vatican from sight; pyramid of Caius Cestius; Protestant burying ground, with the wind sighing through the trees a lullaby over the graves of Shelley and Keats; distant view of Rome, slumbering artistically, and not manufacturingly, in the sunlight of that morning—ye taught one man of the two wild hopes for Rome of the future.

At the foot of the mountain, and adjoining the Protestant

burying ground, there is a powder magazine. Here a French soldier, acting as sentry, paced his weary round. It was not long before a couple of Roman women passed him. They saluted him; he saluted them. They passed behind the magazine. The sentry, with the courtesy which distinguishes Frenchmen, evidently desired to make his compliments and pay his addresses to the *dames*. How could this be done? Before long, two of his compatriots, evidently out for a holiday, passed him. He beckoned to one of them, who at once took his gun and turned sentry, while the relieved guard flew to display to the *dames* his national courtesy. Before Caper had time to smoke a second cigar, the soldier returned to duty, and the one who had relieved him sprung to pay his addresses. During the two hours that Caper and Rocjean studied the scenery, guard was relieved four times.

"Ah!" said Rocjean, "we are a gallant nation. Let us therefore descend and mingle with what the high-minded John Bulls call "the lower orders."

Down they went, and at the first table they came to they found their shoemaker, the Signore Eugenio Calzolajo, artist in leather, seated with three Roman women. They all resembled each other like three pins. The eldest one held a baby, the *caro bambino*, in her arms. She was probably twenty years old. The next one was not over eighteen; while the youngest had evidently not passed her sixteenth year.

The artist in leather saluted Caper and Rocjean with the title of *Illustrissimi* (they both paid their bills punctually), and, as he saw that the other tables were full, he at once made room for them, introducing them to his wife and her two sisters. Caper, who saw that the party had just arrived, and had not as yet had time to order anything from the waiters, told them that the day being his birthday, it was customary among the North American Indians always to celebrate it with a feast of roast dogs and bottled porter; but, as neither of these articles were to be found at Monte Testaccio, he should command what they had; and arresting a waiter, he ordered such a supply of food and wine, that the eyes of the three Roman girls opened wide as owls'. Their tongues were all unloosened at once, as if by magic, and Caper had the satisfaction of seeing, that for what a bottle of hotel champagne costs in the United States, he had provided joy unadulterated, and happy memories for many days, for several descendants of the Cæsars.

While the wine circulated freely, the eldest of the unmarried girls, named Elisa, began joking Caper about his being a heretic, and "a little devil," and asked him to take off his hat, to see if he had horns. Caper told her he was as yet unmarried, . . . and that, among the Indians, bachelors were never allowed to take their hats off before maidens. "But," said he, "what makes you think I am a heretic? Wasn't I at St. Peter's yesterday, and at the confessionals?"

"Yes, you were at them, like an old German gentleman I once knew," said Elisa. "Some of his friends saw him one morning at the German confessional box, and knowing that he was a heretic, asked him what he was doing there? '*Diavolo!*' said he, 'can't a man have a comfortable mouthful of German, without changing religions?'"

"For my part," said Rita, the youngest sister, "I only go to confessional, because I *have* to; and I only confess what I want to."

"Bravo!" exclaimed Rocjean; "I must *paint your portrait.*"

"*Benissimo!* and who will paint mine?" asked Elisa.

"I will," said Caper, "but on condition that you let me keep a copy of it." . . .

Arrangements completed, Rocjean ordered more wine; and then the artist in leather ordered more; then Caper's turn came. After this, the party, which had been gradually growing jolly and jollier, would have danced, had they not all had a holy horror of the prison of San Angelo. The married sister, Doménica, was a full-blooded *Trasteverina*, in her gala dress, and had one of those beautiful-shaped heads that Caper could only compare to a quail's. Her jet-black hair, smoothed close to her head, was gathered in a large roll that fell low on her neck behind, and held by a silver *spadina*, or pin, that, if occasion demanded, would make a serviceable stiletto. Her full face was brown, while the red blood shone through her cheeks, and her lips were full and ripe. Her eyes of deep gray, shaded with long black lashes, sparkled with light when she was aroused. Her sisters resembled her strikingly, except Rita, the youngest, whose face was of that singularly delicate hue of white, the color of the magnolia flower, as one of our American writers has it; or like the white of a boiled egg next to the yolk, as Caper expressed it. Be this as it may, there was something very attractive in this pallor, since it was accompanied by an *embonpoint* indicating anything but romantic meagreness of constitution.

Doménica had, without exaggeration, the value of a dozen or two pairs of patent-leather boots hung on her neck, arms, fingers, ears, and bosom, in the shape of furious-sized pieces of gold jewelry; and it was solid gold. The Roman women, from the earliest days—from the time when Etruscan artists made those ponderous chains and bracelets, down to the present date—have had the most unbridled love for jewelry. Do we not know* that

Sabina's garters were worth	$200,000
Faustina's finger ring,	200,000
Domitia's ring,	300,000
Cæsonia's bracelet,	400,000
Poppæa's earrings,	600,000
Calpurina's (Cæsar's wife) earrings, "above suspicion,"	1,200,000
Sabina's diadem,	1,200,000

And after this, is it at all astonishing that the desire remains for it, even if the substance has been plundered and carried off by those *forestieri*, the Huns, Vandals, Goths, Visigoths, Norsemen, and other heretics who have visited Rome?

While they were all busily drinking and talking, Caper had noticed that the wine was beginning to have its effects on the large crowd who had assembled at the Osterias and Trattorias around the foot of the Bacchic mountain. Laughing and talking, shouting and singing began to be in the ascendant, and gravity was voted indecent.

"Ha!" said Rocjean, "for one hour of the good old classic days!"

"What!" answered Caper; "with those seventy thousand old Jews you were preaching about the other day?"

"Never!—with the Bacchante. But here, our friends are off. Let us help them into the carriage."

As the sun went down, the *minenti* began to crowd toward Rome. More than one *spadina* flashed in the hands of the

---

* Vide *Gems and Jewels*. By Madame de Barrera.

slightly-tight maidens who were on foot. Those of the men who had carriages, foreseeing the inflammable spirit aroused, packed the women in by themselves, gave them lighted torches, and cut them adrift, to float down the Corso; they following in separate carriages.

. . . .

"Ah! really, and pray, Mrs. Jobson, don't you think that it's—ah! a beau-ti-ful sight; they tell me—ah! it's the peasants returning from visiting the shrine of the—ah! Madonna—ah?"

"And I think it is *most* charming, Mister Lushington; and I remember me now that Lady Fanny Errol—poor thing!—said it would be a *charming* sight. And the poor creatures seem *much* happier than our own lower orders; they do, to be sure."

. . . .

"O Lord!" groaned Caper, as he overheard the above dialogue; "allow me to retire."

As an animal-painter, Mr. Caper was continually hunting up materials for sketches. He made excursions into the Campagna, to see the long-horned gray oxen and the hideous buffaloes; watching the latter along the yellow Tiber, when, in the springtime, they coquetted in the mud and water. He sketched goats and sheep, tended by the picturesquely-dressed shepherds, and guarded by the fierce dogs that continually encircled them. In four words, he studied animal-ated nature.

On his first arrival in Rome, he had purchased one of those sprightly little *vettura* dogs, all wool and tail, that the traveller remarks mounted on top of the travelling carriages that enter and leave Rome. With a firm foothold, they stand on the very top of all the baggage that may be piled on the roof of the coach; and there, standing guard and barking fiercely, seem to thoroughly enjoy the confusion attendant on starting the horses, or unloading the baggage. They are seen around the carriage-stands where public hacks are hired, and as soon as one **moves off,** up jumps the *vettura* dog alongside the driver, and never leaves the vehicle until it stops. Then, if he sees another hack returning to the city, he will jump into that, and be carried back triumphant. This sounds like fiction; but its truth will be confirmed by any one who has ever noticed the peculiarities of this breed of dogs, which love to ride.

Caper kept this dog in his studio, and had already made several very lifelike studies of him. One morning, leaving his lodgings earlier than usual, **he met on the stairway of** his house a countryman driving a goat up stairs to be milked; the Romans thus having good evidence that when they buy goat's milk, they don't purchase water from the fountains. As Caper was going out of the door that led into the street, he saw, among the flock of goats assembled there, a patriarchal old billy, whose beard struck him with delight. He was looking at him in silent veneration, when the goats'-milk man came down stairs, driving the ewe before him. He asked the man if he would sell the patriarch; but found that he would not. He promised, however, to lend him to Caper until the next day for a good round sum, to be paid when the goat was delivered at the studio, which the man said would be in the course of an hour.

Our artist **then went down** to the Greco, where he breakfasted; and there met Rocjean, **who proposed to** him **to go** that morning to the Piazza Navona, as it was market day, and they would have a fine chance to take notes of the country people, their costumes, &c. They first went around to Caper's studio, where they had only to wait a short time before the milkman came, driving the old billy goat up stairs before him. Caper made him fast with a cord to a heavy table, the top of which was a vast receptacle of sketch books, oil colors, books, and all kinds of odds and ends.

Rocjean and he then strolled down to the Piazza Navona, where, while walking around, Caper suddenly stumbled over the smallest and most comical specimen of a donkey he had ever seen. The man who owned him, and who had brought in a load of vegetables on the donkey's back, offered to sell him very cheap. The temptation was great, and our animal-artist bought him at once for five *scudi*, alias dollars; but with the understanding that the countryman would deliver him at his studio at once. In twenty minutes' time, the donkey was climbing up a long flight of stairs to Caper's studio, as seriously as if he were crossing the *pons asinorum*. Once in his studio, Caper soon made arrangements to have the donkey kept in a stable near by, when he was not sketching him. This matter finished, Rocjean helped Caper pen him up in a corner of the studio, where he could begin sketching him as soon as he had finished portraying the billy goat. The patriarch had made several attempts to rush at the *vettura* dog; but the string held him fast to the table. Rocjean mentioned to Caper that he ought to feed his menagerie; and the porter, being called and sent out for some food for the goat and donkey, soon returned with a full supply.

Both artists now set to work in earnest—Caper, with paints and brushes, and Rocjean with crayons and sketch book

—determined to take the patriarch's portrait while he was in a peaceful frame of body and spirit.

With an intermission for luncheon, they worked until nearly four o'clock in the afternoon, when Rocjean proposed taking a walk out to the Villa Borghese, and as they returned, on their way to dinner, they could stop in at the studio, and see that the donkey and goat were driven out to the stable, where they could be kept until wanted again. Accordingly, both artists walked out to the villa, and had only taken a short turn toward the Casino, when they met a New-York friend of theirs, alone in a carriage, taking a ride. He ordered the driver to stop, and begged them both to get in with him, and, after passing through the villa and around the Pincio, to come and take dinner with him sociably in his room in the Via Frattina. They accepted; and at ten o'clock that night, while going home in a very happy frame of mind, it suddenly occurred to Caper that his menagerie ought to have been attended to. Rocjean consoled him with the reflection that, having the key in his pocket, they could not possibly get out; so the former thought no more about it.

Early in the morning, having met as usual at the Greco, and breakfasted together, Caper and Rocjean walked round to the former's studio. Before they entered the door of the building, they noticed a small assembly of old women surrounding the porter; and as Caper entered the passage way, they poured a broadside into him.

"*Accidente, Signore*, nobody around here has been able to sleep a wink all night long. *Santa Maria!* such yells have come from your studio, such groans, such horrible noises, as if all the devils had broken loose. We are going to the police; we are going to the *gendarmeria;* we are going to——"

"Go there—and be hanged!" shouted Caper, breaking through the crowd, and, running up stairs two steps at a time, he nearly walked into the lap of a tall female model, named Giacinta, dressed in Ciociara costume, who was calmly seated on the staircase, glaring at another female model, named Nina, who stood leaning against the door of his studio.

"Signor Giacomo, good morning!" said Giacinta; "didn't you tell *me* to be here at nine o'clock?"

"To be sure I did," replied he.

"Then," continued she, "what is *that person* there taking the bread out of my mouth for? *Cospetto!*"

"*Iddio giusto!*" cried Nina; "hear her; she calls *me*, ME, a person! I, who have a watch and chain, and wear a hooped petticoat! *I* take the bread out of her mouth! I a person! I'm a lady, *per Bacco!*"

"*Tace!*" said Rocjean to Nina, "or the Signore Giacomo will send you flying. What do you want, Nina?"

"I only wanted to see if the Signore intended to paint the Lady Godeeva, that he told me about the other day."

"Wait till I open the studio door, and get out of this noise. Those old women down below, and you young ones up here, are howling like a lot of hyenas. Here—come in!"

. . . As Caper said this, he unlocked the studio door, and threw it open. The two models were close at his elbows, while Rocjean drew to one side to let them pass in.

In the next minute, Caper, the two models, a he goat, a dirty little donkey, and a yelping dog, were rolling head over heels down stairs, one confused mass of petticoats and animals.

Rocjean roared with laughter. He could do nothing but hold his sides, fearful of having an apoplectic fit, or bursting a blood-vessel.

The small donkey slid down stairs on his back, slowly, gradually, meekly, his long ears rubbing the way before him. But the billy goat was on his feet in an instant, and was charging, next thing, full force into the knot of old women at the foot of the stairs, who, believing that their last hour had come, and that it was Old Nick in person, yelled out: "'Tis he—the devil! the devil!" and fled before the horns to come.

Giacinta was the first one on her legs, and after picking up the *caro* Giacomo, alias Caper, and finding he was not hurt, she then good-naturedly helped Nina to arrange her tumbled garments.

Rocjean rushed to open the studio windows, to air the room, for it had not the odors of the Spice Islands in it. Caper hastened to pick up paints, brushes, books, easel, but they were too many for him; and at last, giving it up in despair, he sat down on a chair.

"*Well!*" said he, "there *has* been a HARD fight here! The dog must have tackled the billy goat; the goat must have upset this table, broken his string, and pitched into that dirty little donkey; and the donkey must have put his heels through that canvas; and all three must have broken loose and upset us. . . . I say, Rocjean, send out for some wine; *I* am dry, and these girls are, I know."

Peace was soon made. Nina was promised that she should sit for Lady Godiva, as soon as the donkey was caught; for she was to be represented seated on him, instead of a horse.

Giacinta poséd for a *contadina* at a fountain. Rocjean passed round the wine, and helped put the studio in order, and Caper, brush in hand, painted away, determining that, under any circumstances, he never would open another menagerie, until he was able to pay a keeper to look after the animals.

CHAPTER IV.

No matter how well and hearty you may be, if you are in Rome, in summer, when the *sciròcco* blows, you will feel as if convalescent from some debilitating fever. In winter, however, this gentle-breathing southeast wind will act more mildly; it will woo you to the country, induce you to sit down in a shady place, smoke, and "muse." That incarnate essence of enterprise, business, industry, economy, sharpness, shrewdness, and keenness—that Prometheus whose liver was torn by the vulture of cent. per cent.—eternally tossing, restless DOOLITTLE, was one day seen asleep, during bank hours, on a seat in the Villa Madama. The *sciròcco* blew that day. Doolittle fell.

At breakfast, one morning in the latter part of the month of March, Caper proposed to Rocjean, and another artist named Bagswell, to attend the fair held that day at Grotto Ferrata.

"What will you find there?" asked Rocjean.

"Find? I remember, in the *Bohemian Girl*, a song that will answer you," replied Caper; "the words were composed by the theatrical poet Bunn":

> "Rank, in its halls, may not find
> The calm of a happy mind;
> So repair
> To the Fair,
> And they may be met with there."

Unsatisfactory, both the grammar and the sentiment," said Bagswell; "it won't work; it's all wrong. In the first place, rank, in its hauls, *may* find the calm of a happy mind; for instance, the captain of a herring smack may find the calm of a very happy mind in his hauls of No. 1 Digbys; more joy, even, than the fair could afford him. Let us go!"

Bagswell was a "funny" Englishman.

They went—taking the railroad. Dashing out of the station, the locomotive carried them, in half an hour, to the station at Frascati, whirling them across the Campagna, past long lines of ruined or half-ruined and repaired aqueducts; past Roman tombs; past *Roma Vecchia*, the name given to the ruins of an immense villa; landing them at the first slope of the mountains, covered at their base with vineyards, olive and fruit trees, and cornfields, while high over them gleamed glistening-white snow-peaks.

The walk from Frascati to the Grotto, about three miles, was beautiful, winding over hills through a fine wood of huge old elms and plane trees. In the warm sunlight, the butterflies were flitting, while the roadside was purple with violets, and white and blue with little flowers. From time to time our three artists had glimpses of the Campagna, rolling away like the ocean, to dash on Rome, crowned by St. Peter's; the dome of which church towers above the surrounding country, so that it can be seen, far and wide, for thirty miles or more. The road was alive with walkers and riders; here a dashing, open carriage, filled with rosy English; there a *contadino*, donkey-back, dressed in holiday suit, with short-clothes of blue woollen, a scarlet waistcoat, his coarse blue-cloth jacket worn on one shoulder, and in his brown conical-shaped hat a large carnation-pink. Then came more of the country people, almost always called *villani* (hence our word, villains!). These poor villains had sacks on their backs, or were carrying in their hands—if women, on their heads—loads of bacon, sides of bacon, flitches of bacon, hams, loaves of bread, cheese, and very loud-smelling *mortadella;* which they had bought, and were bringing away from the fair.

"There was one task," said Rocjean, "that Hercules declined, and that was eating that vile *mortadella*. He was a strong man; but that was stronger. Wait a moment, till I fill a pipe with caporal, and have a smoke; for if I meet another man with that delicacy, I shall have to give up the Grotto—unless I have a pipe under my nose, as counter-irritant."

The three artists tramped along gayly, until they approached the town, when they assumed the proud, disdainful mood, assuring spectators that they who wear it are of gentle blood, and are tired of life, and weary of travelling around with pockets filled with gold. They only looked coldly at the pens filled with cattle for sale: long-horned, mouse-colored oxen were there; groups of patient donkeys, or the rough-maned, shaggy-fetlocked, bright-eyed small horses of the Campagna; countless pigs, many goats; while, above all, the loud-singing jackasses were performing at the top of their lungs. Here were knots of country people, buying provisions or clothing; there were groups of carriages from Rome, which had rolled out the wealthy *forestieri*, or strangers, drawn up by the wayside, in the midst of all sorts and kinds of hucksters. The road leading to the church, shaded by trees, was crowded with country people, in picturesque costumes, busily engaged in buying and selling hams, bacon, bacon and hams, and a few more hams. Here and there, a cheese stand languished, for pork flourished. Now a coppersmith exposed his wares, chief among which were the graceful-shaped *conche*, or water vessels, the same you see so carefully poised on the heads of so many black-eyed Italian girls, going to or coming from so many picturesque fountains, in—paintings, and all wearing such brilliant costumes, as you find at—Gigi's costume class. Then came an ironmonger, whose wares were all made by hand, even the smallest nails; for machinery, as yet, is in its first infancy around Rome. At this stand, Rocjean stopped to purchase a pallet knife; not one of the regular, artist-made tools, but a thin, pliable piece of steel, without handle, which experience taught him was well adapted to his work. As usual, the ironman asked twice as much as he intended to take, and, after a sharp bargain, Rocjean conquered. Then they came to a stand where there were piles of coarse crockery, and some of a better kind, of classical shape.

Caper particularly admired a beautiful white jug, intended for a water pitcher, and holding about two gallons. After asking its price, he offered a quarter of the money for it. To Bagswell's horror, the crockery man took it, and Caper, passing his arm through the handle, was proceeding up the road, when Bagswell energetically asked him what he was going to do with it.

"Enter Rome with it, like Titus with the *spolia opima*," replied Caper.

"Oh! I say, now," said the former, who was an Englishman, and an historical painter, "you aren't going to trot all over the fair with that old crockery on your arm! Why, God bless me! they'll swear we are drunk. There comes the Duchess of Brodneck; what the deuce will she say?"

"Say?" said Caper; "why, I'll go and ask her. This is not court day."

Without another word, with water pitcher on arm, he walked toward the duchess. Saluting her with marked politeness, he said:

"A countryman of yours, madame, has objected to my carrying this *objet de fantaisie*, assuring me that it would occasion remarks from the Duchess of Brodneck. May I have the good fortune to know what she says of it?"

"She says," replied the lady, smiling, and speaking slowly and quietly, "that a young man who has independence enough to carry it, has confidence enough to—fill it." She bowed, and passed on, Caper politely raising his hat, in acknowledgment of the well-rounded sentence. When he returned to Bagswell, he found the historical painter with eyes the size of grapeshot, at the sublime impudence of the man. He told him what she had said.

"Upon my honor, you Americans have a face of brass; to address a duchess you don't know, and ask her a question like that!"

"That's nothing," said Caper; "a little experience has taught me that the higher you fly, in England, the nearer you approach true politeness and courtesy. Believe me, I should never have asked that question of any Englishwoman whose social position did not assure me she was cosmopolitan."

"Come," said Bagswell, "come; after such an adventure, if there is one drop of anything fit to drink in this town, we'll all go and get lushy."

They went. They found a door over which hung a green branch. Good wine needs no bush, therefore Italian wineshops hang it out; for the wine there is not over good. But as luck was with our three artists, in the shop over the door of which hung the green bough, they found that the *padrone* was an old acquaintance of Rocjean; he had married, and moved to Grotto Ferrata. He had a barrel of Frascati wine, which was bright, sparkling, sweet, and not watered. This the *padrone* tapped in honor of his guests, and, at their urgent request, sat down and helped empty a couple of bottles. Moreover, he told them that as the town was over-crowded, they would find it difficult to get a good dinner, unless they would come and dine with him, at his private table, and be his guests; which invitation Rocjean accepted, to the tavern-keeper's great joy, promising to be back at the appointed time.

Our trio then sauntered forth to see the fair. Wandering among the crowded booths, they came suddenly on a collection of *Zingare*, looking like their Spanish cousins, the *Gitañas*. Wild black eyes, coarse black locks of hair, brown as Indians, small hands, small feet—the Gipsies, children of the storm—my Rommani pals, what are you doing here? Only one woman among them was noticeable. Her face was startlingly handsome, with an aquiline nose, thin nostrils, beautifully-arched eyebrows, and eyes like an eagle. She was tall, straight, with exquisitely rounded figure, and the full drapery of white around her bosom fell from the shoulders in large hanging sleeves; over her head was thrown a crimson and green shawl, folded like the *pane* of the *ciociare*, and setting off her raven-black hair and rich red and swarthy complexion.

Rocjean stood entranced, and Caper, noticing his rapt air, forbore breaking silence; while the gipsy, who knew that she was the admiration of the *forestieri*, stood immovable as a statue, looking steadily at them, without changing a feature.

"*Piu bellissima che la madonna!*" said Rocjean, loud enough for her to hear. Then turning to Caper, "Let's *andiammo*" (travel), said he; "that woman's face will haunt me for a month. I've seen it before; yes, seen her shut up in the Vatican, immortal on an old Etruscan vase. Egypt, Etruria, the Saracen hordes who once overrun all this Southern Italy, I find, every hour, among live people, some trace of you all; but of the old Roman, nothing!"

"You find the old Roman cropping out in these church processions, festivals, shrines, and superstitions, don't you?" asked Caper.

"No! something of those who made the seal, nothing of the impression on the wax remains for me. Before Rome was, the great East was, and shall be. The Germans are right to call the East the Morning Land; thence came light. . . . The longer you live along the wave-washed shore of the Mediterranean, the more you will see what a deep hold the East once had on the people of the coast. The Romans, after all, were only opulent tradesmen, who could buy luxuries without having the education to appreciate them. So utterly did they ignore the Etruscans, who made them what they were, that you seek in vain to find in Roman history anything but the barest outline of the origin of a people so graceful and refined, that the Roman citizen was a bootblack in comparison to one of them. The Saracens flashed light and life, in later days, once more into the Roman leaven. What a dirty, filthy page the whole Gothic middle age is at best! It lies like a huge body struck with apoplexy, and only restored to its sensual life by the sharp lancet, bringing blood, of these same infidels, these stinging Saracens. Go into the mountains back of us, hunt up the costumes that still remain, and see where they all come from—the East. Look at the crescent earrings and graceful twisted gold-work, from—the East. All the commonest household ware, the agricultural implements, the manner of cooking their food, and all that is picturesque in life and religion—all from the East."

"Strikes me," quoth Caper, "that this question of food touches my weakest point; therefore, let us go and dine, and continue the lecture at a more un-hungry period. But where is Bagswell?"

"He is seeking adventures, of course."

"Oh! yes, I see him, down there among the billy goats. Let's go and pick him up; and then for mine host of the Green Bough."

Having found Bagswell, our trio at once marched to the Green Bough, which they saw was filled to overflowing with country people, eating and drinking, sitting on rough benches, and stowing away food and wine as if in expectation of being very soon shipwrecked on a desert island, where there would be nothing but hard-shell clams and lemons to eat. The landlord at once took the trio up stairs, where, at a large table, were half a dozen of his friends, all of the cleanly order of country people, stout, and having a well-to-do look that deprecated anything like famine. A young lady of twenty and two hundred, as Caper summed up her age and weight, was evidently the cynosure of all eyes; two other good-natured women, of a few more years and a very little less weight, and three men, made up the table. Any amount of compliments, as usual, passed between the first six and the last three comers, prefacing everything with desires that they would act without ceremony. But Caper and Rocjean were on a high horse, and they fairly pumped the spring of Italian compliments so dry, that Bagswell could only make a squeaking noise when he tried the handle. This verbifuge of our three artists put their host into an ecstasy of delight, and he circulated all round, rubbing his hands, and telling his six friends that his three friends were *milordi*, in very audible whispers, *milordi* of the most genial, courtly, polite, complimentary, cosmopolitan, and exquisite description.

After all this, down sat our trio; and for the sake of future ages which will live on steam bread, electrical beef, and magnetic fish, let us give them the bill of fare set before them:

ALL THE WINE THEY COULD DRINK.

Maccaroni (*fettucia*) à la Milanese—dish two feet in diameter, one foot and a half high.

Mutton chops, with tomato sauce (*pomo d'oro*).

Stewed celery, with Parmesan cheese.

Stewed chickens.

Mutton chops, bird fashion (*Uccélli di Castrato*. They are made of pieces of mutton rolled into a shape like a bird, and cooked, several at a time, on a wooden spit. They are the *kibaubs* of the East.)

Baked pie of cocks' combs and giblets.

Roasted pig, a twelve-pounder.

Roast squashes, stuffed with minced veal.

Apples, oranges, figs, and *finocchio*.

Crostata di visciola, or wild-cherry pie, served on an iron plate the size of a Roman warrior's shield; the dish evidently having been one formerly.

MORE WINE!

The stout young lady rejoicing in the name of Angeluccia, or large angel, was fascinated by Rocjean's conversational powers and Caper's attentions. The rest of the company, perfectly at ease on finding out that the *milordi* were not French —Rocjean turning American to better please them—and that they were moreover full of fun, talked and laughed as if they were brother Italians. A jollier dinner Caper acknowledged he had never known. One of the Italians was farmer-general for one of the Roman princes. He was a man of broad views, and, having travelled to Paris and London, came home with ultra-liberal sentiments, and, to Bagswell's astonishment, spoke his mind so clearly on the Roman rulers, that our Englishman's eyes were slightly opened at the by no means complimentary expressions used toward the wireworkers of the Papal Government. One Italy, and Rome its capital, was the only platform our princely farmer would take, and he was willing to stake his fortune—a cool one hundred thousand *scudi*—on regenerated Italy.

Conversation then fell on the fair; and one of the Italians told several stories which were broad enough to have shoved the generality of English and American ladies out of the window of the room. But Angeluccia and the two wives of the stout gentlemen never winked; they had probably been to confession that morning, had cleared out their old sins, and were now ready to take in a new cargo. In a little while Rocjean sent the waiter out to a café, and he soon returned with coffee for the party; upon which Caper, who had the day before bought some Havana cigars of the man in the Twelve Apostles, in the Piazza Dódici Apostoli, where there is a government cigar store for the sale of them, passed them around, and they were thoroughly appreciated by the diners. The farmer-general gave our three artists a hearty invitation to visit him, promising them all the horses they could ride, all the wine they could drink, and all the maccaroni they could eat. The last clause was inserted for Rocjean's benefit, who had played a noble game with the grand dish they had had for dinner, and at which Angelucia had made great fun, assuring Rocjean he was Italian to the heart, *e piu basso*.

Then came good-by, and our artists were off—slowly, meditatively, and extremely happy, but, so far, quite steady. They walked to the castellated monastery of San Basilio, where, in the chapel of Saint Nilus, they saw the celebrated frescoes of Domenichino, and gazed at them tranquilly, and not quite so appreciatingly as they would have done before dinner. Then they came out from the gloom and the air heavy with the incense of the chapel, to the bright light and lively scenes of the fair, with renewed pleasure. They noticed that every one wore in the hat or in the lappel of the coat, if men—in their hair or in their bosom, if women—artificial roses; and presently coming to a stand where such flowers were for sale, our trio bought half-a-dozen each, and then turned to where the crowd was thickest and the noise greatest. Three or four donkeys loaded with tinware were standing near the crowd, when one of them, ambitious of distinction, began clambering over the tops of the others in an insane attempt to get at some greens, temptingly displayed before him. Rattle, bang! right and left, went the tins, and in rushed men and women with cudgels; but donkey was not to be stopped, and for four or five minutes the whole fair seemed gathered around the scene, cheering and laughing, with a spirit that set Caper wild with excitement, and induced him to work his way through the crowd, and present one old woman, who had finally conquered the donkey, with two large roses; an action which was enthusiastically applauded by the entire assembly.

"Bravo! bravo! well done, O Englishman!" went up the shout.

A little farther on they came to a large travelling van, one end of which was arranged as a platform in the open air. Here a female dentist, in a sea-green dress, with her sleeves rolled up, and a gold bracelet on her right arm, held in both hands a tooth extractor, bound round with a white handkerchief—to keep her steady, as Caper explained, while she pulled a tooth from the head of a young man who was down in front of her on his knees. Her assistant, a good-looking young man, in very white teeth and livery, sold some patent toothache drops: *Solo cinque baiocchi il fiasco, S'gnore.*

Caper, having seen the tooth extracted, cried, "*Bravissima!*" as if he had been at the opera, and threw some roses at the *prima donna dentista*, who acknowledged the applause with a bow, and requested the Signore to step up and let her draw him out. This he declined, pleading the fact that he had sound teeth. The *dentista* congratulated him, in spite of his teeth.

"But come!" said Bagswell; "look at that group of men and women in Albano costume; there is a chance to make a deuced good sketch."

Two men and three women were seated in a circle; they were laughing and talking, and cutting and eating large slices of raw ham and bread, while they passed from one to another a three-gallon keg of wine, and drank out of the bung. As one of the hearty, laughing, jolly, brown-eyed girls lifted up the keg, Caper pulled out sketch book and pencil to catch an outline sketch—of her head thrown back, her fine full throat and breast heaving as the red wine ran out of the barrel, and the half-closed, dreamy eyes, and pleasure in the face—as the wine slowly trickled down her throat. One of the men noted the artist making a *ritratto*, and laughing heartily, cried out: "Oh! but you'll have to pay us well for taking our portraits!" . . . And the girl, slowly finishing her long draught, looked merrily round, shook her finger at the artist, laughed, and—the sketch was finished. Then Caper, taking Rocjean's roses, went laughingly up to the girl with brown eyes and fine throat, in Albano costume, and begged that she would take the poor flowers, and, putting them next her heart, keep them where it is forever warm—" as the young man on your left knows very well!" he concluded. This speech was received amid loud applause and cheers, and thanks for the roses, and an invitation to take a pull at the barrel. Caper waved them *Adio;* and as our trio turned Rome-ward from the fair, the last things he saw as he turned his head to take a farewell look, were the roses that the Italian girl had placed next her heart.

The exceedingly interesting amusement known as the Tombola, is nothing more than the game of Loto, or *Lótto*, "Brobdignagified," and played in the open air of the Papal States, in Rome on Sundays—and in the Campagna on certain saints' days, come they when they may.

The English have made holiday from holy day, and call the

Lord's day Sunday; while the Italians call Sunday Lord's day, or *Doménica*. Their way of keeping it holy, however, with tombolas, horse races, and fireworks, strikes a heretic, to say the least, oddly.

The Roman tombola should be seen in the Piazza Navona democratically; in the Villa Borghese, if not aristocratically, at least middle-class-ically, or bourgeois-istically.

In the month of November, when the English drown themselves, and the Italians sit in the sun and smile, our friend Caper, one Sunday morning, putting his watch and purse where pickpockets could not reach them, walked with two or three friends down to the Piazza Navona, stopping, as he went along, at the entrance of a small street leading into it, to purchase a tombola ticket. The ticket-seller, seated behind a small table, a blank book, and piles of blank tickets, charged eleven *baiocchi* (cents) for a ticket, including one *baioccho* for registering it. We give below a copy of Caper's ticket:

No. 17 D'ORDINE, LETTERA C.				
CARTELLA DA RITENERSI DAL GIUOCATORE.				
8	12	32	87	60
20	4	76	30	11
45	3	90	55	63

The numbers on this ticket the registrar filled up, after which it was his duty to copy them in his book, and thus verify the ticket should it draw a prize.

The total amount to be played for that day, the tombola being for the benefit of the Cholera Orphans, was one thousand *scudi*, and was divided as follows:

Terno,	$50
Quaterno,	100
Cinquina,	200
Tombola,	650
	$1,000

How many tickets were issued, Caper was never able to find out; but he was told that for a one-thousand-dollar tombola the number was limited to ninety thousand.

The tickets, as will be seen above, are divided into three lines, with five divisions in each line, and you can fill up the fifteen divisions with any numbers, running from one to ninety, that you may see fit. Ninety tickets, with numbers from one to ninety, are put in a revolving glass barrel, and after being well shaken up, some one draws out one number at random (the slips of paper being rolled up in such a manner that the numbers on them cannot be seen). It is passed to the judges, and is then read aloud, and exposed to view, in conspicuous figures, on a stand or stands; and so on until the tombola is won or the numbers all drawn.

Whoever has three consecutive figures on a line, beginning from left hand to right, wins the *Terno;* if four consecutive figures, the *Quaterno;* if five figures, or a full line, the *Cinquina;* and whoever has all fifteen figures, wins the tombola. It often happens that several persons win the *Terno,* &c., at the same time, in which case the amount of the *Terno,* &c., is equally divided among them. These public tombolas are like too many thimble-rig tables, ostensibly started for charitable objects, and it is popularly whispered that the Roman nobility and heads of the Church purchase vast numbers of these tickets, and never fill them up; but then again, they are not large enough for shaving, and are too small for curl papers; besides, six hundred and fifty *scudi!* Whew!

The Piazza Navona, bearing on its face, on week-days, the most terrible eruptions of piles of old iron, rags, paintings, books, boots, vegetables, crockery, jackdaws, *contadini*, and occasional dead cats; wore, on the Sunday of the tombola—it was Advent Sunday—a clean, bright, and even joyful look. From many windows hung gay cloths and banners; the three fountains were making Roman pearls and diamonds of the first water; the entire length (seven hundred and fifty feet) and breadth of the square was filled with the Roman people; three bands of military music played uncensurable airs, since the public censor permitted them; and several companies of soldiers, with loaded guns, stood all ready to slaughter the *plebs*. It was a sublime spectacle.

But the curtain rose; that is to say, the tombola commenced. At a raised platform, a small boy, dressed in black, popularly supposed to be a cholera orphan, rolled back his shirt cuffs—he had a shirt—plunged his hand into the glass barrel, and produced a slip of paper; an assistant carried it to the judges—one resembled Mr. Pecksniff—and then the crier announced the number, and—presto!—on a large blackboard the number appeared, so that every one could see it.

Caper found the number on his ticket, and was marking it off, when a countryman at his side asked him if he would see if the number was on his ticket, as he could not read figures.

Caper accordingly looked it over, and finding that it was there, marked it off for him.

"*Padrone mio*, thank you," said the man, evidently determined, since he had found out a scholar, to keep close by him.

"Seventeen!" called out the tombola crier.

"C—o!" said the *contadino*, with joy in his face; "seventeen is always my lucky number. My wife was seventeen years old when I married her. My donkey was killed by the railroad cars the other day, and he gave just seventeen groans before he died. I shall have luck to-day."

We refrain from writing the exclamation the *contadino* prefaced his remarks with, for fear the reader might have a good Italian dictionary—an article, by the way, the writer has never yet seen. Suffice it to say, that the exclamations made use of by the Romans, men and women, not only of the lower, but even the middling class, are of a nature exceedingly natural, and plainly point to Bacchic and Phallic sources. The *bestémmia* of the Romans is viler than the blasphemy of English or Americans.

It happened that the countryman had a seventeen on his ticket, and Caper marked it off, at the same time asking him how much he would take for his pantaloons. These pantaloons were made of a goat's skin; the long white wool, inches in length, left on, and hanging down below the knees of the man, gave him a Pan-like look, and, with the word tombola, suggested the lines of that good old song—save the maledictory part of it:

> "Tombolin had no breeches to wear,
>   So he bought him a goat's skin, to make him a pair."

These breeches were not for sale; they were evidently the

joy and the pride of the countryman, who had no heart for trade, having by this time two numbers in one line marked off, only wanting an adjoining one to win the *terno*.

"If you were to win the *terno*, what would you do with it?" Caper asked him.

"*Accidente!* I'd buy a barrel of wine, and a hog, and a——"

"Thirty-two!" shouted the crier.

"It's on your paper," said Caper to him, marking it off; "and you've won the *terno!*"

The eyes of the man gleamed wildly; he crossed himself, grasped the paper, and the next thing Caper saw was the crowd dividing right and left, as the excited owner of the goatskin breeches made his way to the platform. When he had climbed up, and, stepping forward, stood ready to receive the *terno*, the crowd jeered and cheered the *villano*, making fine fun of his goatskin, and not a little jealous that a *contadino* should take the money out of the city.

"It's always so," said a fat man next to Caper; "these *villani* take the bread out of our mouths; but *ecco!* there is another man who has the *terno;* blessed be the Madonna, there is a third! Oh! *diavolo*, the *villano* will only have one third of the *terno;* and may he die of apoplexy!"

A vender of refreshments passing along, the fat man stopped him, and purchased a *baioccho's* worth of—what?

Pumpkin seeds! These are extensively eaten in Rome, as well as the seeds of pine cones, acorns, and round yellow chickpeas; they supply the place occupied by groundnuts in our more favored land.

There is this excitement about the tombolas in the Piazza

Navona, that occasionally a panic seizes the crowd, and, in the rush of people to escape from the square, some have their pockets picked, and some are trampled down, never to rise again. Fortunately for Caper, no stampede took place on Advent Sunday, so that he lived to attend another grand tombola in the Villa Borghese.

This was held in the spring time, and the promise of the ascension of a balloon added to the attractions of the lottery. To enter the villa, you had to purchase a tombola ticket, whereas, in the Piazza Navona, this was unnecessary. At one end of the amphitheatre of the villa, under the shade of the ilex trees, a platform was erected, where the numbers were called out and the awards given.

Caper, Rocjean, and another French artist, not of the French Academy, named Achille Légume, assisted at this entertainment. Légume was a very pleasant companion, lively, good natured, with a decided penchant for the pretty side of humanity, and continually haunted with the idea that a princess was to carry him off from his mistress in spectacles, Madame Art, and convey him to the land of Cocaigne, where they never make, only buy, paintings—of which articles, in parenthesis, Monsieur Achille had a number for sale.

"Rocjean," said Légume, "do you notice that distinguished lady on the platform; isn't she the Princess Faniente? She certainly looked at *me* very peculiarly a few minutes since."

"It is the princess," answered Rocjean; "and I also noticed, a few minutes since, when I was on the other side of the circus, that she looked at ME with an air."

"Don't quarrel," spoke Caper; "she probably regards you both equally, for—she squints."

This answer capsized Achille, who, having a small red rosebud in his buttonhole, hoped that at a distance he might pass for a chevalier of the Legion of Honor, and had conquered something, say something noble.

A wandering cigar-seller, with *zigarri scelti*, next demanded their attention, and Rocjean commenced an inspection of the selected cigars, which are made by government, and sold at the fixed price of one and a half *baiocchi* each; even at this low price, the stock of the tobacco factory paid thirteen per cent. under Antonelli's direction.

"Antonelli makes a pretty fair cigar," said Rocjean; "but I wish he would wrap the ends a little tighter. I'm sorry to hear he is going out of the business."

"Why, he would stay in," answered Caper, "but what with baking all the bread for Rome, and attending to all the firewood sold, and trying to make Ostia a seaport, and having to fight Monsieur About, and looking after his lotteries and big pawnbroker's shop, and balancing himself on the end of a very sharp French bayonet, his time is so occupied, he cannot roll these cigars so well as they ought to be rolled. . . . But they have called out number forty-nine; you've got it, Légume; I remember you wrote it down. Yes, there it is."

"Forty-nine!"

"I wonder they dare call out '49 in this villa; or have the people forgotten the revolution already—forgotten that this spot was made ready for a battle ground for liberty? The public censor knows his business: give the Romans bread, and the circus or tombola, they will be content—forever!"

"*Au diable* with politics," interrupted Achille. "What a very pretty girl that is alongside you, Caper. Look at her:

how nicely that costume fits her, the red boddice especially! Where, except in Italy, do you ever see such fine black eyes, and such a splendid head of coal-black hair? This way of having Italian nurses dressed in the Albano costume is very fine. That little boy with her is English, certainly."

"Och! Master Jamey, come in out of that grane grass; d'yiz want ter dirty the clane pinafore I've put on yiz this blissed afthernoon?" spoke the nurse.

"In the name of all that's awful, what kind of Italian is she speaking?" asked Légume of Caper.

"Irish-English," he answered; "she is not the first woman out of Old Ireland masquerading as an Albanian nurse. She probably belongs to some English family who have pretensions."

"Ah, bah!" said Légume; "it's monstrous—perfectly atrocious! ugh! Let us make a little tour of a walk. The tombola is finished. An Irish dressed up as an Italian—execrable!"

CHAPTER V.

THE Café Greco, like the belle of many seasons, lights up best at night. In morning, in *deshabille*, not all the venerability of its age can make it respectable. Caper declares that on a fresh, sparkling day, in the merry spring time, he once really enjoyed a very early breakfast there; and that, with the windows of the Omnibus room open, the fresh air blowing in, and the sight of a pretty girl at the fourth-story window of a neighboring house, feeding a bird and tending a rosebush, the café was rose colored.

This may be so; but seven o'clock in the evening was *the* time when the Greco was in its prime. Then the front room was filled with Germans, the second room with Russians and English, the third room—the Omnibus—with Americans, English, and French, and the fourth, or back room, was brown with Spaniards. The Italians were there, in one or two rooms, but in a minority; only those who affected the English showed themselves, and aired their knowledge of the Anglo-Saxon tongue and habits.

"I habituate myself," said a red-haired Italian of the Greco to Caper, "to the English customs. I myself lave with hot water from foot to head, one time in three weeks, like the English. It is an idea of the most superb, and they tell me I am truly English for so performing. I have not yet arrive to perfection in the lessons of box, but I have a smart cove of a booldog."

Caper told him that his resemblance to an English "gent" was perfect, at which the Italian, ignorant of the meaning of that fearful word, smiled assent.

The waiter has hardly brought you your small cup of *caffè nero*, and you are preparing to light a cigar, to smoke while you drink your coffee, when there comes before you a wandering bouquet-seller. It is, perhaps, the dead of winter; long icicles are hanging from fountains, over which hang frosted oranges, frozen myrtles, and frost-nipped olives. Alas! such things are seen in Rome; and yet, for a dime, you are offered a bouquet of camellia japonicas. By the way, the name camellia is derived from *Camellas*, a learned Jesuit; probably *La Dame aux Camélias* had not a similar origin. You don't want the flowers.

"Signore," says the man, "behold a ruined flower-merchant!"

You are unmoved. Have you not seen or heard of, many a time, the heaviest kind of flour merchants ruined by too heavy speculations, burst up so high the crows couldn't fly to them; and heard this without changing a muscle of your face?

"But, signore, do buy a bouquet to please your lady."

"Haven't one."

"*Altro!*" answers the man, triumphantly, "whom did I see the other day, with these eyes (pointing at his own), in a magnificent carriage, beside the most beautiful *Donna Inglesa* in Rome? *Iddio giusto!*" . . . At this period, he sees he has made a ten strike, and at once follows it up by knocking down the tenpin boy, so as to clear the alley, thus: "For *her* sake, signore."

You pay a *paul* (and give the bouquet to—your landlady's daughter), while the departing *mercante di fiori* assures you that he never, no, never expects to make a fortune at flowers; but if he gains enough to pay for his wine, he will be very tipsy as long as he lives!

Then comes an old man, with a chess board of inlaid stone, which he hasn't an idea of selling; but finds it excellent to "move on," without being checkmated as a beggar without visible means of s'port. The first time he brought it round, and held it out square to Caper, that cool young man, taking a handful of coppers from his pocket, arranged them as checkers on the board, without taking any notice of the man; and, after he had placed them, began playing deliberately. He rested his chin on his hand, and, with knitted brows, studied several intricate moves; he finally jumped the men, so as to leave a copper or two on the board; and bidding the old man good night, continued a conversation with Rocjean, commenced previous to his game of draughts.

Next approaches a hardware merchant, for, in Imperial Rome, the peddler of a colder clime is a merchant, the shoemaker an artist, the artist a professor. The hardware man looks as if he might be "touter" to a broken-down brigand. All the razors in his box couldn't keep the small part of his face that is shaved from wearing a look as if it had been blown up with gunpowder, while the grains had remained embedded there. He tempts you with a wicked-looking knife, the pattern for which must have come from the *lituus* of Etruria, the land called the *mother of superstitions*, and have been wielded for auguries amid the howls and groans of lucomones and priests. He tells you it is a Campagna knife, and that you must have one if you go into that benighted region; he says this with a mysterious shake of his head, as if he had known Fra Diavolo in his childhood, and Fra 'Tonelli in his riper years. The crescent-shaped handle is of black bone; the pointed blade long and tapering; the three notches in its back catch into the spring with a noise like the alarum of a rattlesnake. You conclude to buy one—for a curiosity. You ask why the blade at the point finishes off in a circle? He tells you the government forbids the sale of sharp-pointed knives; *but*, signore, if you wish to *use it*, break off the circle under your heel, and you have a point sharp enough to make any man have an *accidente di freddo* (death from cold—steel).

Victor Hugo might have taken his character of Quasimodo from the wild figure who now enters the Greco, with a pair of horns for sale; each horn is nearly a yard in length, black and white in color; they have been polished by the hunchback until they shine like glass. Now he approaches you, and with deep, rough voice, reminding you of the lowing of the large gray oxen they once belonged to, begs you to buy them. Then he facetiously raises one to each side of his head, and you have a figure that Jerome Bosch would have rejoiced to transfer to canvas. His portrait has been painted by more than one artist.

Caper, sitting in the Omnibus one evening with Rocjean, was accosted by a very seedy-looking man, with a very peculiar expression of face, wherein an awful struggle of humor to crowd down pinching poverty gleamed brightly. He offered for sale an odd volume of one of the early fathers of the Church. Its probable value was a dime, whereas he wanted two dollars for it.

"Why do you ask such a price?" asked Rocjean; "you never can expect to sell it for a twentieth part of that."

"The moral of which," said the seedy man, no longer containing the struggling humor, but letting it out with a hearty laugh, "the moral of which is—give me half a *baiocco!*"

Ever after that, Caper never saw the man, who henceforth went by the name of *La Morale é un Mezzo Baiocco!* without pointing the moral with a copper coin. Not content with this, he once took him round to the *Lepre* restaurant, and ordered a right good supper for him. Several other artists were with him, and all declared that no one could do better justice to food and wine. After he had eaten all he could hold, and drank a little more than he could carry, he arose from the table, having during the entire meal sensibly kept silence, and, wiping his mouth on his coat sleeve, spoke:

"The moral, this evening, signori, I shall carry home in my stomach."

As he was going out of the restaurant, one of the artists asked him why he left two rolls of bread on the table; saying they were paid for, and belonged to him.

"I left them," said he, "out of regard for the correct usages of society; but, having shown this, I return to pocket them."

This he did at once, and Caper stood astonished at the seedy beggar's phraseology.

In addition to these characters, wandering musicians find their way into the café, jugglers, peddlers of Roman mosaics and jewelry, plaster casts and sponges, perfumery and paint brushes. Or a peripatetic shoemaker, with one pair of shoes, which he recklessly offers for sale to giant or dwarf. One morning he found a purchaser—a French artist—who put them on, and threw away his old shoes. Fatal mistake. Two hours afterward, the buyer was back in the Greco, with both big toes sticking out of the ends of his new shoes, looking for that *cochon* of a shoemaker.

To those who read men like books, the Greco offers a valuable circulating library. The advantage, too, of these artistical works is, that one needs not be a Mezzofanti to read the Russian, Spanish, German, French, Italian, English, and other faces that pass before one panoramically. There sits a relation of a hospodar, drinking Russian tea; he pours into a large cup a small glass of brandy, throws in a slice of lemon, fills up with hot tea. Do you think of the miles he has travelled, in a *telega*, over snow-covered steppes, and the smoking *samovar* of tea that awaited him, his journey for the day ended? Had he lived when painting and sculpture were in their ripe prime, what a fiery life he would have thrown into his works! As it is, he drinks cognac, hunts wild boars in the Pontine marshes —and paints Samson and Delilah, after models.

The Spanish artist, over a cup of chocolate, has lovely dreams, of burnt umber hue, and despises the neglected treasures left him by the Moors, while he seeks gold in— castles in the air.

The German, with feet in Italy and head far away in the Fatherland, frequents the German club in preference to the Greco; for at the club is there not lager beer? . . . In Imperial Rome, there are lager-beer breweries! He has the profundities of the aesthetical in art at his finger ends; it is deep-sea fishing, and he occasionally lands a whale, as Kaulbach has done; or very nearly catches a mermaid with Cornelius. Let us respect the man—he *works*.

The French artist, over a cup of black coffee, with perhaps a small glass of cognac, is the lightning to the German thunder. If he were asked to paint the portrait of a potato, he would make eyes about it, and then give you a little picture fit to adorn a boudoir. He does everything with a flourish. If he has never painted Nero performing that celebrated violin solo over Rome, it is because he despaired of conveying an idea of the tremulous flourish of the fiddle bow. He reads Nature, and translates her, without understanding her. He will prove to you that the cattle of Rosa Bonheur are those of the fields, while he will object to Landseer that his beasts are those of the guinea cattle-show. He blows up grand facts in the science of art with gunpowder, while the English dig them out with a shovel, and the Germans bore for them. He finds Raphael, king of pastel artists, and never mentions his discovery to the English. He is more dangerous with the *fleurette*, than many a trooper with broadsword. Everything that he appropriates, he stamps with the character of his own nationality. The English race-horse at Chantilly has an air of curl papers about his mane and tail.

The Italian artist—the night season is for sleep.

The English artist—hearken to Ruskin on Turner! When one has hit the bull's eye, there is nothing left but to lay down the gun, and go and have—a whitebait dinner.

The American artist—there is danger of the youthful giant kicking out the end of the Cradle of Art, and "scatterlophisticating rampageously" over all the nursery.

"I'd jest give a hun-dred dol-lars t'morrow, ef I could find out a way to cut stat-tures by steam," said Chapin, the sculptor.

"I can't see why a country with great rivers, great mountains, and great institutions generally, cannot produce great sculptors and painters," said Caper, sharply, one day to Rocjean.

"It is this very greatness," answered Rocjean, "that prevents it. The aim of the people runs not in the narrow channel of a mountain stream, but with the broad tide of the ocean. In the hands of Providence, other lands in other times have taken up painting and sculpture with their whole might, and have wielded them to advance civilization. They have played—are playing their part, these civilizers; but they are no longer chief actors, least of all in America. Painting and sculpture may take the character of subjects there; but their rôle as king is—played out."

"Much as you know about it," answered Caper, "you are all theory!"

"That may be," quoth Rocjean; "you know what ΘΕΟΣ means in Greek, don't you?"

There came to Rome, in the autumn, along with the other travellers, a caravan of wild beasts, ostensibly under charge of Monsieur Charles, the celebrated Tamer, rendered illustrious and illustrated by Nadar and Gustave Doré, in the *Journal pour Rire*. They were exhibited under a canvas tent in the Piazza Popolo, and a very cold time they had of it during the winter. Evidently, Monsieur Charles believed the climate of Italy belonged to the temperance society of climates. He erred, and suffered with his "*superbe et manufique* ÉLLLLLÉ-

PHANT!" "And when we reflec', ladies *and* gentlemen, that there *are* persons, forty and even fifty years old, who have never seen the Ellllephant!!! . . . and who DARE TO SAY SO!!! . . ." Monsieur Charles made his explanations with teeth chattering.

Caper, anxious to make a sketch of a very fine Bengal tiger in the collection, easily purchased permission to make studies of the animals during the hours when the exhibition was closed to the public; and as he went at everything vigorously, he was before long in possession of several fine sketches of the tiger, and other beasts, besides several secrets only known to the initiated, who act as keepers.

The royal Bengal tiger was one of the finest beasts Caper had ever seen; and what he particularly admired, was the jet-black lustre of the stripes on his tawny sides, and the vivid lustre of his eyes. The lion curiously seemed laboring under a heavy sleep at the very time when he should have been awake; but then his mane was kept in admirable order. The hair round his face stood out like the bristles of a shoe brush, and there was a curl in the knob of hair at the end of his tail that amply compensated for his inactivity. The hyenas looked sleek and happy, and their teeth were remarkably white; but the elephant was the constant wonder of all beholders. Instead of the tawny, blue-gray color of most of his species, he was black, and glistened like a patent-leather boot; while his tusks were as white as—ivory; yea, more so.

"I don't understand what makes your animals look so bright," said Caper, one day, to one of the keepers.

"Come here to-morrow morning early, when we make their toilettes, and you'll see," replied the man, laughing.

"Why, there's that old hog of a lion, he's as savage and snaptious, before he has his medicine, as a corporal; and looks as old as Methusaleh, until we arrange his beard, and get him up for the day. As for the Elllephant . . . ugh!"

Caper's curiosity was aroused, and the next morning, early, he was in the menagerie. The first sight that struck his eye was the elephant, keeled over on one side, and weaving his trunk about, evidently as a signal of distress; while his keeper and another man were—blacking pot and shoe brushes in hand—going all over him from stem to stern.

"Good day," said the keeper to him; "here's a pair of boots for you! put outside the door to be blacked every morning, for five francs a day. It's the dearest job I ever undertook . . . and the boots are ungrateful! Here, Pierre," he continued to the man who helped him, "he shines enough; take away the breshes, and bring me the sand paper, to rub up his tusks. Talk about polished beasts! I believe, myself, that we beat all other shows to pieces on this 'ere point. Some beasts are more knowing than others; for example, them monkeys in that cage there. Give that big fool of a shimpanzy that bresh, Pierre, and let the gen'leman see him operate on tother monkeys."

Pierre gave the large monkey a brush, and, to Caper's astonishment, he saw the animal seize it with one paw, then, springing forward, catch a small monkey with the other paw, and, holding him down, in spite of his struggles, administer so complete a brushing over his entire body, that every hair received a touch. The other monkeys in the cage were in the wildest state of excitement, evidently knowing from experience that they would all have to pass under the large one's hands; and when he had given a final polish to the small one, he commenced a vigorous chase for his mate, an aged female, who, evidently disliking the ordeal, commenced a series of ground and lofty tumblings that would have made the fortune of even the distinguished—Léotard. In vain: after a prolonged chase, in which the inhabitants of the cage flew round so fast that it appeared to be full of flying legs, tails, and fur, the large monkey seized the female, and, regardless of her attempts to liberate herself, he brushed her from head to foot, to the great delight of a Swiss soldier, an infantry corporal, who had entered the menagerie a few minutes before the grand hunt commenced.

"*Ma voi!*" said the Swiss, pronouncing French with a broad German accent; "it would keef me krate bleshur to have dat pig monkey in my gombany. He would mak' virst rait brivate."

The keeper, who was still polishing away with sand paper at the elephant's tusks, and who evidently regarded the soldier with great contempt, said to him:

"He would have been there long since—only he knows too much."

"*Ma voi!* that's the reason you're draining him vor a Vrench gavalry gombany. Vell, I likes dat."

"Oh! no," said the keeper; "his principles an't going to allow him to enter our army."

"Vell, what are his brincibles?"

"To serve those who pay best!" quoth the Frenchman, who, in the firm faith that he had said a good thing, called Pierre to help him adorn the lion, and turned his back on the Swiss, who, in revenge, amused himself feeding the monkeys with an old button, a stump of a cigar, and various wads of paper.

The keeper then gave the lion a narcotic, and, after this medicine, combed out his mane and tail, waxed his moustache, and thus made his toilette for the day. The tiger and leopards had their stripes and spots touched up once a week with hair dye, and as this was not the day appointed, Caper missed this part of the exhibition. The hyenas submitted to be brushed down; but showed strong symptoms of mutiny at having their teeth rubbed with a tooth brush, and their nails pared.

In half an hour more, the keeper's labors were over, and Caper, giving him a present for his inviting him to assist as spectator at *la toilette bien bête*, or beastly dressing, walked off to breakfast, evidently thinking that *Art* was not dead in that menagerie, whatever Rocjean might say of its state of health in the world at large.

"To think," soliloquized Caper, "to think of what a bootless thing it is, to shoe-black o'er an elephant!"

The traveller visiting Rome notices in the Piazza di Spagna, along the Spanish steps, and in the Condotti, Fratina, and Sistina streets, either sunning themselves or slowly sauntering along, many picturesquely-dressed men, women, and children, who, as he soon learns, are the professional models of the artists. For a fee of from fifty cents to a dollar, they will give their professional services for a sitting four hours in length; and those of them who are most in demand find little difficulty, during the "business season," say from the months of November to May, in earning from one and a half to two dollars, and even more, every day. Many of them, living frugally, manage to make what is considered a fortune among the *contadini* in a few years; and Hawks, the English artist, who spent a summer at Saracenesca, found, to his astonishment, that one of the leading men of the town, one who loaned money at very large interest, owned property, and who was numbered among the heavy wealthy, was no other than a certain Gaetano he had more than once used as model, at the price of fifty cents a sitting.

The government prohibiting female models from posing nude in the different life schools, it consequently follows that they pose in private studios, as they choose. This interdiction does not extend to the male models; and when Caper was in Rome, he had full opportunities offered him to draw from these in the English Academy, and in the private schools of Gigi and Giacinti. Supported by the British Government, the English artist has, free of all expense, at this truly National Academy, opportunities to sketch from life, as well as from casts, and has, moreover, access to a well-chosen library of books. With a generosity worthy of all praise, American artists are admitted to the English Academy, with full permission to share with Englishmen the advantages of the life school, free of all cost; a piece of liberality that well might be copied by the French Academy, without at all derogating from its high position—on the Pincian Hill.

If Gigi's school is still kept up (it was in a small street near the Trevi fountain), we would advise the traveller in search of the picturesque by all means to visit it, particularly if it is in the same location it was when Caper was there. It was over a stable, in the second story of a tumbledown old house, frequented by dogs, cats, fleas, and rats; in a room say fifty feet long by twenty wide. A semicircle of desks and wooden benches went round the platform, where stood the male models nude, or, on other evenings, male and female models in costumes, Roman or Neapolitan. Oil lamps gave enough light to enable the artists who generally attended there to draw, and color, in oils or water colors, the costumes. The price of admittance for the costume class was one *paul* (ten cents), and as the model only posed about two hours, the artists had to work very fast to get even a rough sketch finished in that short time. Americans, Danes, Germans, Spaniards, French, Italians, English, Russians, were numbered among the attendants, and, more than once, a sedate-looking English-woman or two would come in quietly, make a sketch, and go away unmolested, and almost unnoticed.

More than three quarters of the sketches made by Caper at Gigi's costume class were taken from models in standing positions. At the end of the first hour, they had from ten to fifteen minutes allowed them to rest; but these minutes were seldom wasted by the artist, who improved them to finish the lines of his drawing, or dash in color. The powers of endurance of the female models were better than those of the men; and they would strike a position and keep it for an hour, almost immovable. Noticeable among these women was one named Minacucci, who, though over seventy years old, had all the animation and spirit of one not half her age, and would keep her position with the steadiness of a statue. She had, in her younger days, been a model for Canova; had outlived two generations; and was now posing for a third. If you have ever seen many figure paintings executed in Rome, your chance is good to have seen Minacucci's portrait over and over again. Caper affirms that of any painting made in Rome from the years 1856 to 1860, introducing an Italian head, whether a Madonna or sausage seller, he can tell you the name of the model it was painted from nine times out of ten! The fact is, they do want a new model for the Madonna badly in Rome; for Giacinta is growing old and fat, and Stella, since she married that cobbler, has lost her angelic expression. The small boy who used to pose for angels has smoked himself too yellow, and the man who stood for Charity has gone out of business.

"I have," said Caper to me the other day, "too much respect for the public to tell them who the man with red hair and beard used to pose for; but he has taken to drinking, and it's all up with him."

Spite of fleas, rats, squalling cats, dog fights, squealing of horses, and braying of donkeys, lamp smoke, and heat or cold, the hours passed by Caper in Gigi's old barracks were among the pleasantest of his Roman life. There was such novelty, variety, and brilliancy in the costumes to be sketched, that every evening was a surprise; save those nights when Stella posed, and these were known and looked forward to in advance. She always insured a full class, and, when she first appeared, was the beauty of all the models.

Caper was sitting one afternoon in Rocjean's studio, when there was a tap at the door.

"*Entrate!*" shouted Rocjean, and in came a female model, called Rita. It was the month of May; business was dull; she wanted employment. Rocjean asked her to walk in, and rest herself.

"Well, Rita, you haven't anything to do, now that the English have all fled from Rome before the malaria?"

"Very little. Some of the Russians are left up there in the Fratina; but since the Signore Giovanni sold all his paintings to that rich Russian banker, *diavolo!* he has done nothing but drink champagne, and he don't want any more models."

"What is the Signore Giovanni's last name?" asked Caper.

"Who knows, Signore Giacomo? I don't. We others (*noi altri*) never can pronounce your queer names, so we find out the Italian for your first name, and call you by that. Signore Arturo, the French artist, told me once that the English and Russians and Germans had such hard names, they often broke their front teeth out trying to speak them; but he was joking. *I* know the real, true reason for it."

"Come, let us have it," said Rocjean.

"*Accidente!* I won't tell you; you will be angry."

"No, we won't," spoke Caper; "and what is more, I will give you two *pauls* if you will tell us. I am very curious to know this reason."

"*Bene*, now the *prete* came round to see me the other day; it was when he purified the house with holy water; and he asked me a great many questions, which I answered so artlessly, yes, *so* artlessly! whew! [here Miss Rita smiled artfully]. Then he asked me all about you heretics, and he told me you were all going to—be burned up, as soon as you died; for the Inquisition couldn't do it for you in these degenerate days. After a great deal more twaddle like this, I asked him why you heretics all had such hard names, that we others never could speak them? Then he looked mysterious—so! [here Miss Rita diabolically winked one eye,] and said he, 'I will tell you, *per Bacco!* hush—it's because they are so abominably wicked, never give anything to OUR Church, never have no holy water in their houses, never go to no confession, and are such monsters generally, that their police are all the time busy trying to catch them; but their names are so hard to speak, that when the police go and ask for them, nobody knows them, and so they get off; otherwise, their country would have jails in it as large as St. Peter's, and they would be full all the time!"

"H'm!" said Rocjean; "I suppose you would be afraid to go to such horrible countries, among such people?"

"Not I," spoke Rita. "Didn't Ida go to Paris, and didn't she come back to Rome with such a magnificent silk dress, and gold watch, and such a bonnet! all full of flowers, and lace, and ribbons? Oh! they don't eat 'nothing but maccaroni' there! And they don't have priests all the time sneaking round to keep a poor girl from earning a little money honestly, and haul her up before the police if her *carta di soggiorno* [permit to remain in Rome] runs out. I wish [here Rita stamped her foot, and her eyes flashed] Garibaldi would come here! Then you would see these black crows flying, *Iddio giusto!* Then we would have no more of these *arciprete* making us pay them for every mouthful of bread we eat, or wine we drink, or wood we burn."

"Why," said Caper, "they don't keep the baker shops, and wineshops, and woodyards, do they?"

"No," answered Rita, "but they speculate in them, and Fra 'Tonelli makes his cousins, and so on, inspectors; and they regulate the prices to suit themselves, and make, oh! such tre-men-du-ous fortunes. [Here Rita opened her eyes, and spread her hands, as if beholding the elephant.] Don't I remember, some time ago, how, when the Pope went out riding, he found both sides of the way, from the Vatican to San Angelo, crowded with people on their knees, groaning, and calling to him. Said he to Fra 'Tonelli:

"'What are these poor people about?'

"'Praying for your blessed holiness,' said he, while his eyes sparkled.

"'But,' said the Pope, 'they are moaning and groaning.'

"'It's a way the *poblaccio* have,' answered 'Tonelli, 'when they pray.'

"The Pope knew he was lying, so, when he went home to the Vatican, he sent for one of his faithful servants, and said he:

"'Santi, you run out and see what all this shindy is about.'

"So Santi came back, and told him 'Tonelli had put up the price of bread, and the people were starving. So the Pope took out a big purse with a little money in it, and said he:

"'Here, Santi, you go and buy me ten pounds of bread and get a bill for it, and have it receipted!'

"So Santi came back with bread, and bill all receipted, and laid it down on a table, and threw a cloth over it. By and by, in comes 'Tonelli. Then the Pope says to him, kindly, and smiling:

"'I am confident I heard the people crying about bread to-day; now, tell me truly, what is it selling for?'

"Then 'Tonelli told him such a lie! [Up went Rita's hands and eyes.]

"Then the Pope says, while he looked so [knitting her brows]:

"'Oblige me, if you please, by lifting up that cloth.'

"And 'Tonelli did.

"Bread went down six *baiocchi* next morning!"

"By the way, Rita," asked Rocjean, "where is your little brother, Beppo?"

"Oh! he's home," she answered; "but I wish you would ask your friend Enrico, the German sculptor, if he won't have him again, for his model."

"Why, I thought he was using him for his new statue?"

"He was; but, oh! so unfortunately, last Sunday, father went out to see his cousin John, who lives near Ponte Mole, and has a garden there, and Beppo went with him; but the dear little fellow is so fond of fruit, that he ate a pint of raw horse-beans!"

"Of all the fruit!" shouted Caper.

"*Si, signore*, it's splendid; but it gave Beppo the colic next day, and when he went to Signore Enrico's studio to pose for Cupid, he twisted and wrenched around so with pain, that Signore Enrico told him he looked more like a little devil than a small love; and when Beppo told him what fruit he had been eating, Signore Enrico bid him clear out for a savage that he was, and told him to go and learn to eat them boiled! before he came back again."

"I will speak to the Signore Enrico, and have him employ him again," said Rocjean.

"Oh! I wish you would, for the Signore Enrico was very good to Beppo; besides, his studio is a perfect palace for cigar stumps, which Beppo used to pick up and sell—that is, all those he and father didn't smoke in their pipes."

"Make a sketch, Caper," said Rocjean, "of Cupid filling up his quiver with cigar stumps, while he holds one between his teeth. There's a model love for you! Now, give Rita those two *pauls* you promised her, and let her go. *Adio!*"

GIULIA DI SEGNI.

(Lines found written on the back of a sketch in Caper's portfolio.)

By Roman watch-tower, on the mountain top,
We stood, at sunset, gazing like the eagles
From their cloud-eyrie, o'er the broad Campagna,
To the Albanian hills, which boldly rose,
Bathed in a flood of red and pearly light.
Far off, and fading in the coming night,
Lay the Abruzzi, where the pale, white walls
Of towns gleamed faintly on their purple sides.

The evening air was tremulous with sounds—
The thrilling chirp of insects, twittering birds,
Barking of shepherds' fierce, white, Roman dogs;
While from the narrow path, far down below,
We heard a mournful rondinella ring,
Sung by a home-returning mountaineer.

Then, as the daylight slowly climbed the hills,
And the soft wind breathed music to their steps,
O'er the old Roman watch-tower marched the stars,
In their bright legions—conquerors of night—
Shedding from silver armor shining light;
As once the Roman legions, ages past,
Marched on to conquest o'er the Latin way,
Gleaming, white stoned, so far beneath our gaze.

GIULIA DI SEGNI, 'mid the Volscians born,
Streamed in thy veins that fiery, Roman blood,
Curled thy proud lip, and fired thy eagle eyes.
Faultless in beauty, as the noble forms

> Painted on rare Etrurian vase of old;
> How life, ennobled by thy love, swept on,
> Serene, above the mean and pitiful!
> Stars! that still sparkle o'er old Segni's walls,
> Oh! mirror back to me one glance from eyes
> That yet may watch you from that Roman tower.

Caper's uncle, from St. Louis, Mr. William Browne, one day astonished several artists who were dining with him:

"My young men," said he, "there is one thing pleases me very much about you all, and that is, you never mention the word Art; don't seem to care anything more about the old masters, than I would about a lot of old wornout broomsticks; and if I didn't know I was with artists in Rome, the crib—no, what d'ye call it?"

"The manger?" suggested Rocjean.

"Yes," continued Uncle Bill, "the manger of art—I should think I was among a lot of smart merchants, who had gone into the painting business determined to do a right good trade."

"Cash on delivery," added Caper.

"Yes, be sure of that. Well, I like it; I feel at home with you; and as I always make it a point to encourage young business men, I am going to do my duty by one of you, at any rate. I shan't show favor to my nephew, Jim, any more than I do to the rest. And this is my plan: I want a painting, five feet by two, to fill up a place in my house in St. Louis. It's an odd shape, and that is so much in my favor, because you haven't any of you a painting that size under way, and can all start even. I'll leave the subject to each one of you, and I'll pay five hundred dollars to the man who paints the best picture, who has his done within seven days, *and puts the most work on it!* Do you all understand?"

They replied affirmatively.

"But what the thunder," asked Caper, "are those of us who don't win the prize, going to do with paintings of such a size, left on our hands? Nobody, unless a steamboat captain, who wants to ornament his berths, just that size, and relieve the tedium of his passengers, would ever think of buying them."

"Well," replied Uncle Bill, "I don't want smart young men like you all, to lose your time and money; so I'll buy the balance of the paintings for what the canvas and paints cost, and give two dollars a day for the seven days employed on each painting. Isn't that liberal?"

"Like Cosmo de Medici," answered Rocjean; "and I agree to the terms in every particular, especially as to putting the most work on it! There are four competitors—put down their names. Légume, you will come in, won't you?"

"Certainly I will, by jing!" answered the French artist, who prided himself on his knowledge of English, especially the interjections.

"Then," continued Rocjean, "Caper, Bagswell, Légume, and I, will try for your five-hundred-dollar prize. When shall we commence?"

"To-day is Tuesday," replied Uncle Bill; "say next Monday—that will give you plenty of time to get your frames and canvases. So that ends all particulars. There are two friends of mine here from the United States—one, Mr. Van Brick, of New York, and the other, Mr. Pinchfip, of Philadelphia—whom I think you all met here last week."

"The thin gentleman with hair very much brushed, be gad?" asked Légume.

"I don't remember as to his hair," answered Uncle Bill, "but that's the man. Well, these two, I know, will act as vampires, and I am sure you will be pleased with their verdict. Monday after next, therefore, we will all call; so be ready."

The four artists took the whole thing as a joke, but determined to paint the pictures; and, at Caper's suggestion, each one agreed, as there was a play of words in the clause, "most work on it," to puzzle Uncle Bill, and have the laugh on him.

On the day appointed to decide the prize, Uncle Bill, accompanied by Messrs. Van Brick and Pinchfip, called first at Légume's studio. They found him in the Via Margutta (in English, Malicious street), in a light, airy room, furnished with a striking attention to effect. On his easel was a painting of the required size, representing Louis XV. at Versailles, surrounded by his lady friends. By making the figures of the ladies small, and crowding them, Légume managed to get a hundred or two on the canvas. A period in their history to which Frenchmen refer with so much pleasure, and with which they are so conversant, was treated by the artist with professional zeal. The merits of the painting were carefully canvassed by the two judges. Mr. Pinchfip found it exceedingly graceful, neat, and pretty. Mr. Van Brick admired the females, remarking that he should like to be in old Louis's place. To which Légume bowed, asserting that he was sure he was in every way qualified to fill it. Mr. Van Brick determined in his mind to give the artist a dinner, at Spillman's, for that speech.

Mr. Pinchfip took notes in a book; Mr. Van Brick asked

for a light to a cigar. The former congratulated the artist; the latter at once asked him to come and dine with him. Mr. Pinchfip wished to know if he was related to the Count Légume whom he had met at Paris. Mr. Van Brick told him he would bring his friend Livingston round to buy a painting. Mr. Pinchfip said that it would afford him pleasure to call again. Mr. Van Brick gave the artist his card, and shook hands with him . . . and the judges were passing out, when Légume asked them to take one final look at the painting, to see if it had not the *most work* on it. Mr. Van Brick instantly turned toward it, and running over it with his eye, burst into an uncontrollable fit of laughter.

"If the others beat that, I am mistaken," said he. "Look at there!" calling the attention of Uncle Bill and Mr. Pinchfip to a fold of a curtain, on which was painted, in small letters:

"MOST WORK."

"I say, Browne," continued Mr. Van Brick, "he is too many for you; and if the one who puts 'most work' on his painting is to win the five hundred dollars, Légume's chance is good."

"Very ingenious," said Mr. Pinchfip, "very; it's a legitimate play upon words. But legally, I cannot affirm that I am aware of any precedent for awarding Mr. Browne's money to Monsieur Légume on this score."

"We will have to make a precedent, then," spoke Van Brick, "and do it illegally, if we find that he deserves the money. But time flies, and we have the other artists to visit."

They next went to Bagswell's studio, in the Viccolo dei Greci, and found him in a large room, well furnished, and having a solidly comfortable look; the walls ornamented with paintings, sketches, costumes, armor; while, in a good light under its one large window, was his painting. They found he had left his beaten track of historical subjects, and in the *genre* school had an interior of an Italian country inn—a kitchen scene. It represented a stout, handsome country girl, in Ciociara costume, kneading a large trough of dough, while another girl was filling pans with that which was already kneaded, and two or three other females were carrying them to an oven, tended by a man who was piling brushwood on the fire. The painting was very lifelike, and, for the short time employed on it, well finished. It wanted the fire and dash of Légume's painting, but its truthfulness to life evidently made a deep impression on Uncle Bill. Stuck on with a sketching tack to one corner was a piece of paper, on which was marked the number of hours employed each day on the work; it summed up fifty-four hours, or an average each day of nearly eight hours' work on it.

Mr. Pinchfip's note book was again called into play. Mr. Van Brick had another cigar to smoke, remarking that the artist had triple work in his picture—head, bread, and prize work: his picture representing working in, over, and for bread!

They next went to see Rocjean, in the Corso. They found him in a bournouse, with a fez on his head, a long chibouk in his mouth, smoking away, extended at full length on a settee, which he insisted was a divan. There was a glass bottle holding half a gallon of red wine on a table near him; also a bottle of Marsala, and half a dozen glasses. There was a roaring wood-fire in his stove—for it was December, and the day was overcast and cool.

"This is the most out-and-out comfortable old nest I've seen in Rome," said Mr. Van Brick, as they entered; "and as for curiosities and plunder, you beat Barnum. *Will I take a glass of wine?* I am there!"

Rocjean filled up glasses. Mr. Pinchfip declining, as he never drank before dinner, neither did he smoke before dinner. He told them that the late Doctor Phyzgig, who had always been their (the Pinchfips') family physician, had absolutely forbidden it.

No one made any remark to this, unless Mr. Van Brick's expressive face could be translated as observing, in a quiet manner, that the late Doctor was possibly dyspeptic, and probably nervous. Rocjean's painting represented a view of the Claudian aqueduct, mountains in the distance; bold foreground, shepherd with flocks, a wayside shrine, peasants kneeling in front of it. Over all, bold cloud effects. A very ponderous volume, balanced on top of the picture and leaning against the easel, invited Uncle Bill's attention, and he asked Rocjean why he had put it there? The artist answered, that it was a folio copy of *Josephus*, his works; and, as he was anxious to comply with the terms of Mr. Browne, he had placed it there in order to put the *most work* on it.

Mr. Pinchfip having asked Rocjean why, in placing that book there, he was like a passenger paying his fare to the driver of an omnibus?

The latter at once answered:

"I give it up."

"So you do," replied Pinchfip. "You are quick, sir, at answering conundrums."

Mr. Brick saw it. Finally Uncle Bill was made to comprehend.

"Very excellent, sir; very ingenious! Philadelphians may well be proud of the high position they have as punsters, utterers of *bon mots* and conundrums," said Rocjean. "I have had the comfort of living in your city, and thoroughly appreciating your—markets."

After Rocjean's, the judges and Uncle Bill went to Caper's. As they entered his room, they found that ingenious youth walking, in his shirt sleeves, in as large a circle as the room would permit, bearing on his head a large canvas, while a quite pretty female model, named Stella, sat on a sofa, marking down something on a piece of paper, using the sole of her shoe for a writing desk.

"We-ell!" said Uncle Bill.

"One more round," quoth Caper, with unmoved countenance, "and I will be with you. That will make four hundred and fifty, won't it, Stella?"

"*Eh, Gia!* one more is all you want." And making an extra scratch with a pencil, the female model surveyed the newcomers with a triumphant air, plainly saying: "See there! I can write, but I am not proud."

"What are you about, Jim?"

"Look at that painting!" answered Caper. "The Blessing of the Donkeys, Horses, &c.; it is one of the most imposing ceremonies of the Church. As my specialty is animal, I have chosen it for my painting; and not contented with laboring faithfully at it, I have determined, in order to put the thing beyond a doubt as to my gaining the prize, to put the *most work* on it of any of my rivals; so I have actually, as Stella will tell you, carried it bodily four hundred and fifty times round this studio."

"Instead of a painting, I should think you would have made a panting of it," spoke Mr. Van Brick.

"The idea seems to me artful," added Mr. Pinchfip; "but after all, this pedestrian work was not on the painting, but under it; therefore, according to Blackstone on Contracts, this comes under the head of a consideration *do, ut facias,* see vol. ii. page 360. How far moral obligation is a legal consideration, see note, vol. iii. p. 249 Bossanquet & Puller's Reports. The principle *servus facit, ut herus det,* as laid down by . . ."

"Jove!" exclaimed Uncle Bill; "couldn't you stop off the torrent for one minute? I'm drowning—I give up—do with me as you see fit."

.   .   .   .   .   .

"And now," said Mr. Van Brick, "that we have seen the four paintings, let us, Mr. Pinchfip, proceed calmly to discover who has won the five hundred dollars. Duly, deliberately, and gravely, let us put the four names on four slips of paper, stir them up in a hat. Mr. Browne shall then draw out a name, the owner of that name shall be the winner."

It was drawn, and, by good fortune for him, Bagswell won the five hundred dollars. Thus Uncle Bill Browne bought one painting for a good round sum, and three others at the stipulated price. Which one of the four had the *most work* on it, is, however, an unsettled question among three of the artists, to this day.

CHAPTER VI.

WITH that wise foresight, shared by all European rulers, the Roman Pincio was undoubtedly wedded to its purpose of keeping the idle ones very busy at the very time of day when revolutionary plots find the best hearing—before dinner. Whirling around its walks in carriages, or gently promenading under trees, among rose bushes, and by fountains, while a large band of musicians play with spirit fine selections from the last operas, or favorite airs from old ones; the eye gratified by the sight of pleasant faces, or dwelling enraptured on the beautiful landscape spread before it—how can the brain disengage itself to think of Liberty, won through toil and battle, only to be preserved by self-denial and moral strength?

But the traveller who travels only to travel, and has the means and spirit to find pleasure wherever he goes, thinking only of what he sees, enjoys to its fullest extent the luxurious seat of the hired, white-damask-lined carriage, drawn by stalwart, heavy-limbed, coal-black horses, with sweeping tails, the white foam flying from the champed silver bits, the whole turn-out driven by a handsome, white-gloved, black-coated Roman. In solemn state and swiftly, he winds up the zigzag road leading from the Piazza Popolo (so called from *popolo*, a poplar tree, and not, as the English will have it, from *popolo*, the people), and at last reaches the summit of Roman ambition—the top of the Pincian Hill. He passes other carriages filled with other strangers like himself, or with titled and fashionable Romans, and finally, his carriage drawn up to one side of the broad drive in front of the semicircle where the band plays, he descends, to walk around and chat with the friends he may find there.

Toward sunset the scene is full of animation. The sabres of the cavalry soldiers, on guard to prevent infraction of rules, gleam brightly; the old infantry soldiers are darting here and there, chasing away sundry ownerless dogs, who always make it a point to promenade the Pincio; the Italian nurses from Albano, or at least dressed in Albanese costume, shine conspicuous in their crimson-bodiced dresses; Englishmen going through their constitutional; Frenchmen mourning for the Champs Elysées; artists in broadbrim hats smoking cigars; Americans observing Italy, so as to be like Italians; ladies of all nations commanding the attention of mankind as they sweep along the hard-rolled gravel walks; smiles, bows, looks of love, indignation, affection, coquetry; faces reflective of great deeds and greater dinners . . . every face bright in the lambent amber light that streams from the sun dipping his head preparatory to putting on his nightcap, and bidding Rome *felicissima notte!*—a most happy night.

Over the irregular walls of the subdued white and mellow gray houses and palaces, beyond the Tiber running red in the dying sunlight, over the round-walled castle of San Angelo, the dome of St. Peter's rises full in the midst of the twinkling, hazy, red and golden light. Passing the stone pines crowning Monte Mario, there gleam away to the left the far waters of the sea, over which the purple mist of young night tenderly, softly falls. Once thoughtfully noted, you will remember this glowing scene years after sublimer and wilder views are lost to memory, or grown so faint that they are to you but as dull colors seen in dreams of old age compared to the flashing brightness of those presented to the closed eyes of youth.

As the sun sets, and those in carriages and on foot slowly leave the heights of the Pincio, and descend once more to the old city, you will hear, as the evening star shines brighter and brighter, the first liquid, thrilling notes of the nightingales; then, as you lean over the stone parapet, dreamily looking into the dense foliage of trees and shrubs beneath you, you will feel the beauty of those lines:

> "Seek the nightnigale's sequestered bower,
>   Who with her lovelorn melody
> So bewitched thee in the vernal hour :
>   When she ceased to love, she ceased to be."

It is from the months of May to November, when travellers have left Rome, and the city is in the hands of the Romans, that your walks on the Pincio will prove something more than a mere repetition of a stroll in Baden-Baden, or a revival of ideas common to the Prado or Prater. No longer the little prettinesses of the Medicean Venus flirt by you in the nervous silks that flutter along these walks, but something nobly womanly, of a solid past, slow and stately, moves solemnly by. We know the life of these copies of the Venus of Milos; we know its most commonplace and vulgar attributes, but we know, too, its strength! The city of Rome holds in its women the mothers of heroes, when Providence shall withdraw the black veil now hung over their rude minds, and let in the light of knowledge. We who laugh at their sad ignorance, think what we would be without liberty—our minds enslaved, geography tabooed! Egypt is a paradise compared to Rome.

The advantages of foreign travel to an intelligent American are to teach him . . the disadvantages of living anywhere save in America. And though the artistic eye dwells with such loving repose on the soothing colors of Italy, and particularly on the subdued white and gray tones of Roman ruins and palaces, walls and houses, yet the owner of that artistic eye should restrain his wrath at the fiery-red bricks of our own cities; for let him reflect, that this color goads him on, as it doth a bull, to make valorous efforts—to do something!

Looking down from the stone balustrade of the Pincio on the Piazza Popolo, we note two churches, one on either side of the Corso; their architecture is neither more nor less hideous than nine tenths of the other three hundred and odd churches of Rome; the same heavy, half-cooked look about doors and windows, suggesting cocked hats of the largest size on the heads of dwarfs of no size at all; the same heavy scroll-work, reminding one of the work of a playful giant of a green grocer who has made a bouquet of sausages and cabbages, egg plants and legs of mutton, and exhibits it to a thick-headed public as a—work of art. O Roman *Plebs!* lay this flattering unction to your soul—we did not do that!

The history of all nations seems to indicate successive ages of grub and butterfly-life; certainly Rome has been a grub long enough. Let us hope the sun of Victor Emanuel, the King of Gallant Men, will hasten the time when the Romans shall wing their way to the light of Liberty. These mockeries of architecture shall then stand as warning fingers to the Romans of the sad days that were; the days when mind and body were enslaved, and the grinning monkey held the dove tight-clutched in his brutal grasp. Through sword and fire public taste must pass before it is purified: the mountain stream, dashing along with bounding steps, is clear and sparkling, but in the long stretch of level pasture-land or prairie it is still and—dirty.

It may be well to descend and wander through those close and narrow streets where the waste water of old Roman aqueducts makes green and damp the foundation stories of gloomy houses, and where the carefully-nurtured traveller sees sights of smoked interiors, dirt and rubbish in the streets, that terrify him; but let him remember that in the worst of these kennels the inhabitants have never forgotten that they had a Past, and the "I am a Roman citizen!" still rings in their ears, eats into their hearts, and is at their tongue's end. Monsieur About was in Rome when Caper was there; he saw these Romans through Napoleonic spectacles: while one foot was trying to stamp on Antonelli gently, the other was daintily ascending the shining steps leading to the temple of Gallic fame. He is impressed with the idea that the Romans are hangers-on of hangers-on to patricians, from which we are to infer, if the patricians are ever hung, there will be a heavy weight to their feet!

Rocjean, one afternoon, after a walk on the Pincio, was returning to his studio, when, as he descended to the Via Babuino, he met a Roman artist named Attonito, who cultivated the English.

"Ow arr you toe-day, my dear?" he asked Rocjean.

"Quite well, except a slight attack of bad English, from which I hope to recover in a few minutes."

"Pray tell unto me th-hat weech is bad Englis."

"Haven't you been on the Pincio?"

"Yas, I tak' consteetutionails up there avery afternoons; it is a costume Englis' th-hat I vary moche cotton to." . . .

"W-hat! Cotton to? Why, that is a clear Americanism; where did you pick it up?"

"Meester Caper of Noo-York, he told unto me it am more elegant as to say, I love, or I affection. Bote, 'ave you saw that bu-tee-fool creechure with 'air of flags?" . . .

"What!"

"'Air of flags; 'ow you name eet? *Capellatura di lino?*"

"Oh! you mean tow-head?"

"Toe! no, no! I mean *lino.*"

"Ah! yes; flaxen hair."

"*Benissimo!* Vary well, flagson 'air and blue eyze. Shhe was in carri-adge with Lady Blumpudy. I go avery afternoons to inspect her as she takes the airs on the Pincio. Eet would gife me great pleasures to ally myself to her in marriage compact, bote I do not know eef she has a fortune. Do you know anytheengs?"

"Yes, a great many; one of which is, that it is my dinner time; and as I turn down the Condotti—good afternoon."

"Goo-ood by, my dear," answered Attonito, as he slowly wandered up the Piazza di Spagna.

"Another example of the beneficial effects of the Pincio on the *bourgeoisie,*" thought Rocjean. "When will the alarm bell in the clock of Roman time ring out its awaking peal?"

If one would realize the romantic side of Rome in all its stately grandeur, and receive a solemn and ineffaceable impression of its beauty, by all means let him, like Quevedo's hero, sleep "a-daytime," and do his sight-seeing by moonlight or starlight; for, save in some few favored quarters, its inspection by gaslight would be difficult. Remember, too, that all that is grandly beautiful of Rome, the traveller has seen before he reaches the Imperial City—with the eyes of understanding, with the eyes of others—in books.

Nothing but a heap of old stones, bricks, and mortar, is there here for the illiterate tourist. He can have six times as jolly a time in Paris for half the money that he pays "in that old hole where a fellow named Culius Jæsar used to live."

As if the night were not sufficiently dark in this city, there are always those who stand ready with the paint brush of fancy to make it even of a darker hue; whisperings among the travellers in hotels of certain Jim Joneses or Bill Smiths who have been robbed. Yes, sir; early in the evening, right there in the Corso; grabbed his watch and chain, struck him on the head. You know he was a powerfully built man; but they came behind him, and if he hadn't have done so and so, the rascally Italians would have killed him, and so forth.

"Re-al-ly; well, you won't catch me out at nights!"

There rises up, as I write, the figure of a slim young man, of the daytime negro-minstrel style of beauty, who once dwelt three weeks in Rome. I know that he was profound in knowledge of trick and vice, and that he had an impediment in his speech—he could never speak the truth. He told a fearful tale of a midnight robbery in the Piazza di Spagna—himself the victim. It was well told, and I ought to know, for I read it years before in a romance; only the scene was, in type, laid in Venice. According to this negro-minstrel style of youth, he had been seized from behind, held, robbed of watch and elegant gold chain, red coral shirt studs, onyx sleeve buttons, and a portemonnaie containing fifty *scudi*, &c., &c. He was the theatrical hero of the hotel for two days, and the recipient of many drinks. Time, the eater of things, never digested this falsehood, and months after the youth had left, I learned that he had lost all his jewelry and money at—twenty-deck poker.

A few nights after Caper was domiciled in the Via Babuino, Rocjean called on him, and, as he entered his room, carefully extinguished a taper, and was putting it in his pocket, when Caper asked him what that was for?

"That? it's a *cerina*. Have you been two weeks in Rome, and not found out that? Why, how did you get up stairs at night?"

"There was a lamp in the entry."

"None there to-night, so I had to light this. It's only a long piece of wick, dipped in wax. You see, you can roll it up in a ball, and carry it in your pocket, so! Without this, and a box of matches, you can never hope to be a good Roman. You must have seen, that where the houses have any front doors, three quarters of them are open all night long; for, as on every floor of a house there live different families, they find it saves trouble—trouble is money in Rome—to leave the door unclosed. These dark entries—for they are seldom lighted—offer a grand chance for intrigues; and when you have lived here as long as I have, you will find out that they —improve the chances. A *cerina*, in addition to keeping you from breaking your neck by tumbling down stone stairs, gives light to avoid the stray dogs that sleep around loose, and to see if there is any enemy around who wants to give you a few inches of cold steel. You may laugh at robbers here; but you may cry for mercy in vain to a Roman who seeks *vendetta* —revenge, you know. Bad way to use foreign words; but we all do it here. Speak an Italianized English after a time— the effect of bad examples. But come; if you want to see Rome by moonlight, it's time we were off."

As they reached the street, Caper asked Rocjean where he could buy the *cerina*.

"At any *drogheria*," said the latter.

"Good! there is a druggist's store up the street—Borioni's."

"A *drogheria* means a grocery store in Rome. If you want molasses, however, you must go to the *farmacia* for it (that is the Roman for druggist's shop), and you will buy it by the ounce."

"Live and learn," said Caper, as they entered the grocery, and bought the *cerina*—price, one *baioccho* a yard.

"And now let us walk out to St. Peter's, and see the church by moonlight."

"The want of sidewalks in this city," remarked Rocjean, "compelling the Romans to walk over cobble stones, undoubtedly is the cause of the large feet of the women, added to their dislike of being in pain from tight shoes or boots. For genuine martyrdom from tight shoes, French, Spanish, and Americans—but chiefly Cubans—next to Chinese women, are ahead of the world."

"But apart from the fact that they do walk on the narrow sidewalks in the Corso, I have noticed that in the side streets, even where there is a footwalk, nobody takes advantage of it at night."

"For a good reason, as we shall probably see," said Rocjean, "before we reach the bridge of San Angelo. But keep close to me in the middle of the street."

The moonlight shone brightly down the narrow street they were then walking through, which, but for this, the occasional dim light of an oil lamp hung in front of a shrine, the light from a wine or grocery shop, and the ruddy blaze of a charcoal fire, where chestnuts were roasting for sale, would have been dark indeed. The ground floor of very few Roman houses is ever occupied as a dwelling place; it is given up to shops, stables, &c., the families residing, according to their wealth, on the lowest up to the highest stories; the light purses going up, and the heavy ones sinking. They had walked nearly to the end of this street, when, happening to look up at the fourth story of a house, Caper saw something white being reversed in the moonlight, and the next instant a long stream of water, reminding him of the horse-tail fall in Switzerland, came splashing down where a sidewalk should have been.

"What do you think of the middle of the street now?" asked Rocjean.

"Let's stick to it, even if we stick in it. I'm going to buy an umbrella, *and spread it, too*, when I go out of nights, after this."

They reached the bridge of San Angelo, and studied for a short time the fine effect of the moonlight shining on the turbid, slow-flowing Tiber, and lighting up the heavy pile of the castle of San Angelo. Then they reached the Piazza of St. Peter's, and here the scene was imperial. Out and in through the semicircular arcade of massive pillars the moonlight stole to sleep upon the soft-toned, gray old pavement, or was thrown in dancing, sparkling light from the two noble jets of water tossed in the clear night air by the splashing fountains. In all its gigantic proportions rose up, up into the clear blue of the spangled sky, the grand thought of Michael Angelo—the dome of St. Peter's.

Returning from St. Peter's, Rocjean proposed to walk through the Trastevere, the other side of the Tiber, and to cross over the river by the Ponte Rótto, or Broken Bridge. They found the street along the river very quiet. Here and there a light showed, as on the other side, a wineshop or coffee room; but the houses had few lights in them, and, spite of the moonlight, the streets looked gloomy and desolate.

"They seem to keep dark this side of the river," said Caper.

"Yes," answered Rocjean, "and live light. They go to bed for the most part early, and rise early; they economize fifty-one weeks in the year, in order to live like lords for the fifty-second—that is Carnival Week. Then you shall see these queenly Trasteverine in all their bravery, thronging the Corso. But here is a clean-looking wineshop; let us go in and have a *foglietta*."

They found the shop full of thirsty Romans—it is safe to say that—although the number of small flasks showed they could not indulge their taste so deeply as they wished to. The centre of the listening group of Romans was a bright-eyed, curly-haired man, who was reciting, with loud emphasis:

THE LIFE AND DEATH,

OF THE PERFIDIOUS ASSASSIN,

ARRIGO GARBETINGO OF TRENTO,

Who slew nine hundred and sixty-four grown persons, and six children.

He had already got through his birth and wicked childhood, and had arrived at that impressive part where he commences his career of brigand at large, accompanied by a "bool-dog":

> "He had a bull-dog of the English breed, oh!
>   More savage than all others that we've seen, oh!
> Close at his side it always walked, indeed, oh!
>   And never barked! but then, his bite was keen, oh!
> When on some poor man straight he sprung—take heed, oh!
>   His soul from body quickly fled, I ween, oh!
> Because with cruel, gnashing teeth he tore, oh!
>   Him all to pieces, in a manner sore, oh!"

The reciter here stopped to drink another tumbler of wine, upon which Caper and Rocjean, having finished their pint, paid their scot, and departed.

"Was that an improvisatore?" asked Caper.

"He might pass for such with a stranger of inflammable imagination, who didn't know the language," answered Rocjean. "He is, in fact, a reciter, and you can buy the poh, poh-em he was reciting, at any of the country fairs, of the man who sells rosaries and crucifixes. It is one of the cent-songs of the Papal States, published *con licenza*—with license; and a more cruel, disgusting, filthy, and demoralizing tendency than it must have on the people, cannot well be imagined; and there are hundreds of worse."

While Rocjean was talking, they had crossed the Ponte Rótto, and as he finished his sentence, they stood in front of the ruined house of—Cola di Rienzi! "Redeemer of dark centuries of shame—the hope of Italy, Rienzi, last of Romans!"

"Well," said Rocjean, as he halted in front of the ruined

house, and looked carefully at the ornamental stones still left, "when St. Peter's church shall be a circus, this house shall be a shrine."

"That being the state of the case," spoke Caper, "let us walk up to the Trevi fountain, and see the effect by moonlight of its flashing waters, and inhale the flavor of fried fish from the adjacent stands."

They stood in front of the wild waters, dashing, sparkling over the grand mass of tumbled rocks reared behind the wall of a large palace. Neptune, car, horses, tritons, all, stone as they were, seemed leaping into life in the glittering rays of the moonlight; and the rush and splash of the waters in the great basin below the street, contrasted with the silence of the city, left a deep impression of largeness and force on the minds of the two artists.

"Let us go down and drink the water; for he who drinks of it shall return again to Rome!"

"With all my heart," said Caper; "for if the legend has one word of truth in it, Garibaldi will be back again some *bello giorno*——"

"*Bello giorno* means fine day; *giorno di bello* means a day for war: I drink to both!" spoke Rocjean, dipping water up in his hand.

They returned to the street, and were walking toward the Piazza di Spagna, when they overtook two well-dressed men, evidently none the better for too much wine. As they passed them, one of the men said to the other:

"J-im! I don't see but what we-we-'ll have to r-r-roost out-tall night. I don't know 'ny 'talian—*you* don't know 'ny 'talian—we-we-'re nonpl'sh'd, I'm th-think'ng."

"Ary borry boutére spikinglish?" said the other one to the two artists, as they were walking on.

"Yes," said Caper; "four of 'em. If you've lost your way, we'll set you right. Where's your hotel?"

"'Tel? Why, 'Tel Europe p'aza Spanya. Are you English?"

"No, sir; I'm an American born, bred and—buttered," said Caper.

"B-bullyf'ryou! We'resame spishies—allrite—d-driv'on!"

"Look here," said the one of the two men who was least tipsy, "if this tother g-gen'leman and I could stick our heads into c-cold water, we'd come out tall right."

"It's only a block or two back to the Trevi fountain," answered Caper, "and if your friend will go with you, you'll find water enough there."

They went back to the fountain, and, descending the steps with some difficulty, the two men soon had their heads pretty well cooled off, and came up with cleared intellects and improved pronunciation. In the course of conversation, it appeared that the two travellers—for such they were—after rather too much wine at dinner in their hotel, had been invited to the German Club, where Rhine wine, &c, had finished them off. Attempting to return to their hotel alone, they had lost their way. As the four walked along, it came out that one of them owned a painting by Rocjean; and when he discovered that one of his guides was no other than that Americanized Frenchman, the whole party at once fraternized, and, disregarding any more moonlight effects, walked at once to Caper's rooms, where, over cigars and a bottle of Copalti's wine, they signed, sealed, and delivered a compact to have a good time generally for the week the two travellers intended devoting to Rome. The moral of which is . . . that you make more friends than meet enemies—walking round Rome by night.

They were in the presence of a man with flowing hair, flowing beard, and flowing language, in a studio, all light from which was excluded by heavy curtains, except enough to display an easel on which was placed a painting, a background of dark blue, where were many apparently spider and crow tracks.

"Those who, in the profundity of their darkness, incline to the belief that the vitality of art, butterfly-like, has fled from this sunny world, have made the biggest kind of a mistake," said Mr. Artaxerxes Phlamm, the Mystic Artist, to Caper. The hit was evidently intended for Rocjean, but that descendant of the Gauls, for some reason, did not smite back again; he contented himself with the remark:

"Art is long."

"Yes, sir," continued Mr. Phlamm; "not only it has length, but breadth, breadth, broadness; it extends from— yes—from—pole to pole."

"Like a clothes line," said Caper.

"Ah!" continued Phlamm, with a pickled smile, "Fancy, ever Fancy; but it is Imagination that, as it were, brings man to a level with his destiny, and elevates him to the Olympium heights of the True, and all that rises much above the meedy-ochre. But I must not forget that this is your first visit to me studeeyoh. The painting on the easel is a view of Venice on the Grand Canal."

"But," said Rocjean, "I do not see the canal."

"When you are gazing at the stars, do you see your boots?" asked Phlamm.

"I always do," spoke Caper, quickly; "always gaze at 'em at night; smoke a cigar—put my feet higher than my head—sit in a chair—stars reflected in boots—big thing!"

"You are full of life and spirits, Caper," continued Phlamm; "full of 'em; but Rocjean is more serious—more imbued with his nobil calling. My illustration, as he understands, would convey the idea that such a thing as foreground in a painting is false; it's a sham, it's a delusion, and all that. It may do for pre-Raffleites, but for a man who looks Naychure in the face, he sees her operating diversely, and he works accordingly. I repeat it again: when I was on the Grand Canal in Venice, I didn't see the Grand Canal."

"Neither did I," spoke Caper; "we're just alike. I kept my head all the time out of the gondola window, looking for pretty girls—and I saw them!"

"May I ask why you dead-color your canvas blue, and then make your drawing in black outline?" asked Rocjean.

"What is the color of the sky? Is it not blue? Is not blue a cold color? Is it not the negative to the warmth, the balance to the scales, the one thing needed on which to rear the glorious fabric that Naychure reveals to the undimmed vision of man? I know your answer, and I refute it. I have studied Art from its roots, and now I'm in the branches, and I grasp the fruit. My manner is peculiar. I have no patent for it; I ask for none. The illimitable passes the legitimate, and the sw-word is carried by the hero—for me the bruzh, the paint bruzh. You see that painting before you?—it is my child. I lavish on it my intentions. I am going to work three years on that picture!"

"I bet you a new hat you sell it, and a dozen more, and send 'em off before six months. You're all the rage now, since you sold old Goldburg a picture," quoth Caper.

"I don't bet; I am opposed to betting. But look that picture of mine in the face—in the face! Here is a finished painting, The Lake of Zurich. See those clouds floating mistily away into the far distance—there's atmosphere for you! there's air! You can't cut those clouds into slices of cheese, as you can them of that humbug of a Cloud Lowrain. Cloud Lowrain! he's a purty painter! Naychure is my teacher. I go out mornings, and hear the jackdaws chatter, and see trees, and all that. Sometimes I walk around in a garden for ten minutes, and commune with Naychure—that's the way to do it. Look at clouds before you paint 'em. I know it's hard, when the sun's in your eyes; but do it. I've spent a week at a time outdoors, like Wordsworth, and the great, the grand, the colossal Ruzking."

"I like that water," said Rocjean, alluding to that of the painting.

"Water is my peculiar study. I am now engaged experimenting on it—see there!" Here Phlamm pointed to a basin.

"Been washing your hands?" asked Caper.

"Scientifically experimenting, not manually. Water is soup-or-fish-all; earth is not soup-or-fish-all."

"Our dinners are, during Lent," quoth Caper, "unless we're heretics."

"I don't understand your frivolity. What do you mean?"

"Didn't you say, 'Soup or all fish?'"

"Pshaw! You will never make an artist—never, never! *You* are too—too superficiall—too much of the earth—dirty."

"Oh! now I understand," answered Caper. "Give it to me; I deserve it."

"I was studying water, its shadows and its superficiality, in that basin," continued Phlamm; "and I study the ocean there, and have devolved great principles from it. What makes my pictures sought for by the high and the low—wealthy? What? It's the Truth in 'em, the Mystery, the Naychure. The old masters were humbugs; they weren't mysterious; they had no inner sight into the workings of Naychure. Who'd buy one of their pictures, when he might have a Turner for the same price? Nobody."

"Wouldn't he?" asked Caper. "Try him with a Raphael —just a small one."

"Raphael? You mean Raffaele. Ah! he *was* a painter; he wasn't one of the old masters, however; he was a middle-age master. What sweetness! what a kind of—sweetness generally! what a blending of the prayerful infant with the enthusiastic beauty! the—the polished chastity of his Madonnas! the folds of his drapery, and—the drapery of his folds! Truly enchanting, and so very uncommonly gentlemanly in his colors."

"The Chesterfield of oil colors?" suggested Rocjean. "But à propos of Nature; you never paint a picture directly from her, do you?"

"Never! Does a great historical painter use the model? No, sir; he draws on his imagination for his figures. He scorns to copy from a model. I convey the impression of mystery that Naychure gives me; I am no servile copyist. And I claim to leave an impression on the minds of the beholders of my works. Why, even Caper, I believe, can see what I wish to tell, and read my poems on canvas. Tell me, Caper, what idea does even that rough sketch of Venice awake in your imaginative faculties, and all that?"

Caper's face wore a deeply thoughtful look, as he answered: "I do see it; I do claim to read the lesson you would teach——"

"Speak it out," interrupted Phlamm; "I knew you would feel the deep, mysterious sentiment as is in it."

"Spider tracks and crows' feet on the blue mud of a big marsh," spoke Caper, resolutely.

"Pshaw!" exclaimed Phlamm, impetuously; "you have no faith; and without that, all Art is a sealed thing. Goldburg, to whom I lately sold a painting, had faith. He saw the grand idea which I explained to him in that picture. He knew that the Earl of Bigbarns had purchased a work of mine, and he said to me: 'The opinion of such a man is an opinion as should be a valuable opinion to a business man, and govern the sentiments of those who worship Art.' Other artists see Naychure, but *how* do they see her? I answer, blindly! They don't feel her here!" (Phlamm struck his waistcoat in fearful proximity to a pocket in it, and altogether too low for his heart.)

"Nay-chure," said Caper to Rocjean, as they left this studio of the mysterious one, "ruined a good Barnum to make a poor Phlamm, when she made him."

It is a mournful sight to see a city of one hundred and eighty thousand five hundred and thirty-nine inhabitants, including one thousand three hundred and thirty-one priests, two thousand four hundred and four monks, and eight hundred and fifty-four Jews, Turks, and heretics, as the census had it, attacked with hydrophobia. But it is so. A preternatural dread of water rages among all the inhabitants of Rome, from the untitled down to the titled.

"Madame," said Rocjean to a distinguished female model, "I assure you that, in the sixth century (or, as Sir Gardiner Wilkinson has it, in the five hundred), there were nine thousand and twenty-five baths in this city."

"Those must have been good times," replied she, "for the washerwomen, *seguro!* There are a good many clothes of the *forestieri* (strangers) washed here now; but not so many different places to wash them in."

"I mean places to bathe one's self all over in."

"*Mai!* Never, never!" exclaimed the woman, with horror; "never! 'twould give them the fever—kill them dead!"

Mr. Van Brick, of New York, arriving in Rome early in the morning, demanded of the porter at the hotel where he could find a *bagno*, or place where he could get a bath. He was directed to go down the Babuino, and at such a number he would find the establishment. Forgetting the number before he was three steps from the hotel, he inquired of a man who was driving a she jackass to be milked, where the bath was. As he spoke very little Italian, he had to make up by signs what he wanted in words. The man, probably believing he wanted a church, and that his motions signified being sprinkled with water, pointed to the Greek church; and Van Brick, thinking it was a solemn looking old *bagno*, strode in, to his astonishment finding out, as soon as he entered, that he was by no means in the right place. As he turned to go out, he saw an amiable-looking young man, with a black cocked hat in his hand, and a black serge shirt on that came down to his heels, and had a waistband drawing it in over his hips. He asked the young man, as well as he could in Italian, where there was a *bagno*.

"The signore is English?" asked the youth in the black shirt.

"I want a bath," said Van Brick; "which way?"

"Have patience, signore. There are a great many English in Rome."

"Farewell!" quoth Van Brick, turning on his heel, reflecting: "That youth talks too much. He does it to conceal his ignorance. He don't know what a bath is." Coming out of the church, he met a good-natured looking Roman girl, without any bonnet, as usual, going along with a bottle of wine and a loaf of bread.

"Can you tell me where the bath is?"

"*Chi lo sa*, signore."

This CHI LO SA, or, "who knows?" of the Romans, is a shaft that would kill Paul Pry. It nearly throws an inquisitive man into convulsions. He meets it at every turn. The simplest question is knocked to pieces by it. So common is it for a Roman of the true *plebs* breed to give you this for an answer to almost every question, that Rocjean once won a hat from Caper in this wise: They stood, one evening, in front of a grocer's store, down by the Pantheon. It was brilliantly illuminated with hundreds of candles, displaying piles of hams, cheese, butter, eggs, &c., &c. Chandeliers constructed of eggshells, where candles shone brightly, particularly struck Caper.

"You see," said Rocjean, "as any one else can see, that those chandeliers are made of egg shells. Now, I will bet you a hat that I will ask four men, one after another, who may come to look in this window, what those chandeliers are made of, and three at least, if not all four of them, will answer, 'Who knows?' (*Chi lo sa*)."

"Done!" said Caper.

Rocjean asked four men, one after another. All four answered: "Who knows?"

But to continue the bath hunt. Van Brick was thrown over by the girl's answer, and next asked an old woman, who was standing at the door of a house, buying broccoli from a man with a handcart.

"Can *you* tell me where the bath is?"

"The bath?"

"Yes; the bath."

"Is it where they boil water for the English?"

"That must be the shop," quoth Brick.

"That is the place," pointing with her finger to a house on the opposite side of the way.

Van Brick crossed over, and, after five minutes' hunt over the whole house, was coming down disheartened, when he saw a pretty girl, about eighteen years old, standing by the doorway.

"Can you tell me where the bath is?"

"*Seguro!* I attend to them. You can't have a warm bath for two or three hours yet, for there is no fire; but you can have a cold one."

"Well, let me have it as quickly as possible."

"Yes, sir. We have no soap for sale, but you can get it two doors off."

Van Brick went out, and after a time returned with a cake of soap.

"Signore," said the girl, when he went back, "the water is all running out of the hole in the bottom of the tub, and I can't stop it."

"H'm! Show me the tub; I am a splendid mechanic."

The hole being stopped, the tub was rapidly filling with water. Van Brick, in anticipation, was enjoying his bath, when in rushed the attendant.

"Signore, you will have to wait a few minutes—until I wash some towels."

Van Brick was *in extremis*. Taking a gold *scudo*—one of those dear little one-dollar pieces the Romans call *farfälle* (butterflies)—from his pocket, he thus addressed her:

"Maiden, rush round the corner, and buy me a yard of anything that will dry me. I don't care what it is, except salt fish."

"Oh! but these English are bursting with money," thought the girl; and thus thinking, she made great haste, only stopping to tell three or four friends about the crazy man that was round at her place, who didn't want salt fish to make him dry.

"Behold me back again!" said the girl; "I flew."

"Yes," said Van Brick, "and so did time; and he got ahead of you about half an hour. Give me the towels."

"Si, signore, behold them! See how fine they are! What an elegant fringe on them; and only twenty-five *baiocchi* apiece, fringe and all included."

Van Brick, at last left in peace, plunged into the bath.

When he came out, he found he had half a *scudo* to pay for the water, half a *scudo* for towels, quarter of a *scudo* for soap, and another quarter *scudo* for a *buona mano* to the bath girl. Total, one dollar and a half.

"Now," soliloquized Van Brick, as he dressed himself, "I have an arithmetical question to solve. If a Roman, by hard scratching, can earn twenty cents a day, and it costs him twenty-five cents for board and lodging, how long will it be before he saves up a dollar and a half to take a bath? But that intelligent maiden will tell me, I know?" He asked her.

"Signore, the Romans never bathe."

"You mean the Catholic Romans; for the pagan Romans didn't do anything else."

"They're all burning up in the *inferno, seguro!*" said the maiden.

"But they had fifteen aqueducts to keep them cool when they were alive," spoke Van Brick.

"*Chi lo sa.* We have three aqueducts, we Romans, and we have more water—yes, more water than we can—drink."

"Yes, while there's wine about. *Adio, bella ninfa!*"

CHAPTER VII.

THERE was a shop occupied by a dealer in paintings, engravings, intaglios, old crockery, and *Bric-à-brac*-ery generally, down the Via Condotti, and into this shop Mr. William Browne, of St. Louis, one morning found his way. He had been induced to enter by reading in the window, written on a piece of paper,

"A REEL TITIANO FOR SAL,"

and as he wisely surmised that the dealer intended to notify the English that he had a painting by Titian, for sale, he went in to see it.

Unfortunately for Mr. Browne, familiarly known as Uncle Bill, he had one of those faces that invariably induced Roman tradesmen to resort to the Oriental mode of doing business, namely, charging three hundred per cent. profit; and as this dealer, having formerly been a courier, commissionaire, and pander to English and American travellers, naturally spoke a disgusting jargon of Italianized English, and had what he believed were the most distinguished manners—*he* charged five hundred per cent.

"I want," said Uncle Bill to the "brickbat" man, "to see your Titian."

"I shall expose 'im to you in one moment, sare; you walk this way. He's var' fine pickshoor, var' fine. You ben long time in Rome, sare?"

No reply from Uncle Bill. His idea was, even a wise man may ask questions, but none but fools answer fools.

Brickbat man finds that his customer has ascended the human scale one step; he prepares "to spring dodge" Number Two on him.

"Thare, sare, thare is Il Tiziano! I s'pose you say you see notheeng bote large peas board: zat peas board was one táble for two, tree hundret yars; all zat time ze pickshoor was unbeknounst undair ze táble. Zey torn up ze táble, and you see a none-doubted Tiziano. Var' fine pickshoor!"

"Do you know," asked Uncle Bill, "if it was in a temperance family all that time?"

"I am not acquent zat word, demprance—wot it means?"

'Sober," was the answer.

'Yas, zat was in var' sobair fam'ly — in convent of nons."

"That will account for its being undiscovered so long; all the world knows they are not inquisitive! If it had been in a drinking house, somebody falling under the table would have seen it—wouldn't they?"

Brickbat reflects, and comes to the conclusion that the "eldairly cove" is wider awake than he believed him, at first sight.

"Now I torne zis board, you see, on ze othaire side, ze Bella Donna of Tiziano. Zere is one in ze Sciarra palace, bote betwane you and I, I don't believe it is gin'wine."

"I don't know much about paintings," spoke Uncle Bill,

"but I know I've seen seventy-six of these Belli Donners, and each one was sworn to as the original picture!"

"Var' true, sare, var' true; Tiziano Vermecellio was grate pantaire, man of grate mind; and when he got holt onto fine subjick, he work him ovair and ovair feefty, seexty times. Ze chiaro-'scuro is var' fine, and ze depfs of his tone somethings var' deep, vary. Look at ze flaish, sare—you can pinch him; and, sare, you look here, I expose grand secret to you. I take zis pensnife, I scratgis ze pant. Look zare!"

"Well," said Uncle Bill, "I don't see anything."

"You don't see anne theengs! Wot you see under ze pant?"

"It looks like dirt."

"*Cospetto!* zat is ze gr-and prep-par-ra-tion zat makes ze flaish of Tiziano more natooral as life. You know grate pantaire, Mistaire Leaf, as lives in ze Ripetta? Zat man has spend half his lifes scratging Tiziano all to peases, for find out 'ow he mak's flaish: now he believes he found out ze way, bote, betwane you and I——" Here the brickbat man conveyed, by a shake of his head and a tremolo movement of his left hand, the idea that "it was all in vain."

"What do you ask for the picture?" asked Uncle Bill.

The head of the brickbat man actually disappeared between his shoulders as he shrugged them up, and extended his hands at his sides like the flappers of a turtle. Uncle Bill looked at the man in admiration; he had never seen such a performance before, save by a certain contortionist in a travelling circus; and in his delight he asked the man, when his head appeared, if he wouldn't do that once more—only once more!

In his surprise at being asked to perform the trick, he actually went through it again; for which Uncle Bill thanked him kindly, and again asked the price of the Titian.

"I tak' seex t'ousand *scudi* for him; not one *baiocch*, less."

"It an't dear, 'specially for those who have the money to scatterlophisticate," replied Uncle Bill, cheerfully.

"No, sare; it ees dogs chip—var' chip. I have sev'ral Englis' want to buy him bad. I shall sell him some days to somebodies. Bote, sare, will you 'ave ze goodniss to write down on peas paper zat word—var' fine word—you use him minit 'go—scatolofistico sometheengs. I wis' to larn ze Englis' better as I spiks him."

"Certainly; give me a pencil and paper. I'll write it down, and you'll astonish some Englishman with it, I'll bet a hat."

So it was written down; and if any one ever entered a shop in the Condotti where there was a Titiano for Sal, and was "astonished" by hearing that word used, they may know whence it came.

Mr. Browne, after carefully examining the usual yellow marble model of the column of Trajan, the alabaster pyramid of Caius Cestius, the verd-antique obelisks, the bronze lamps, lizards, marble *tazze*, and paste gems of the modern-antique factories, the ever-present Beatrice Cenci on canvas, and the water-color costumes of Italy, made a purchase of a Roman mosaic paperweight, wherein there was a green parrot with a red tail and blue legs, let in with minute particles of composition resembling stone, and left the brickbat man alone with his Titiano for Sal.

Rocjean came into Caper's studio one morning, evidently having something to communicate.

"Are you busy this morning? If not, come along with me; there is something to be seen—something that beats the Mahmoudy Canal of the Past, or the Suez Canal of the Present, for wholesale slaughter; for I do assure you, on the authority of Hassel, that nine hundred and thirty-six million four hundred and sixty-one thousand people died before it was finished!"

"That must be a work worth looking at. Why, the pyramids must be as ant-hills to Chimborazo in comparison to it! Nine hundred and odd millions of mortals! Why, that is about the number dying in a generation—and these have passed away while it was being completed? It ought to be a masterpiece."

"Can't we get a glass of wine round here?" asked Rocjean, looking at his watch; "it is about luncheon time, and I have a charming little thirst."

"Oh! yes, there is a wineshop only three doors from here, pure Roman. Let us go; we can stand out in the street, and drink, if you are afraid to go in."

Leaving the studio, they walked a few steps to a house that was literally all front-door; for the entrance was the entire width of the building, and a buffalo team could have passed in without let. Outside stood a winecart, from which they were unloading several small casks of wine. The driver's seat had a hood over it, protecting him from the sun, as he lazily sleeps there, rumbling over the tufa road, to or from the Campagna, and around the seat were painted, in gay colors, various patterns of things unknown. In the autumn, vine branches, with pendent, rustling leaves, decorate hood and horse; while in spring or summer, a bunch of flowers often ornaments this gay-looking winecart.

The interior of the shop was dark, dingy, sombre, and dirty enough to have thrown an old Flemish Interior-artist into hysterics of delight. There was an *olla-podrida* browniness about it that would have entranced a native of Seville; and a collection of dirt around, that would have elevated a Chippewa Indian to an ecstasy of delight. The reed mattings hung against the walls were of a golden ochre color, the smoked walls and ceiling the shade of asphaltum and burnt sienna, the unswept stone pavement a warm gray, the old tables and benches very rich in tone and dirt; the back of the shop, even at midday, dark, and the eye caught there glimpses of arches, barrels, earthen jars, tables, and benches, resting in twilight, and only brought out in relief by the faint light always burning in front of the shrine of the Virgin, that hung on one of the walls.

In a wineshop, this shrine does not seem out of place—it is artistic; but in a lottery office, open to the light of day, and glaringly commonplace, the Virgin hanging there looks much more like the goddess Fortuna than Santa Maria.

But they are inside the wineshop, and the next instant a black-haired, gypsy-looking woman, with flashing black eyes, warming up the sombre color of the shop by the fiery-red and golden silk handkerchief which falls from the back of her head, Neapolitan fashion, illuminating that dusky old den like fireworks, asks them what they will order?

"A *foglietta* of white wine."

"Sweet or dry?"

"Dry" (*asciùtto*), said Rocjean.

There it is, on the table, in a glass flask brittle as virtue, light as sin, and fragile as folly. They are called Sixtusses, after that pious old Sixtus V. who hanged a publican and wine-seller sinner in front of his shop for blasphemously expressing his opinion as to the correctness of charging four times as much to put the fluoric acid government stamp on them as the glass cost. However, taxes must be raised, and the thinner the glass, the easier it is broken, so the Papal government compel the wine sellers to buy these glass bubbles, forbidding the sale of wine out of anything else, save the *bottiglie;* and as it raises money by touching them up with acid, why, the people have to stand it. These *fogliette* have round bodies and long, broad necks, on which you notice a white mark made with the before-mentioned chemical preparation; up to this mark the wine should come, but the attendant generally takes thumbtoll, especially in the restaurants where foreigners go, for the Roman citizen is not to be swindled, and will have his rights: the single expression, "I AM A ROMAN CITIZEN," will at times save him at least two *baiocchi*, with which he can buy a cigar. There was a time when these words would have checked the severest decrees of the highest magistrate; now, when they fire off "that gun," the French soldiers stand at its mouth, laugh, and say, "*Boom!* you have no balls for your cartridges!"

The wine finished, our two artists took up their line of march for the object that had outlived so many millions on millions of human beings, and at last reached it, discovering its abode afar off by the crowd of fair and unfair, or red-haired Saxons, who were thronging up a staircase of a house near the

Ripetta, as if a steamboat were ringing her last bell, and the plank were being drawn in.

"And pray, can you tell me, Mister Buller, if it's a positive fact that the man has been so long as they say, at work on the thing?"

"And ah! I haven't the slightest doubt of it, myself. I've been told that he has worked on it, to be sure, for full thirty years; and I may say I am delighted that he has it done at last, and that it is to be packed up and sent away to St. Petersburg next week. And how do you like the Hotel Minerva? I think it's not a very dirty inn, but the waiters are very demanding, and the fleas——"

"I beg you won't speak of them; it makes my blood run cold. Have you seen the last copy of *Galignani?* The Americans, I am glad to see, have had trouble with us, and I hope they will be properly punished. Do you know the Duke of Bigghed is in town?"

"Really! and when did he come?—and where is the duchess? Oh! she's a very amiable lady; but here's the picture!"

Ushered in, or preceded by this rattle-headed talk, Caper and Rocjean stood at last before Ivanhof's celebrated painting —finished at last! Thirty years' work, and the result?

A very unsatisfactory stream of water, a crowd of Orientals, and our Saviour descending a hill.

The general impression left on the mind after seeing it, was like that produced by a wax-work show. Nature was travestied; ease, grace, freedom, were wanting. Evidently the thirty years might have been better spent collecting beetles or dried grasses.

Around the walls of the studio hung sketches painted during visits the artist had made to the East. Here were studies of Eastern heads, costumes, trees, soil by riverside, sand in the desert, copied with scrupulous care and precise truth; yet, when they were all together in the great painting, the combined effect was a failure.

The artist, they said, had, during this long period, received an annual pension of so many roubles from the Russian government, and had taken his time about it. At last it was completed; the painting that had outlasted a generation was to be sent to St. Petersburg to hibernate, after a lifetime spent in sunny Italy. Well! after all, it was better worth the money paid for it, than that paid for nine tenths of those kingly toys in the baby-house Green Chambers of Dresden. *Le Roi s'amuse!*

And the white-haired Saxons came in shoals to the studio to see the painting with thirty years' labor on it, and accordingly as their oracles had judged it, so did they: for behold! gay colors are tabooed in the mythology of the Pokerites, and are classed with perfumes, dance music, and jollity, and art earns a precarious livelihood in their land, where all knowledge of it is supposed to be tied up with the enjoyers of primogeniture.

The Apollo, where grand opera, sandwiched with moral ballets, is given for the benefit of foreigners, principally, would be a fine house if you could only see it; but when Caper was in Rome, the oil lamps, showing you where to sit down, did not reveal its proportions, or the dresses of the box beauties, to any advantage; and as oil lamps will smoke, there settled a veil over the theatre toward the second act, that draped Comedy like Tragedy, and then set her to coughing.

During Carnival, a melancholy ball or two was given there. A few wild foreigners venturing in masked, believed they had mistaken the house; for, although many women were wandering around in domino, they found the Roman young men unmasked, walking about dressed in canes and those dress coats familiarly known as tail coats, which cause a man to look like a swallow with the legs of a crane, and wearing on their impassive faces the appearance of men waiting for an oyster supper—or an earthquake.

The commissionaire at the hotel always recommends strangers to go to the Apollo: "I will git you lôge, sare, first tier—more noble, sare."

The Capranica Theatre is next in size and importance. It is beyond the Pantheon, out of the foreign quarter of Rome, and you will find in it a Roman audience—to a limited extent. Salvini acted there in *Othello*, and filled the character admirably. It is needless to say that Iago received even more applause than Othello; Italians know such men profoundly—they are Figaros turned undertakers. Opera was given at the Capranica when the Apollo was closed.

The Valle is a small establishment, where Romans, pure blood, of the middle class, and the nobility who did not hang on to foreigners, were to be found. Giuseppina Gassier, who has since sung in America, was prima donna there, appearing generally in the *Sonnambula*.

But the Capranica Theatre was the resort for the Roman *minenti*, decked in all their bravery. Here came the shoemaker, the tailor, and the small artisan, all with their wives or women, and with them the wealthy peasant who had ten cents to pay for entrance. Here the audience wept and laughed, applauded the actors, and talked to each other from one side of the house to the other. Here the plays represented Roman life in the rough, and were full of words and expressions not down in any dictionary or phrase book; nor in these local displays were forgotten various Roman peculiarities of accentuation of words, and curious intonations of voice. The Roman people indulge in chest notes, leaving head notes to the Neapolitans, who certainly do not possess such smoothness of tongue as would classify them among their brethren in the old proverb: "When the confusion of tongues happened at the building of the tower of Babel, if the Italian had been there, Nimrod would have made him a plasterer!"

You will do well, if you want to learn from the stage and audience, the Roman *plebs*, their customs and language, to attend the Capranica Theatre often; to attend it in "fatigue dress," and in gentle mood, being neither shocked nor astonished if a good-looking Roman youth should call your attention to the fact that there is a beautiful girl in the box to the left hand, and inquire if you know whether she is the daughter of Santi Stefoni, the grocer? And should the man on the other side offer you some pumpkin seeds to eat, by all means accept a few; you can't tell what they may bring forth, if you will only plant them cheerfully.

Do not think it strange, if a doctor on the stage recommends conserve of vipers to a consumptive patient; for these poisonous reptiles are caught in large numbers in the mountains back of Rome, and sold to the city apothecaries, who prepare large quantities of them for their customers.

When you see, perhaps the hero of the play, thrown into a paroxysm of anger and fiery wrath by some untoward event, proceed calmly to cut up two lemons, squeeze into a tumbler their juice, and then drink it down—learn that it is a common Roman remedy for anger.

Or if, when a piece of crockery, or other fragile article, may be broken, you notice one of the actors carefully counting the pieces, do not think it is done in order to reconstruct the article, but to guide him in the purchase of a lottery ticket.

When you notice that on one of his hands the second finger is twined over the first, of the Rightful-heir in presence of the Wrongful-heir, you may know that the first is guarding himself against the Evil Eye supposed to belong to the second.

And—the list could be extended to an indefinite length—you will learn more, by going to the Capranica.

At the Metastasio Theatre there was a French vaudeville company, passably good, attended by a French audience, the majority officers and soldiers. Here were presented such attractive plays as *La Femme qui Mord*, or "The Woman who Bites;" *Sullivan*, the hero of which gets *bien gris*, very gray —that is, blue—that is, very tipsy; and, at the close, astonishes the audience with the moral: To get tight, is human! *Dalilah*, &c., &c. The French are not very well beloved by the Romans pure and simple; it is not astonishing, therefore, that their language should be laughed at. One morning Rome woke up to find placards all over the city, headed:

FRENCH

TAUGHT IN THIRTY-SIX LESSONS!

Apply to Monsieur So-and-so.

A few days afterward appeared a fearful woodcut, the

head of a jackass, with his tongue hanging down several inches, and under it these words, in Italian: "The only tongue yet learnt in less than thirty-six lessons!"

Caper, seated one night in the parquette of the Metastasio, had at his side a French infantry soldier. In conversation, he asked him:

"How long have you been in Rome?"

"Three years, *Mossu*."

"Wouldn't you like to return to France?"

"Not at all."

"Why not?"

"Wine is cheap here, tobacco not dear, the ladies are extremely kind: *voila tout!*"

"You have all these in France."

"*Oui, Mossu!* but when I return there, I shall be a farmer again; and it's a frightful fact, that you may plough your heart out, without turning up but a very small quantity of these articles there!"

French soldiers still protect Rome—and "these articles there."

"Can you tell me," said Uncle Bill Browne to Rocjean, with the air of a man about to ask a hard conundrum, "why beards, long hair, and art, always go together?"

"Of course, art draws out beards along with talent. Paints and bristles must go together; but high art drives the hair of the head in, and clinches it. Among artists, first and last, there have been men with giant minds, and they have known it was their duty to show their mental power: the beard is the index."

"But the beard points downward," suggested Caper, "and not upward."

"That depends——"

"On *pomade Hongroise*—or beeswax," interrupted Caper.

"Exactly; but let me answer Uncle Bill. To begin, we may safely assert that an artist's life—here in Rome, for instance—is about as independent a one as society will tolerate. Its laws, as to shaving especially, he ignores; and, caring very little for the Rules of the Toilette, as duly published by the *bon ton* journals, uses his razor for mending lead pencils, and permits his beard to enjoy long vacation rambles. Again: those who first set the example of long beards, Leonardo da Vinci, for example, who painted his own portrait with a full beard a foot long, were men who moved from principle; and I have the belief, that were Leonardo alive to-day, he would say:

"My son, and well-beloved Rocjean, *zitto!* and let ME talk. Know, then, that I did permit my beard luxuriant length—for a reason. Thou dost not know, but I do, that among the ancient Egyptians they worshipped in their deity the male and female principle combined; so the exponents of this belief, the Egyptian priests, endeavored in their attire to show a mingling of the male and female sex; they wore long garments, like women, *vergogna!* they wore long hair, *guai!* and they SHAVED THEIR FACES! It pains me to say, that their indecent example is followed even to this day, by the priests of what should be a purer and better religion.

"*Silenzio!* I have not yet said my say. Among Eastern nations, their proverbs, and, what is better, their customs, show a powerful protest against this impure old faith. You have seen the flowing beards of the Mohammedans, especially the Turks, and their short-shaved heads of hair, and you may have heard of their words of wisdom:

"'Long hair, little brain.'

"And that eloquent sentence:

"'Who has no beard, has no authority.'

"They have other sayings, which I cannot approve of; for instance:

"'Do not buy a red-haired person; do not sell one either. If you have any in the house, drive them away.'

"I say I do not approve of this, for the majority of the English have red heads; and people who want to buy my pictures I never would drive out of my house, *mai!*"

"Come," said Caper, "Leonardo no longer speaks, when there is a question of buying or selling. Assume the first person."

"Another excellent reason for artists in Rome to wear beards is, that where their foreign names cannot be pronounced, they are often called by the size, color, or shape of this face drapery. This is particularly the case in the Café Greco, where the waiters, who have to charge for coffee, &c., when the artist does not happen to have the change about him, are compelled to give him a name on their books, and in more than one instance, I know that they are called from their beards. I have a memorandum of these nicknames: I am called *Barbone*, or Big-bearded; and you, Caper, are down as *Sbarbato Inglese*, The Shaved Englishman."

"H'm!" spoke Caper; "I an't an Englishman, and I don't shave; my beard has to come yet."

"What is my name?" asked Uncle Bill.

"*Paga Sempre*, or He Pays Always. A countryman of mine is called *Baffi Rici*, or Big Moustache; another one, *Barbetta*, Little Beard; another, *Barbáccia*, Shabby Beard; another, *Barba Nera*, Black Beard; and, of course, there is a *Barba Rossa*, or Red Beard. Some of the other names are funny enough, and would by no means please their owners. There is *Zoppo Francese*, The Lame Frenchman; *Scapiglione*, the Rowdy; *Pappagallo*, the Parrot; *Milordo*; *Furioso*; and one friend of ours is known, whenever he forgets to pay two *baiocchi* for his coffee, as *San Pietro!*"

"Well," said Uncle Bill, "I'll tell you why I thought you artists wore long beards: that when you were hard up, and couldn't buy brushes, you might have the material ready to make your own."

"You're wrong, uncle," remarked Caper. "When we can't buy them, we get trusted for them—that's our way of having a brush with the enemy."

"That will do, Jim, that will do; say no more. None of the artists' beards here can compare with one belonging to a buffalo-and-prairie painter who lives out in St. Louis. It is so long, he ties the ends together, and uses it for a bootjack. Good night, boys! good night!"

Rocjean was finishing his after-dinner-ical coffee and cigar, when, looking up from *Las Novedades*, containing the latest news from Madrid, and in which he had just read *en Roma es donde hay mas mendigos*—Rome, is where most beggars are, found; London, where most engineers, lost women, and rat terriers abound; Brussels, where women who smoke are all round—looking up from this interesting reading, he saw opposite him a young man, whose acquaintance, he knew at a glance, was worth making. Refinement, common sense, and energy were to be read plainly in his face. When he left the café, Rocjean asked an artist with long hair, who was fast smoking himself to the color of the descendants of Ham, if he knew the man?"

"No-o-oo; I believe he's some kind of a calico painter."

"What?"

"Oh! a feller that makes designs for a calico mill."

Not long afterward Rocjean was introduced to him, and found him, as first impressions taught him he would, a man well worth knowing. He was making a holiday visit to Rome, his settled residence being in Paris, where his occupation was designer of patterns for a large calico mill in the United States. A New-Yorker by birth, consequently more of a cosmopolitan than the provincial life of our other American cities will tolerate or can create in their children, Charles Gordon was every inch a man, and a bitter foe to every liar and thief. He was well informed, for he had, as a boy, been solidly instructed; he was polite, refined, for he had been well educated. His life was a story often told: mercantile parent, very wealthy; son sent to college; talent for art, developed at the expense of trigonometry and morning prayers; mercantile parent fails, and falls from Fifth Avenue to Brooklyn, preparatory to embarking for the land of those who have failed and fallen—wherever that is. Son wears long hair, and believes he looks like the painter who was killed by a baker's daughter, writes trashy verses about a man who was wronged, and went off and howled himself to a long repose, sick of this vale of tears, *et cetera*. Finally, in the midst of his despair, long hair, bad poetry and painting, an enterprising friend, who sees he has an eye for color, its harmonies and contrasts, raises him with a strong hand into the clear atmosphere of exertion for a useful and definite end—makes him a "calico painter."

It was a great scandal for the Bohemians of art to find this calico painter received everywhere in refined and intelligent society, while they, with all their airs, long hairs, and shares of impudence, could not enter—they, the creators of Medoras, Magdalens, Our Ladies of Lorette, Brigands' Brides, Madame not In, Captive Knights, Mandoline Players, Grecian Mothers, Love in Repose, Love in Sadness, Moonlight on the Waves, Last Tears, Resignation, Broken Lutes, Dutch Flutes, and other mock-sentimental-titled paintings.

"God save me from being a gazelle!" said the monkey.

"God save us from being utility calico painters!" cried the highminded, dirty cavaliers who were not cavaliers, as they once more rolled over in their smokehouse.

"In 1854," said Gordon, one day, to Rocjean, after their acquaintance had ripened into friendship, "I was indeed in sad circumstances, and was passing through a phase of life when bad tobacco, acting on an empty stomach, gave me a glimpse of the Land of the Grumblers. One long year, and all that was changed; then I woke up to reality and practical life in a 'calico mill;' then I wrote the lines you have asked me about. Take them for what they are worth.

REDIVIVUS.
MDCCCLVI.

He sat in a garret in Fifty-four,
To welcome Fifty-five:
'God knows,' said he, 'if another year
Will find this man alive.

I was born for love, I live in song,
Yet loveless and songless I'm passing along,
    And the world?—Hurrah!
    Great soul, sing on!'

He sat in the dark, in Fifty-four,
    To welcome Fifty-five:
'God knows,' said he, 'if another year
    I'll any better thrive.
I was born for light, I live in the sun,
Yet in darkness, and sunless, I'm passing on,
    And the world?—Hurrah!
    Great soul, shine on!'

He sat in the cold, in Fifty-four,
    To welcome Fifty-five:
'God knows,' said he, 'I'm fond of fire,
    From warmth great joy derive.
I was born warm-hearted, and oh! it's wrong
For them all to coldly pass along:
    And the world?—Hurrah!
    Great soul, burn on!'

He sat in a home, in Fifty-five,
    To welcome Fifty-six:
'Throw open the doors!' he cried aloud,
    'To all whom Fortune kicks!
I was born for love, I was born for song,
And great-hearted MEN my halls shall throng.
    And the world?—Hurrah!
    Great soul, sing on!'

He sat in bright light, in Fifty-five,
    To welcome Fifty-six:
'More lights!' he cried out, with joyous shout;
    'Night ne'er with day should mix.

I was born for light, I live in the sun,
  In the joy of others my life's begun.
    And the world?—Hurrah!
    Great soul, shine on!'

He sat in great warmth, in Fifty-five,
  To welcome Fifty-six,
In a glad and merry company
  Of brave, true-hearted Bricks!
'I was born for warmth, I was born for love,
  I've found them all, thank God above!
    And the world?—Ah! bah!
    Great soul, move on!'

The Roman season was nearly over: travellers were making preparations to fly out of one gate as the malaria should enter by the other; for, according to popular report, this fearful disease enters the last day of April, at midnight, and is in full possession of the city on the first day of May. Rocjean, not having any fears of it, was preparing not only to meet it, but to go out and spend the summer with it. It costs something, however, to keep company with La Malaria, and our artist had but little money: he must sell some paintings. Now it was unfortunate for him, that though a good painter, he was a bad salesman; he never kept a list of all the arrivals of his wealthy countrymen, or other strangers who bought paintings; he never ran after them, laid them under obligations with drinks, dinners, and drives; for he had neither the inclination nor that capital which is so important for a picture merchant to possess in order to drive—a heavy trade, and achieve success—such as it is. Rocjean had friends, and warm ones; so that, whenever they judged his finances were in an embarrassed state, they voluntarily sent wealthy sensible as well as wealthy insensible patrons of art to his aid, the latter going as Dutch galliots laden with doubloons might go to the relief of a poor, graceful felucca, thrown on her beam ends by a squall.

One morning there glowed in Rocjean's studio the portly forms of Mr. and Mrs. Cyrus Shodd, together with the tall, fragile figure of Miss Tillie Shodd, daughter and heiress-apparent and transparent. Rocjean welcomed them as he would have manna in the desert, for he judged, by the air and manner of the head of the family, that he was on picture buying bent. He even gayly smiled, when Miss Shodd, pointing out to her father, with her parasol, some beauty in a painting on the easel, ran its point along the canvas, causing a green streak from the top of a stone pine to extend from the tree some miles into the distant mountains of the Abruzzi—the paint was not dry!

She made several hysterical shouts of horror after committing this little act, and then seating herself in an arm-chair, proceeded to take a mental inventory of the articles of furniture in the studio.

Mr. Shodd explained to Rocjean that he was a plain man:
This was apparent at sight.
That he was an uneducated man:
This asserted itself to the eyes and ears.
After which self-denial, he commenced "pumping" the artist on various subjects, assuming an ignorance of things which, to a casual observer, made him appear like a fool; to a thoughtful person, a knave: the whole done in order, perhaps, to learn about some trifle which a plain, straight-forward ques-

tion would have elicited at once. Rocjean saw his man, and led him a fearful gallop in order to thoroughly examine his action and style.

Spite of his commercial life, Mr. Shodd had found time to "self-educate" himself—he meant self-instruct; and having a retentive memory, and a not always strict regard for truth, was looked up to by the humble ignorant as a very columbiad in argument, the only fault to be found with which gun was, that when it was drawn from its quiescent state into action, its effective force was comparatively nothing, one half the charge escaping through the large touchhole of untruth. Discipline was entirely wanting in Mr. Shodd's composition. A man who undertakes to be his own teacher, rarely punishes his scholar, rarely checks him with rules and practice, or accustoms him to order and subordination. Mr. Shodd, therefore, was—undisciplined: a raw recruit, not a soldier.

Of course, his conversation was all contradictory. In one breath, on the self-abnegation principle, he would say: "I don't know anything about paintings;" in the next breath, his overweening egotism would make him loudly proclaim: "There never was but one painter in this world, and his name is Hockskins; he lives in my town, and he knows more than any of your 'old masters'! *I* ought to know!" Or: "*I* am an uneducated man," meaning uninstructed; immediately following it with the assertion: "All teachers, scholars, and colleges are useless folly, and all education is worthless, except self-education."

Unfortunately, self-education is too often only education of self!

After carefully examining all Rocjean's pictures, he settled his attention on a sunset view over the Campagna, leaving Mrs. Shodd to talk with our artist. You have seen—all have seen—more than one Mrs. Shodd; by nature and innate refinement, ladies; (the "Little Dorrits" Dickens shows to his beloved countrymen, to prove to them that not all nobility is nobly born—a very mild lesson, which they refuse to regard;) Mrs. Shodds who, married to Mr. Shodds, pass a life of silent protest against brutal words and boorish actions. With but few opportunities to add acquirable graces to natural ease and self-possession, there was that in her kindly tone of voice and gentle manner winning the heart of a gentleman to respect her as he would his mother. It was her mission to atone for her husband's sins, and she fulfilled her duty; more could not be asked of her, for his sins were many. The daughter was a copy of the father, in crinoline; taking to affectation—which is vulgarity in its most offensive form—as a duck takes to water. Even her dress was marked, not by that neatness which shows refinement, but by precision, which in dress is vulgar. One glance, and you saw the woman who in another age would have thrown her glove to the tiger for her lover to pick up!

Among Rocjean's paintings was the portrait of a very beautiful woman, made by him years before, when he first became an artist, and long before he had been induced to abandon portrait painting for landscape. It was never shown to studio visitors, and was placed with its face against the wall, behind other paintings. In moving one of these to place it in a good light on the easel, it fell, with the others, to the floor, face uppermost; and while Rocjean, with a painting in his hands, could not stoop at once to replace it, Miss Shodd's sharp eyes discovered the beautiful face, and, her curiosity being excited, nothing would do but it must be placed on the easel. Unwilling to refuse a request from the daughter of a patron of Art in perspective, Rocjean complied, and, when the portrait was placed, glancing toward Mrs. Shodd, had the satisfaction of reading in her eyes true admiration for the startlingly lovely face looking out so womanly from the canvas.

"H'm!" said Shodd the father; "quite a fancy head."

"Oh! it is an exact portrait of Julia Ting. If she had sat for her likeness, it couldn't have been better. I must have the painting, pa, for Julia's sake. I *must*. It's a naughty word, isn't it, Mr. Rocjean? but it's so expressive!"

"Unfortunately, the portrait is not for sale. I placed it on the easel only in order not to refuse your request."

Mr. Shodd saw the road open to an argument. He was in ecstasy; a long argument—an argument full of churlish flings and boorish slurs, which he fondly believed passed for polished satire and keen irony. He did not know Rocjean; he never could know a man like him; he never could learn the truth, that confidence will overpower strength; only at last, when through his hide and bristles entered the flashing steel, did he, tottering backward, open his eyes to the fact that he had found his master—that, too, in a poor devil of an artist.

The landscapes were all thrown aside; Shodd must have that portrait. His daughter had set her heart on having it, he said, and could a gentleman refuse a lady anything?

"It is on this very account I refuse to part with it," answered Rocjean.

It instantly penetrated Shodd's head that all this refusal was only design on the part of the artist to obtain a higher price for the work than he could otherwise hope for; and so, with what he believed was a masterstroke of policy, he at once ceased importuning the artist, and shortly departed from the studio, preceding his wife with his daughter on his arm, leaving the consoler, and by all means his best half, to atone, by a few kind words at parting with the artist, for her husband's sins.

"And there," thought Rocjean, as the door closed, "goes 'a patron of art'—and by no means the worst pattern. I hope he will meet with Chapin, and buy an Orphan and an Enterprise statue; once in his house, they will prove to every observant man the owner's taste."

Mr. Shodd, having a point to gain, went about it with elephantine grace and dexterity. The portrait he had seen at Rocjean's studio he was determined to have. He invited the artist to dine with him—the artist sent his regrets; to accompany him, "with the ladies," in his carriage to Tivoli—the artist politely declined the invitation; to a *conversazione*, the invitation from Mrs. Shodd—a previous engagement prevented the artist's acceptance.

Mr. Shodd changed his tactics. He discovered at his banker's, one day, a keen, communicative, wiry, shrewd, &c., &c., enterprising, &c., "made-a-hundred-thousand-dollars" sort of a little man, named Briggs, who was travelling in order to travel, and grumble. Mr. Shodd "came the ignorant game" over this Briggs; pumped him, without obtaining any information, and finally turned the conversation on artists, denouncing the entire body as a set of the keenest swindlers, and citing the instance of one he knew who had a painting which he believed it would be impossible for any man to buy, simply because the artist, knowing that he (Shodd) wished it, would not set a price on it, so as to have a very high one offered. (!) Mr. Briggs instantly was deeply interested. Here was a chance for him to display before Shodd of Shoddsville his shrewdness, keenness, and so forth. He volunteered to buy the painting.

In Rome, an artist's studio may be his castle, or it may be an Exchange. To have it the first, you must affix a notice to your studio door, announcing that all entrance of visitors to the studio is forbidden except on, say Monday, from twelve M. to three P. M. This is the baronial manner. But the artist who is not wealthy, or has not made a name, must keep an Exchange, and receive all visitors who choose to come, at almost any hours—model hours excepted. So Briggs, learning from Shodd, by careful cross-questioning, the artist's name, address, and a description of the painting, walked there at once, introduced himself to Rocjean, shook his hand as if it were the handle of a pump upon which he had serious intentions, and then began examining the paintings. He looked at them all, but there was no portrait. He asked Rocjean if he painted portraits; he found out that he did not. Finally, he told the artist that he had heard some one say—he did not remember who—that he had seen a very pretty head in his studio, and asked Rocjean if he would show it to him.

"You have seen Mr. Shodd lately, I should think?" said the artist, looking into the eyes of Mr. Briggs.

A suggestion of a clean brickbat passed under a sheet of yellow tissue-paper was observable in the hard cheeks of Mr. Briggs, that being the final remnant of all appearance of modesty left in the sharp man, in the shape of a blush.

"Oh! yes; everybody knows Shodd; man of great talent—generous," said Briggs.

"Mr. Shodd may be very well known," remarked Rocjean, measuredly, "but the portrait he saw is not well known; he and his family are the only ones who have seen it. Perhaps it may save you trouble to know, that the portrait I have several times refused to sell him, will never be sold while I live. The *common* opinion that an artist, like a Jew, will sell the old clo' from his back for money, is erroneous."

Mr. Briggs shortly after this left the studio, slightly at a discount, and as if he had been measured, as he said to himself; and then and there determined to say nothing to Shodd about his failing in his mission to the savage artist. But Shodd found it all out in the first conversation he made with Briggs; and very bitter were his feelings when he learned that a poor devil of an artist dared possess anything he could not buy, and, moreover, had a quiet moral strength which the vulgar man feared. In his anger, Shodd, with his disregard for truth, commenced a fearful series of attacks against the artist, regaling every one he dared to with with the coarsest slanders, in the vilest language, against the painter's character. A very few days sufficed to circulate them, so that they reached Rocjean's ears; a very few minutes passed before the artist presented himself to the eyes of Shodd, and, fortunately finding him alone, told him, in four words, "You are a slanderer;" mentioning to him, besides, that if he ever uttered another slander against his name, he should compel him to give him instantaneous satisfaction, and that, as an American, Shodd knew what that meant.

It is needless to say, that a liar and slanderer is a coward;

consequently Mr. Shodd, with the consequences before his eyes, never again alluded to Rocjean, and shortly left the city for Naples, to bestow the light of his countenance there in his great character of Art Patron.

"It is a heart-touching face," said Caper, as, one morning, while hauling over his paintings, Rocjean brought the portrait to light which the cunning Shodd had so longed to possess for cupidity's sake.

"I should feel as if I had thrown Psyche to the Gnomes to be torn to pieces, if I had given such a face to Shodd. If I had sold it to him, I should have been degraded; for the women loved by man should be kept sacred in memory. She was a girl I knew in Prague, and, I think, with six or eight exceptions, the loveliest one I ever met. Some night, at sunset, I shall walk over the old bridge, and meet her as we parted; *à propos* of which meeting, I once wrote some words. Hand me that portfolio, will you? Thank you. Oh! yes; here they are. Now, read them, Caper; out with them!

ANEZKA OD PRAHA.

Years, weary years, since on the Moldau bridge,
  By the five stars and cross of Nepomuk,
I kissed the scarlet sunset from her lips:
    Anezka, fair Bohemian, thou wert there!

Dark waves beneath the bridge were running fast,
In haste to bathe the shining rocks, whence rose
Tier over tier, the gleaming domes and spires,
Turrets and minarets of the Holy City,
Its crown the Hradschin of Bohemia's kings.
O'er Wyssehrad we saw the great stars shine;

We felt the night wind on the rushing stream;
We drank the air as if 'twere Melnick wine,
And every draught whirled us still nearer Nebe:
   Anezka, fair Bohemian, thou wert there!

Why ever gleam thy black eyes sadly on me?
Why ever rings thy sweet voice in my ear?
Why looks thy pale face from the drifting foam
Dashed by the wild sea on this distant shore—
Or from the white clouds does it beckon me?

My own heart answers: On the Moldau bridge,
Anezka, we will meet to part no more.

CHAPTER VIII.

IF a man's mind and purse were in. such state that he didn't care where he went, and was able to go there; if the weather was fine, and the aforesaid man could eat, drink, and sleep rough, and really loved picturesqueness in all his surroundings for its own sake—that man should travel by *vettura*. Not one of. the *vetture* advertised by a Roman "to go to all parts of the world;" not one of those travelling carriages with a seat for milady's maid and milord's man, with courier beside the driver, and a *vettura* dog on top of the baggage, at the very sight of which beggars spring from the ground as if by magic, and the custom house officers assume airs of state. No, no, NO! What is meant by a *vettura*, is a broken-down carriage, seats inside for four English or six Italians, a seat outside, along with the driver, for one American or three Italians, and places to hold on to, for two or three more Italians. The harness of the horses consists of an originally leather harness, with rope commentaries, string emendations, twine notes, and ragged explanations of the primary work; in plain English, it's an edition of harness with nearly all the original leather expurgated.

Well, you enter into agreement with the compeller of horses, alias *vetturino*, to go to a certain town a certain distance from Rome. The vehicle he drives is popularly reported to leave regularly for that town; you know that regularly means regularly-uncertainly. You go and see the *vetturino*, say in that classic spot, the Piazza Pollajuólo; you find him, after endless inquiries, in a short jacket, in a wineshop, smoking a throat-scorcher of a short pipe, and you arrange with him as regards the fare, for he has different prices for different people. Little children and soldiers pay half price, as you will read on your railroad ticket to Frascati, and priests pay what they please, foreigners all that can be squeezed out of them, and Italians at fixed price.

As for the horses that drag this *vettura*. Olà! I hope the crows will spare them one day longer. The long-suffering traveller pauses here, reader, wipes the dust from his brow, and exclaims:

"Blessed be bull fights; for they use up that class of horses which in pious America drag oysters to their graves, and in Papal Italy drag the natives to their lairs outside of Rome!"

You will toil along the dusty plain—hot, weary, worn out —but anon you begin the ascent of the mountains; then, as you go up, the air grows purer and cooler. You descend from the *vettura*, and on foot tramp up the road, perhaps beside the driver, who is innately thankful to you for saving his horses a heavy pull; and with him, or a fellow traveller, joke off the weary feeling you had in the low grounds. Again you are ascending a still steeper part of the mountain. Now oxen are attached to the old rumbling rattletrap of a carriage, and it is *creak*, pull, yell, and cheer, until you find yourself above the clouds—serene and calm—away from dust, heat, turmoil, bustle, in an old *locanda*, in a shaded room, a flask of cool red wine before you, the south wind rustling the leaves in the lattice, the bell of the old Franciscan convent sending its clear silver notes away over valley and mountain from its sleepy old home under the chestnut trees, the crowing of cocks away down the mountain, the hum of bees in the flower garden under the window—the blessed, holy calm of the country!

It is the end aimed at that makes *vettura* travelling jolly; for it can well be imagined, as an Englishman justly said of it: "It is just as good a vehicle to go to the gallows in, as any I've ever been in, I'm sure." But it is equally certain, that the quiet joys revealed to the man who travels by it—always be it understood, the man who don't care where he goes, or when he gets there—are many. These quiet joys consist of exquisite paintings, sketches, scenes, landscapes, or whatever else you choose to call them, wherein shrines, *osterias* or taverns, *locandas* or inns; costumes; shadow of grand old trees; the old Roman stone sarcophagus turned into a water trough, into which falls the fountain, and where the tired horses thrust their dusty muzzles, drawing up water with a rattling noise, while the south wind plays through the trees, and they switch the flies from their flanks with their tails; the old priest, accosted by the three small boys—"they are asking his blessing," said Miss Hicks—"they are asking him for a pinch of snuff," said Caper—and when she saw him produce his snuff-box, she acquiesced; the winecarts instead of swillcarts; the Italian peasants instead of Paddies; agriculture instead of commerce; churches and monasteries in place of cotton mills; Roman watch towers instead of factory chimneys; trees instead of board yards; vineyards and olive groves in place of blue grass and persimmon trees; golden oranges in place of crab apples and choke pears; *zigarri scelti* instead of Cabañas —but this is the reverse of the medal; let us stop before we ruin our first position.

It was warm in Rome. The English had fled. The Romans, pure blood, once more wandered toward sunset—not after it—on the Pincian Hill, and trod with solid step the gravel of *Il Pincio Liberato*. In the Spanish square around the fountain called Barcaccia, the lemonaders are encamped; a hint of lemon, a supposition of sugar, a certainty of water— what more can one expect for a *baiocco?* From midday until three o'clock in the afternoon, scarcely a place of business, store or shop, is open in Rome. The inhabitants are sleeping, clad as Monsieur Dubufe conceived the original Paradisians should be clad. At sunset, as you turn down the Via Condotti, you see chairs and tables placed outside the Café Greco for its frequenters. The interior rooms are too, too close. Even that penetralia, the "Omnibus," cannot compare with the unwalled room outside, with its star-gemmed ceiling, and the cool breeze eddying away the cigar smoke; so its usual occupants are all outside.

At one of these tables sat Caper, Rocjean, and their mutual friend, Dexter—an animal-painter—the three in council, discussing the question, "Where shall we go this summer?" Rocjean strongly advocated the cause of a little town in the Volscian mountains, called Segni, assuring his friends that two artists of the French Academy had discovered it the summer before.

"And they told me," he said, "that they would have lived there until this time, if they had had it in their power. Not that the scenery around there was any better, if so good, as at Subiaco, or even Gennezzano; but the wine was very cheap, and the cost of boarding at the *locanda* was only forty *baiocchi* a day——"

"We will go! we will go!" chimed in Caper.

"There were festivals in some of the neighboring towns nearly every week, and costumes——"

"Let us travel there," said Caper, "at once!"

"Horses were to be had for a song——"

"I am ready to sing," remarked Dexter.

"There was good shooting; *beccafichi*, woodcock, and quails; also red-legged partridges——"

"Say no more," spoke Caper, "but let us secure seats in the next stage that starts for such game scenes—immediately!"

Matters were so well arranged by Rocjean, that three days after the above conversation, the three artists, with passports properly viséd, were waiting, toward sunset, in the Piazza Pollajuólo, for the time not advertised, but spoken of, by the *vetturino* Francesco as his hour for starting for Segni.

Our trio entered the piazza (every house in the environs of it being gayly decked outside with flying pennants, banners, standards, flags, in the shape of long shirts, short shirts, sheets, and stockings, hanging out to dry). They entered the house, resembling a henhouse, where the *vettura* was reposing, and commenced a rigid examination of the old vehicle, which looked guilty and treacherous enough to have committed all kinds of breakdowns and upsets in its day. While they were thus engaged, the driver and an assistant mounted to the top, and made fast the baggage, covering it all with a rough reed matting, and tying it carefully on with cords except a large-sized basket, which they let fall, striking Caper on one side of the head as it descended.

"*Accidente!*" yelled two voices from the top of the carriage. "Santa Maria! Madonna mia! it isn't anything, merely a bread basket!" cried Francesco, who, delighted to find out he had not killed his passenger, and so lost a *scudo*, at once harnessed in three horses abreast to the *vettura*, interspersing his performance with enough oaths and vulgarity to have lasted a small family of economical *contadine* for a week. One of his team, a mare named Filomena, he seemed to be particularly down on. She was evidently not of a sensitive disposition, or she might have revenged sundry defamations of her character with her heels. As it was, she only whinnied, and playfully took off the driver's cap with her teeth, lifting a few hairs with it.

"*Signora diavola!*" said Francesco, addressing the mare, and grabbing his cap from her teeth; "this is an insult—an insult to ME! Recollect that—when you are going up the mountain!"

"Come, Francesco, come!" said Rocjean; "it's time to be off."

"*Ecco me qua*, Signore; have patience a little minute (*piccolo momento*), and then, whew! but we'll fly!"

The trio were anxious to get off, for every now and then, from some third or fourth story window, down would come waste water thus emptied into the street, and they were fearful that they might be deluged.

"Jump inside," said Francesco, when he had the old *vet-*

tura fairly in the street; "then you may laugh at the cascades of Pollajuólo, *seguro!*"

Creak, bang! rumble, rattle! off they went, and were fairly under way, at last, for Segni. They passed out of Rome by the Porta San Giovanni, where their passports received a *visto;* and this being finished, again started, the *vettura* soon reaching the Campagna. It looked a fair and winning scene, as they saw far away its broad fields of ripe wheat swayed by the wind, and nodding all golden in the setting sun; herds of horses feeding on the bright green grass; the large gray oxen, black eyed and branching horned, following the *mandarina*, or leading ox, with his tinkling bell; the ruined aqueducts and Roman tombs; the distant mountains robed in purple mist; the blue-clothed *contadini* returning homeward. Yet this was where the malaria raged. As the road, after an hour's drive, gradually ascending, carried them into a purer and clearer air, and they felt its freshness invigorating mind and body, there broke out a merry spirit of fun with our trio, as, descending from the carriage, they walked up the steepest part of the ascent, laughing and joking, or stopping to note the glories of sunset over Rome, above which hung the dome of St. Peter's, grand in the golden haze.

They reached Colonna while the west was still flaming away, and found the red wine there cool, if nothing better, as they drank it by the fountain under the old trees. Then they mounted the *vettura* refreshed, and pushed on in the shadow of evening, under a long avenue of trees, and late into the night, until they reached Valmontone; and they knew, by the tinkling of mule bells, and the hoarse shouts of their drivers, with the barking of dogs, and the bars of bright light shooting through darkness from doors and windows, that the *Osteria e Locanda* was near, and supper not far off. The *vettura* stopped.

Descending, they entered the large hall of the inn, with its whitewashed walls and brick floor, its ceiling heavy with rough-hewn rafters, and its long wooden tables and rough benches stained nearly black by use. By the oil lights burning in the graceful long-stemmed Roman lamps, they saw three or four countrymen eating eggs fried with olive oil in little earthenware pipkins—a highly popular dish in the country round Rome, since, by proper management, a great deal of bread, which is not very dear, can be consumed with a few eggs. One of the number was luxuriating in *agrodolce*—meat stewed with preserved prunes or cherries—a dish which many travellers have laughed at in Germany, but have never observed in "classic Italy."

"*E che volete, Signori?*" from the once white-aproned waiter, aroused our artists to a sense of duty; and fried ham, eggs, bread, and wine, with a salad, were ordered, slowly brought, and ham and eggs quickly finished and again furnished, much to the astonishment of a family of peasants who had entered while they were eating, and who watched the plates of ham and eggs disappear as if it were a feat of jugglery. After supper came coffee and cigars, and the sight of one of the soldiers of the patrol, who came in to have a glass of *sambuca*, his blue uniform in good condition, his carbine brightly shining. After the horses were well rested, the *vettura* again started, as the first faint light of day shone in the east. About two miles from Valmontone, they commenced the ascent of the mountains, and shortly had two oxen attached to help drag their vehicle upward. The road wound along a mountain side—a ravine far below them—and from its base arose a high conical mountain opposite to them, as they slowly toiled upward. Again and again they pulled through heavy clouds of mist hanging around the mountain side, emerging above them only again to enter others. Finally it cleared; and over the mountains, beyond the valley yet white with the morning dews, they saw the red sun rise clear and sparkling; while high above their heads, perched on mountain top and side, loomed out the old, gray, timeworn walls of Segni. The *vettura* came to a halt under the shade of some old mulberry trees, and our travellers descended, to leave it where it was, for the town was not built with a view to the entrance of carriages.

Leaving the *vettura*, they mounted the steep road, seeing above them the ruined walls, once the ramparts of the town, crowned by gray old houses with tiled roofs rising one over the other, and soon entered the Maggiore Gate, with its round arch, its architecture noting a time when Segni was not quite the unknown place it now is. As they entered the gate, seeing the cleanly dressed country people seated on the stone benches under its shadow—the women with their blue woollen shawls formed into coifs falling over head and shoulders, loose and pendent white linen sleeves, and black woollen bodices tightly laced, calico or woollen skirts, and dark-blue woollen aprons with broad bands of yellow or red; while the men wore blue knee breeches, brown woollen stockings, and blue jackets, with here and there a short scarlet waistcoat, and all with black conical felt hats, sometimes ornamented with a flower—noting all this, our artists knew it was Sunday, or a festival. It was both.

The main street was very narrow—the houses so close together that a donkey loaded with brushwood could hardly scrape through—and so steep that he had hard work to get a foothold on the smooth, worn stones serving to pave it. The buildings were all of that sombre gray stone so picturesque in paintings, and so pleasant for the eye to rest on, yet withal suggesting no brilliant ideas of cleanliness, or even neatness. The houses were rarely over two stories in height, the majority only one story, and but very few of them boasted glazed window frames, board shutters letting in light or keeping out rain. Two twists through the narrow streets, or rather alleys, a right-angled turn, a wheel to the left, then straight forward thirty steps, and lo! they were in the inn, alias *locanda*, of Gaetano. As soon as rooms could be given them, our artists, spite of its being daylight, took a long nap, induced by travelling all night without sleep.

About noon, the landlord, Gaetano, aroused them with the fact that dinner was ready. They made a hearty meal, the landlord being careful to wish them "good appetite" before they commenced. When it was over, and they were about to rise and go forth to discover if there was a café in the town, the waiter girl appeared with two large dishes, on one of which were green peas in the pod, and on the other goat's-milk cheese.

"I know what the cheese is for," said Caper; "but it seems to me an odd way, to send in peas for the guests to shell for them."

"Perhaps," said Dexter, "as they've no opera house here, it's one of their amusements."

"Can you tell me," asked Rocjean of the stout waiter girl, "what we are to do with those peas?"

"Eh? Why, Signor, they are the fruit. You eat them."

"Pods and all?"

"Certainly; they are very sweet and tender."

"No, thank you. You can take them away. Will you send the *padrone* here?"

In came the landlord, and then and there a bargain was struck. For forty cents a day, he agreed to give them individually:

First: Breakfast—consisting of eggs, bread, butter, fruit in season, one dish of meat, a pint of good wine, and a cup of coffee.

Second: Dinner—soup, boiled meat, roast meat, vegetables, bread, butter, fish occasionally, one pint of wine, salad, dessert.

Third: Supper—one dish of meat, bread, butter, salad, and pint of wine.

Fourth: A bedchamber for each one, with the use of the main room.

It was moreover agreed and covenanted, that for the extra sum of two *baiocchi* each one, he would provide a cup of coffee and sugar after dinner.

This is the Italian mode of proceeding; and when you have done thus, you will rarely find any trouble, either in receiving what you have agreed for, or in being overcharged. Justice to Gaetano Colajamo, keeper of the *locanda* at Segni, demands that it should be here witnessed that he faithfully and truly kept the agreement thus made; that, after six months spent with him by Caper, he found that Gaetano had acted fairly, squarely, honestly, and manfully with him, from the day of his arrival until he shook hands at parting. May his tribe increase!

Leaving the hotel, they found a café near the Maggiore Gate, and learned that coffee was to be had there only on Sundays and festivals, the demand for it on other days being so small that it would not pay to make it. After coffee, Caper proposed a ramble up town; and the trio sallied out, succeeding, by dint of perseverance, and digging their heels firmly in the pavement, in climbing up the main street, which was about ten feet wide, and very steep, an angle of forty-five degrees about describing its inclination; and as it was paved with limestone cubes, worn smooth by the iron shoes of clambering horses and donkeys, it was difficult at times to prevent slipping. The irregularity of the front of the houses, and their evident want of repairs—in fact, their general tumble-down look, relieved here and there by a handsome middle-age doorway or window on the first floor, while the second story would show a confused modern wall of rubble work and poverty-stricken style of architecture generally; all these contrasts brought out the picturesque element in force. As they passed a row of iron-grated windows, a rough, hairy hand was thrust nearly into Rocjean's face, with the request that he would bestow a *baioccho* for charity on the owner.

"What are you doing in there?" asked Dexter.

"Nothing, nothing. Santa Maria! I am an innocent man. I never did anything; I never will do anything so long as I live."

"That's the reason they shut you up, perhaps. You are lazy, an't you?"

"Never. It's because I've been too active. So, Signor, give me a few *baiocchi*, for I am tired of being shut up in this old bottle; and if they will let me out, I will marry her to-morrow."

So Rocjean gave him a few *baiocchi*, asking Caper what he thought of this plan of allowing jail-birds to sit and sing to every one who passed by, permitting the inmates of the prison to converse with and entertain their friends?

They had hardly passed the prison, before three horses, sleekly curried, and with ribbons tied to their manes and tails, were led past them. And in answer to a question from Dexter, he learned that they were being led down to the stretch of road at the foot of the town, the spur connecting the conical mountain on which Segni is built, with the Volscian mountains in its rear. This road was about a quarter of a mile in length, quite level, and lined on both sides with fine old elm trees, giving goodly shade. It was used as a race-course, and the three horses were going down to run a *Carriera*, or race. Four horses were to run barebacked, their riders being well used to dispense with saddles, and managing to guide them with a rope halter in lieu of a bridle. The purse was four *scudi* (four dollars). Two horses were to run at a time, and the race was then to be run off by the two winning horses.

Anxious to conform to the customs of the country, including Sabbath quarter-races, our three artists retraced their steps, and, descending the main street, were soon outside the gate of the town. Selecting a good position in the shade where they could see the race to advantage, they quietly waited for the races to begin. At the firing of a gun, down the course came two flying bay horses, ridden by boys, who urged them on to top speed, accelerated by the shouts of the entire population. The smallest horse won that heat. Again the gun was fired; and now the two other horses, a dark bay and a black, came thundering along, the black going ahead by four lengths, and receiving shouts of applause, as *Il Diavolo Benissimo!* Now came the real pull, for the two winners were to try off; and as the last gun sounded, *Clatter, whiz!* the small bay and the black horse fairly flew by, neck and neck. Unfortunately, the black bolted from the course before he reached the goal, and the last seen of him he was somewhere on top of a hill, with his legs white with lime, which he had picked up darting through a mortar bed where a house was building. The bay horse, *Mortadella*, ridden by a boy named Bruno, won this Sunday quarter race; and though the horse was not timed, it is safe to say the time was good, taking into account the fact that on week days he brought wood down the mountain on his back, and consequently had that peculiar corkscrew motion incident to his profession.

The race over, Caper proposed their once more ascending the main street, and making a bold endeavor to discover the top of the town, from which he argued there must be a fine view. Sturdily mounting up, they found themselves at last on the summit of the mountain, and, passing several houses, an academy, and a church, found before them a pleasant walk called the Pianillo, which was the crown of the conical mountain, and from whence, looking over the valley below and around them, they saw far off the Albanian mountains to their front and left, while away to their right hand, and fading into the clouds, the chain of the Abruzzi showed them the confines of Naples. From this walk they saw the mountains and towns of San Germano, Santo Padre di Regno, L'Arnara, Frosinone, Torrice, Monte San Giovanni, Veroli, Ferentino, Morino, Agnani, Acuto, Piglio, Serrone, Paliano, Roviate, Civitella, Olevano, San Vito, Capranica, Gennazzano, Cave, Palestrina, Valmontone, Montefortino, Lugnano, Zagarolo, Colonna, Rocca Priora, and the neighboring towns of Sgurgola, Gorga, and Gavignano, with that lovely valley, La Villamagna.

Lost in admiration of the splendid panorama before them, our artists were not at first aware that the Pianillo was fast filling up with the people who had lately attended the horse race: believing they were attracted here by the lovely scenery, they only admired their good taste, when Rocjean, overhearing two of the Segnians, discovered that they came there to enjoy a very different spectacle—that of *La Giostra del Porchetto*, or

SMALL-HOG GAME.

What this might be, our artists had yet to learn. It sounded slightly sensual for a Sunday amusement, but as there was a bishop in the town, and nothing could consequently be permitted that would shock, &c., &c., Caper, Rocjean, and Dexter at once agreed to assist the heads of the Church in their pious endeavors to celebrate the day—as the Romans do. Not far from where they were standing, at the foot of wild rocks and the ruins of an old Roman watch tower, was a curious basin cut in the solid rock, its sides lined with large blocks, and its circular form preserved entire; its depth was from five to seven feet, and its bottom was, like the sides, paved with smooth blocks. It was popularly said to have been anciently a cistern, a fish tank, &c., but nothing was known definitely as to its original purpose. It now served for the circus, where the Small-Hog Game was annually indulged in.

About twenty-two o'clock (that is, six in the afternoon), the audience and spectators—for it was an audible as well as visible entertainment—being assembled, and desirous for the performance to commence, whistled and shouted slightly, but not indecorously; for the grand army of the town—seven gendarmes—were around. Our three artists mounted up the rocks overhanging the cistern, and looked down on the heads of the people. They saw a thousand or two female heads, mostly with light hair, all pulled directly back from the forehead, twisted into a knot behind, and tied with a piece of string, while a silver bodkin a foot in length, run in sideways, held it tight. The heads of these silver hairpins indicated the married or unmarried state of the wearers; the former were fashioned as acorns or flower buds, while the latter were full-blown flowers with expanded petals. The faces of these women were tanned, but ruddy health was there, and robust forms; and you saw among them all a very happy, contented, ignorant look, showing a satisfied condition of heart, without endless longings for the unattainable and dim—they always had "the dim" about them in the shape of the one-horse lamps of the country, a saucer of oil, with a piece of twine hanging over the edge for a wick. By the way, the Acadiens on Bayou la Fourche, in Louisiana, have the same "lampion" light!

The dress of these women was plain, but strong and serviceable. White shirts in full folds covered neck and bosom, the sleeves hanging from the shoulder in large folds, a bodice of dark-blue cloth was laced tightly around their waists, while skirts, generally of dark-blue cloth, hung in heavy lines to their ankles.

The men, assembled there to the number of about two thousand, were accoutred in blue cloth jackets (which rarely have the owners' arms in the sleeve, but are worn as cloaks), red waistcoats of startlingly crimson color, and blue small-clothes, while conical black felt hats, adorned here and there with flowers, served for head coverings. A large assemblage of children, dressed and undressed, filled up the gaps.

Suddenly, *Bang, Bangity Bang!* a row of small mortars were fired off in succession, and a small boy, with a banner in his hands, and an Irish pennant in his wake, appeared marching slowly along. On the banner was a painting of a small black hog between two men, each armed with brooms, who seemed bent on sweeping it out of existence; over these were the words:

GIOSTRA DEL PORCHETTO.

Then came six *contadini*, young men, and stout, each armed with a broom three or four feet in length, made of rushes tied together, resembling our birch brooms without their handles. They entered the arena or cistern, and then, each one throwing aside his hat, had a large linen bag, coming to a point at the top, tied over his head and throat, so that it was impossible for him to see. On each of these bags a comical face was roughly painted. To the right leg of each man a cowbell was tied. With their brooms swinging a preparatory flourish, the six stood ready to commence the game. The small hog was then turned into the cistern, announcing his presence by sundry squeals. Now the game fairly begins: *Whish!* sound the brooms as they are whisked here, there, everywhere, in attempts to strike the hog; one man, giving a strong blow, strikes another one, who was stooping down to arrange his garters, where he dislikes to be struck, and instantly the one struck runs a muck, hitting wildly right and left. Two or three men charge on one another, and brooms fly in splinters all round. One champion got a head blow, and had his wind knocked out by another blow simultaneously. Round they go, and at it they go, beating the air and each other, while the wreath of honor, alias small hog, keeps turning up his head, calculating the chances, and making fierce rushes every time he sees a broom approaching him. He must have practised in the game before, he manages so well to avoid being hit. The six men, being unable to hit the hog, grew angry; and one of them, unmindful of the fact that his smallclothes had burst open at the knee, and his stockings were around his shoes, terribly batters another combatant, who strives in vain to dodge him. Then the six shouted truce, and, pulling off their caps, declared that the small hog must have the bell tied to him also, so that, like a beacon (or bacon), he might warn the cruisers of his whereabouts. This arranged, and the caps again being tied on, they recommence the game with renewed spirit. One man ignobly raised his helmet, alias nosebag, to see where the small hog was keeping himself, and then made a rush for him, whereupon one of the three umpires, a very lean man, with nervous twitches, rushed at the man in a great state of excitement, and collared him amid the disapproving shouts of the spectators; he let him go upon this, and the other two umpires, who were fat men, jumping into the cistern to take away their lean brother, received several violent blows on the road, finally leading away the thin man, in a high state of twitches, communicating themselves to his stovepipe hat (only one on the ground), and to a large cane he tried to hold. A lucky blow from one of the gamesters struck the hog, and there was a cessation of hitting, interrupted by an outside *contadino* of the tight-built style breaking through the gendarmes and umpires, and jumping into the middle of the cistern, beginning a fearful battle of words with the man who hit the hog, interrupted, however, by two of the gendarmes, who collared him, and led him off up the steps, his legs very stiff, his body at an angle of forty-five degrees, and his head turned round to give a few last fierce words to the hog hitter. The man would have made a good bandit, on canvas, with his bronzed, bearded face, flashing eyes, conical hat, savage features, broad shirt collar, red sash around his waist, and leather gaiters, showing he rode horses, and came from down in the plain.

The game recommenced, and, by good luck, the broom swinger who hit the hog the first blow, hit him twice more; and the regulation being, that whoever first struck the hog three blows should win him, the successful hog hunter bore off the small hog on his back, having at the same time to carry the standard above described. The cheers of beauty and ugliness accompanied the hog and standard bearer, as, jerking down his head, the umpire pulled off his headbag, showing the face of Bruno, the butcher, who kept a bulldog. A great many friends surrounded him, patting him on the back—*he had a hog to be eaten!*

So ended the Game of the Small Hog.

After this was all over, a Tombola came off in front of the church; and our three artists, having purchased tickets for this Sunday lottery, in order to keep the day as the rest of the people did, and not render themselves liable to the censure of being eccentric, had an opportunity of seeing its beneficial working—for those who got it up!

The Tombola finished, there was a good display of fireworks. In the still night air of the Sabbath, the fiery snakes and red serpents, blue fires and green, darting flames and forked lights, reminded our artists of a large painting over the Maggiore Gate of the town, where a lot of the condemned are expiring in a very vermilion-colored Inferno—condemned, perhaps, for Sabbath breaking!

Returning to their inn to supper, the landlord handed them a note without address, which he said had been sent them by the Gonfaloniere of the city, who had called upon them as soon as he learned that they were strangers there. Caper, opening the envelope, found in it the following printed invitation to attend a concert to be given that night at the Palazzo Comunale, in honor of the day:

"IL GONFALONIERE

"DELLA CITTA' DI SEGNI

"Invita li sigi. Rocjean, Caper e Dexter ad intervenire all' Accademia di Musica che si terrà nella Sala del Palazzo Comunale il giorno 18 Luglio alle ore 9½ pom. per festeggiare la ricorrenza del Protettore S. Bruno."

"It sounds well," said Dexter; "but both of you have seen the tumbledown, ruined look of the old town, or city, as they call it; and the inhabitants, as far as I have seen them, don't indicate a very select audience for the concert."

"Select audience be hanged! It's this very selectness that is no selectness—that makes your English, and a part of our American society, a dreary bore," broke in Caper. "I've come up here in the mountains to be free; and if the Gonfaloniere bids me welcome to a palace where the *nobilità* await me, with music, I shall not ask whether they are select or not, but go."

"I think," spoke Rocjean, "we should go; it will be the easiest way to acknowledge the attention shown us, and probably the pleasantest to the one who sent it. I am going."

It therefore came to pass, that near the hour noted in the invitation, Rocjean and Caper, inquiring the direction to the Palazzo Comunale of the landlord, went forth to discover its whereabouts, leaving Dexter to hunt scorpions in the sitting room of the inn, or study the stars from its balcony.

Climbing up the main street, now quite dark save where the lamp of a stray shrine or two feebly lit up a few feet around it, they soon found the palace, the lower story of which held the postoffice, and various other offices. After passing a gendarme on guard at the door, they found themselves in a not very light hall leading to the second story. Mounting a flight of stairs, there stood another soldier on guard. A door suddenly was thrown open, and then a burst of light showed them a large hall with lofty ceilings, the walls hung with red and golden tapestry, and, with its rich mediæval groined arches and gilded cornices, resembling, after all the ruins and decay of the town, a castle hall in fairy land, rather than a positively real earthly room. Dazzled by the brilliance of the scene, Rocjean and Caper were standing near the door of entrance, when a tall, stout, and very handsome man, leaving a circle of ladies, at once approached them, and introducing himself as the Gonfaloniere of the city, with much courtesy showed them to seats among the "most reserved of the reserved." There sat the

Bishop of the Commune in purple silk robes, with an inch-wide golden chain over his breast, animatedly conversing with a dashing Roman lady, startlingly handsome, with solitaire diamond earrings flashing light, while the lace on her dress would have caused deaths of envy in one of our country villages. The Governor of the Province was there, a quiet, grave gentleman, earnest enough in his duties to be respected, and evidently a favorite with several ladies who also shone in diamonds, and with the "air noble" so much adored by Dexter. A warlike-looking priest, who Caper afterward found out was the chaplain of a regiment of soldiers, and by no means afraid of grape juice, was also there; and with numerous distinguished men and beautiful women, including one or two of the *Stelle d'Anagni*, or Stars of Anagni, as the nobility of that town are called, made, with their rich dresses and courteous manners, such a picture—so startlingly in contrast with the outdoor life that our artists had seen, that they have never forgotten it to this day. The concert for which the invitation was given soon commenced. The selection of vocal and instrumental pieces was made with good judgment; and the singers, who came from Rome, and had been selected for their ability, sang with a skill and grace that proved they knew that their audience had nice judgment and critical ears.

The concert was over : and having made their acknowledgments to the Gonfaloniere for the pleasure they had received through his invitation, our two artists, lighting cigars, walked up to the Pianillo, where the rising moon gave them a splendid view of the Campagna, and mountain-bounded horizon. Thus ended their first day in Segni, and their first Sunday in the Campagna.

The sickles were flashing in the sunlight, felling the ripened wheat in the valley, when our three artists, having previously arranged the matter with a certain Segnian named Bruno, stood one morning early, waiting his appearance with horses, to carry them down the mountain to a farm belonging to Prince Doria, called the Piombinara. There they were going to see a *triglia*, or threshing of wheat with horses.

"Here he comes," said Caper, "with a piebald horse and a bay mare and an iron-gray mule. Let's toss up for a choice."

The mule fell to Caper. Mounting him gayly, and calling to the others to follow, he led the way with their guide down the steep street of the town until they reached the road outside of the gate, when, the others coming up, the party ambled along down the mountain road. In about an hour they reached the plain, and fifteen minutes more brought them to the old, ivy covered, ruined fortress of the middle ages, called the Piombinara. Passing this, they soon reached an open field, in the centre of which, near a small cabin, they found quite a number of harvesters engaged piling up sheaves of wheat in a circle on a spot of ground previously levelled and hardened until it presented a surface as even as a barn floor.

While they were inquiring of the harvesters as to the time when the threshing would commence, a fine-looking man, mounted on a fiery, full-blooded chestnut horse, rode up, and, politely saluting the three artists, inquired of them if they were not desirous of seeing the *triglia*.

Rocjean answered that it was for that purpose they had come there, having learned in Segni that the horses would begin the threshing that morning.

The horseman then introduced himself as Prince Doria's agent for the Piombinara and farmer of the estate, and gave them a warm welcome; being very glad, he said, that the *triglia* would not begin until the afternoon, since he hoped it would give him, in the mean time, the pleasure of showing them the estate, and extending the rough hospitality of the Campagna to them.

Our artists, acknowledging his politeness, accepted the invitation of Signor Ercole, as he was generally called, and, upon his proposing a ride around the estate, accompanied him. They first visited the old ruin, riding in through what was formerly its main entrance. Once inside, they found the lower walls sufficiently entire to give them an idea of the size and form of the old fortress. At one end they found the ruins of a small chapel, where even yet the traces of fresco painting could be seen on its walls; near this arose a tall, square tower, ivy clad to its very summit, from whence a flock of hawks were flying in and out. The lightning had so shattered its walls, that it threatened every moment to fall; yet in this dilapidated state it had remained for years, and was regarded, therefore, as an "un-tumbling" curiosity. After some time spent here, which Dexter improved by making a pencil sketch of the valley and adjacent mountains, Signor Ercole leading the way, they rode through a small wood, where herds on herds of black hogs were feeding, to the pasture grounds, where the brood mares and colts of the prince were seen grazing together. Over a hundred head of the purest blood stock were here; and Dexter, who was thoroughly conversant with horseflesh, passed the highest encomiums of praise on many of the animals. Riding on, they next saw quite a number of oxen; but the superintendent informed them that these were only a few kept to perform the farm work, the large herds belonging to the estate being at this season of the year driven miles away to feed upon other lands of the prince. Continuing their ride, the party next came to the wheatfields, extending far and wide, like those of Illinois, for a hundred acres or more. Here the harvesters, most of whom were from the Abruzzi, were busily engaged, men and women, in loading the large carts with wheatsheafs, the grain being all cut, and consequently many of the laborers having returned to their distant homes. Returning from the fields, Signor Ercole now invited them to enter the farmhouse. This was a very large stone house, whitewashed, looking, as they approached it, more like a garrison for several regiments than a residence for a few families and a storehouse for agricultural implements and crops. The lower floor of this long building was taken up with stables and offices; but mounting a wide stone staircase, our artists found themselves in a large room scrupulously neat, with whitewashed walls, very high ceilings, and whips, guns, dogs, tables, account books, stone floors, and rough seats, making a curious mingling of monastery, squire's office, sportsman's chamber, and social hall; for no sooner had Signor Ercole seen his guests comfortably seated, than his servant brought in cigars, with a brass dish of live coals to light them, several bottles of wine, and one of capital old Sambuca di Napoli—a liquor that is refreshing, drank, as it should be, with a good allowance of water.

Dinner was served at an early hour, with a profusion of each dish that would have frightened an economical Yankee housewife. Six roast chickens were not considered at all too many for the five persons at table—the fifth being a jolly old gentleman, an uncle to the Signor Ercole. The plate of maccaroni looked as if Gargantua had ordered it—the salad might have been put in a bushel measure, the bread been carried in a donkey cart, and the wine—ahem! in the expressive language of the Celts, there was "lashings of it."

But even a Campagna dinner with a Farmer-General will have an end; and when our friends had finished theirs, they arose and went dreamily forth to the before-mentioned squire's office, where they lighted cigars, while they drank small cups of black coffee, and gazed out of the open windows to the distant mountains, rising far above the plain sleeping in the summer sun, and hushed to sleep by the unceasing song of the cicalas sharply crying from leaf and blade of grass.

About three o'clock in the afternoon, a man came to inform the Signor Ercole that the mares and colts had been driven into the corral, and our party accordingly walked out to see them lassoed prior to their performance in the ring. As they approached the corral, they saw the blooded animals circling around the inclosure, apparently aware that they would soon be called on to do some work—the only work, in fact, the majority of them had to do the whole year through. Taking a lasso from one of the men, Signor Ercole entered the inclosure, and singling out a fine-looking bay mare, he threw the lasso— the noose encircling her neck as she dashed forward, bringing her up all standing. Satisfied with this performance, he handed her over to one of the herdsmen, who, fastening her with a halter, again and again swung the lasso, catching at last twelve horses and mares. One long halter was now attached to six of the animals, and a driver, taking it in hand, led them toward the spot where the beaten earth was covered with sheaves of wheat standing on end one against the other in a circle of say thirty or forty feet in diameter; another driver, fastening six others, horses and mares, to another long halter, led them to the side opposite the first six. As soon as they were stationed, waving long-lashed whips, plunge! ahead went the wild horses, jumping into the wheatsheaves breast high, rearing, squealing, kicking, lashing out their hoofs, their eyes starting from their heads, while each driver stood firm in one spot, whirling his whip-lash, and keeping his team within a circle one half of which was in the wheat, and the other half outside. Thus there were three circles—one of wheat, and the other two described by the horses as they dashed wildly around, the drivers shouting, the wheat flying, and being quickly threshed under the swift-moving hoofs of the twelve four-legged flails!

Caper and Dexter were meanwhile as busy as they could be sketching the scene before them, and endeavoring to catch notes of the first plunges and excited motions of the horses. The active motive-power of the foreground finished, with a hasty sketch of the Piombinara at the right hand, in the middle ground the Campagna, with its cornfields and ruined towers, while in the distance the Lepini mountains stretched away into cloudland—all afforded a sketch from which both Caper and Dexter afterward made two very excellent paintings.

The sketches finished, Signor Ercole insisted upon the artists taking a stirrup cup with him before they left for Segni; and accordingly, accompanying him to the house, they drank success to their hospitable entertainer, and departed highly pleased with this Representative Man. It is his class—the intelligent producers of the Papal States—to whom we must look for all the life that will keep that wornout old body sufficiently animated to last until Regenerated Italy can take it in hand, see it decently buried, and over its tomb achieve a brilliant future.

Segni might well boast of her hogs and donkeys. As the sun rose, a wild-looking fellow stood by the Maggiore Gate, and blew on a long horn many rough blasts; then from all the streets and alleys rushed out black hogs tumultuously, to the number of one hundred or more, and followed their pastor with the horn to the field or forest. There he guarded them all day, and at sunset brought them back to the town; when, as soon as they reached the gate, the herd separated, and right and left, at top speed, every hog hastened to his own house. Poor as the inhabitants were, yet among the five thousand of them living in the town, besides countless black hogs, they owned over two hundred and fifty donkeys and mules, the majority donkeys of the longest-eared, smallest-body breed you can conceive. Costing little, if anything, to support them, they were excellent labor-saving machines, and did three quarters of the work that in our country would have been done by hod and wheelbarrow labor. Very surefooted, they were well calculated for travelling the mountain roads around; and with their enormous saddles, a direct copy of those now used in Egypt, of course attracted the attention of the two animal-painters, who determined to secure a good specimen, and make a sketch of donkey and saddle.

The most comical-looking one in the town belonged to a cross, ill-tempered, ugly brute of a hunchback, who, as soon as he learned that the artists wanted to paint him, asked such a price for his loan, that they found themselves obliged to give up all hopes of taking his portrait. One morning, as Caper was walking out of the inn door, he nearly tumbled over a little, sunburnt, diminutive donkey that had a saddle on his back, resembling, with this on him, a broken-backed rabbit. Caper was charmed; and, as he stood there lost in admiration, a poor little lame boy came limping up, and, catching Long Ears by the rope halter, was leading him away, when the artist stopped him, and asked him whom it belonged to. The small boy, probably not understanding Caper, or afraid of him, made no answer, but resolutely pulled away the donkey to a gateway leading into a garden, at the end of which was a half-ruined old house. Our artist followed him in, when, raising his eyes toward the house, he saw leaning from one of the windows, her figure marked boldly against the dark gray of the house, a strikingly beautiful woman. There was an air of neatness in her dress, a certain care of her hair, that was an improvement over any of the other female Segnians he had yet seen.

"Can you tell me," said Caper, pointing to the donkey, "who owns that animal?"

"*Padrone mio*, I own him," said the woman.

"I want to paint him."

"*Do* you?" replied the beauty, whose name Caper learned was Margarita; and she asked this with a very astonished look.

"I do, indeed I do. It will not hurt him."

"No, I don't believe it will. He is very ugly and sunburnt. I think it will improve him," said Margarita, confidently.

Caper didn't see how the mere taking his portrait would improve the animal; but thinking it might be meant for a compliment, he assented, adding that he would pay a fair price for himself and his friend to be allowed to have the donkey, all saddled, for two or three hours every day when he was not used.

That very day, about four o'clock in the afternoon, Caper and Dexter, having prepared their sketching paper, with colors on pallet, mallsticks in hand, and seated on camp stools in the shade of a wall, were busy sketching, in Margarita's garden, the donkey, held by the little lame boy, and fed from time to time with cornmeal in order to keep him steady. Margarita was seated, with a little child in her arms, on a flight of old wooden steps leading to the second story of her house; and with her bright crimson bodice, and white falling linen sleeves, and shirt gathered in folds over her bosom, while her dark-blue skirts, and dark apron with brilliant gold and red stripes, were draped around her as she sat on the stairs, looked exactly like one of Raphael's *Madonne alla Fornarina*. Her large eyes followed seriously every moment of the painters. Caper, learning that she was a widow, did not know but what her affections were straying his way.

"I say, Dexter, don't you think, now, she's regarding us pretty closely?"

"I am sure it's the donkey is next her heart, and it is more than probable she's there on watch to keep us from stealing it. D'ye notice the manner she's eying the paints? Every time my brush goes near the vermilion, and I move my stool, her eyes brighten. I wonder what's up around the gate there? Hanged if half the old women and children around town aren't assembled there! Look."

Caper looked, and, sure enough, there was a crowd of heads; and, not content with standing at the gateway, they began soon to enter the garden, crowding around our two artists, getting in front of the donkey, and being generally in the way.

Once or twice Dexter drove them off with words, until, at last, an unlucky urchin striking his elbow and making him mar his sketch, he laid down his sketching box, and, clubbing his camp stool, made a rush at the crowd. They fled before him, in their hurry tumbling one over the other, and then, scrambling to their feet, were soon out of sight. Returning to his sketch, he was no sooner busily at work than they were all back again, but now keeping at respectful distance.

After about two hours' work, Caper proposed knocking off sketching, and continuing it next day; to which Dexter assenting, they put up their sketches. Caper agreeing to pay Margarita for the afternoon's study, he went up to her, and handing over the amount agreed upon, she seemed by no means satisfied.

"Won't that pay you?" asked he.

"Certainly, but——"

"But what?"

"When are you going to paint the donkey? Here I've told all my friends that you were to paint the little old fellow all over, perhaps a nice red color, or bright yellow; and here we've all been waiting hours to see you begin, and you haven't put the first brush to him yet!"

This was too much for the gravity of Caper, who fairly roared with laughter; and Dexter, who had listened to the talk, joining in as chorus, made the garden ring.

"They are crazy," said one old woman, who was holding a distaff in one hand, while she was making woollen thread with the other.

"*Eh, Giá,*" said another, who had once been to Rome, and therefore was great authority, "they are Englis', and all the Englis' is crazy. Didn't I once live with an Englis' family? and they were that mad that they washed themselves every day! And they had white sticks with hair on the end of them, what they scrubbed their mouth and teeth with two and three times a day!"

"Now, Maricuccia, that is too much; what could they do that for?"

"*Ma che!* I tell you it was so; and their maid told me it was to kill the little devils that are always jumping in and out of the throats of all heretics."

"Santa Maria!"

The next day, after they had finished their sketch of the donkey, Caper proposed that they should oblige Margarita by giving the donkey a little of that painting the owner seemed so anxious to have bestowed on him. Dexter accordingly drew bright yellow circles of cadmium and yellow ochre round his eyes, giving him a peculiarly owly look; painted white rings round his tail, black streaks round his body, and touched the ends of his ears with vermilion. A more striking looking object you never saw; and when Margarita proudly led him forth and showed him to the surrounding multitude, there were storms of applause for the *Inglese* who painted donkeys!

CHAPTER IX.

It was a warm day in October when Caper engaged rooms in the Babuino. The sun shone cheerfully, and he took no heed of the cold weather to come: in fact, he entertained the popular idea, that the land half-way between the tropics and paradise, called Italy, stood in no need of pokers and coal hods. He was mistaken. Awaking one morning to the fact that it was cold, he began an examination of his rooms for a fireplace: there was none. He searched for a chimney—in vain. He went to see his landlady about it. She was standing on a balcony, superintending the engineering of a bucket in its downward search for water. The house was five stories high, and from each story what appeared to be a lightning rod ran down into what seemed to be a well, in a small garden. Up and down these rods, tin buckets, fastened to ropes, were continually running, rattling, clanking down, or being drawn splashing, dripping up; and as they were worked assiduously, it made lively music for those dwelling in the back part of the house.

Having mentioned to the landlady that he wanted a fire, the good woman reflected a moment, and then directed the servant to haul out a sheet iron vessel mounted on legs. This was next filled with charcoal, on which was thrown live coals, and the entire arrangement being placed outside the door on the balcony, the servant bent over and fanned it with a turkey feather fan. Caper looked on in astonishment.

"Are you going to embark in the roast chestnut trade?" he asked.

"*Ma che!*" answered madame; "that is your fire."

"It will bring on asphyxia."

"We are never asphyxied in Rome with it. You see, the girl fans all the venom out of it; and when she takes it into your room, it will be just as harmless as—let me see—as a baby without teeth."

This comparison settled the question, for it proved it wouldn't bite. Caper managed to worry through the cold weather with this poor consoler. It gave him headaches, but it kept his head otherwise cool, and his feet warm; and, as he lived mostly in his studio, where he had a good wood stove, he was no great loser.

"But," said he, descanting on this subject to Rocjean, "how can the Romans fight for their firesides, when they haven't any?"

"They will fight for their *scaldine*, especially the old women and the young women," answered Rocjean, "to the last gasp. There is nothing they stick to like these. Even their husbands and lovers are not so near and dear to them."

"What are they? and how much do they cost?" asked Caper, artistically.

"Crockery baskets with handles; ten *baiocchi*," replied Rocjean. "You must have noticed them. Why, look out of that window; do you see that girl in the house opposite? She has one on the window sill, under her nose, while her hands are both held over the charcoal fire that is burning in it. If there were any proof needed that the idea of a future punishment by fire did not originate in Rome, the best reply would be the bitter hatred the Romans have of cold. I can fancy the income of the Church twice as large, if they had only thought to have filled purgatory with icebergs, and a corresponding state of the thermometer. A Roman, in winter time, would pay twice as many *baiocchi* for prayers to get a deceased friend out of the cold, as he could otherwise be induced to. The English and other foreigners have, little by little, induced hotel and boarding house keepers to introduce grates and stoves, with good coal and wood fires, wherever they may hire lodgings; but the old Romans still stand by *brasero's* and *scaldina's*."

"I caught a bad cold yesterday, thanks to this barbarous custom," said Caper. "I was in the Vatican, looking at a pretty girl copying a head of Raphael's, and depending on imagination and charcoal to warm me: the results were, chills and the snuffles."

"Let that be a warning to you against entering art galleries during cold weather. To visit the Borghese collection, with the thermometer below freezing point, and see all those semi-nude paintings, whether of saints or sinners, chills the heart; not only that they have no clothes, but that the artists who made the pictures were so radically vulgar—because they were affected!"

"But," spoke Caper, "they probably painted them in the merry spring time, when they had forgotten all about frozen fountains and oranges iced; or, it may be, in their day wood was cheaper than it is now, and money plentier."

"Yes, in the days when three million pilgrims visited Rome in a year. But would you believe it? within thirty miles of this city I have seen enough timber lying rotting on the ground, to half warm the Eternal City? The country people, in the commune where I lived one summer, had the privilege of gathering wood in the forest that crowns the range of mountains backing up from the sea, and separating the Pontine Marshes from the higher lands of the Campagna: but the trunks of the hewn trees, after such light branches as the women could hack off were carried away, were left to rot; for there was no way to get them to Rome—an hour's distance by railroad. Cold? The Romans are numbed to the heart. Wait until they are warmed up; wait until they have a chance to make money—there will be no poets like Casti in those days—Casti, who wrote two hundred sonnets against a man who dunned him for—thirty cents! Talk about knowing enough to go into the house when it rains! Why, the Roman shopkeepers of the poorer class don't know enough to shut their shop doors when they are starved with cold. You will find this to be the fact. Look, too, at the poor little children! do they ever think of playing fire engine, and thus warming themselves in a wholesome manner? No! One day I was painting away, when I heard a poor, thin little voice, as of a small dinner bell with a croup; and hoping at last I might see the little ones having a good frolic, I went to the window and looked out. What did I see? A small boy with a large, tallow-colored head, carrying a large black cross in the pit of his stomach; another small boy ringing a bell; and five others following along, in a crushed, despondent manner—inviting other boys to hear the catechism explained in the parish church. Meat for babes! I don't wonder the Roman women all want to be men, when I see the men without half the spirit of the women, and, such as they are, loafing away the winter evenings for warmth in wineshops or cafés. Poor Roman women, huddled together in your dark rooms, feebly lighted with a poor lamp, and hugging *scaldine* for better comfort! Would that the American woman could see her Italian sister, and bless her stars that she did not live under the cap and cross keys."

"The cold has one good effect," interrupted Caper; "the forcible gesticulation of the Italians, which we all admire so much, arises from the necessity they have to do so—in order to keep warm. I have, however, an idea to better the condition of the wood sawyers in the Papal States, by introducing a saw buck or saw horse. As it is, they hold the wood in their hands, putting the saw between their knees, and then fairly rubbing the wood through the saw, instead of the saw through the wood. How, too, the Romans manage to cut wood with such axes as they have, is passing strange. It would be well to introduce an American axe here, handle and all."

"We have an old, old saying in France," spoke Rocjean:

"' *Jamais cheval n'y homme
S'amenda pour aller a Rome.*'

' Never horse or man mended, that unto Rome wended.' Your American axe is useless without American energy, and would not, if introduced here, mend the present shiftless style of wood chopping. Evidently the people will one day take it up and try it—when their minds and arms are free. As it is, the genuine Romans live through their winters without wood in a merry kind of humor; taking the charcoal sent them by chance for cooking with great good nature; and, without words, blessing God for giving them vigorous frames and sturdy bodies to withstand cold and heat. After all, the want of fixed firesides by no manner of means annoys the buxom Roman woman of the people: she picks up her moving stove, the *scaldina*, and trots out to see her nearest gossip, knowing that her reception will be warm, for she brings warmth with her. There is a copy of Galignani, a round of bull beef, and a dirty coal fire, even in Rome, for every Englishman who will pay for them; but why, oh why! forever hoist the banner of the Blues over the gay gardens of every earthly paradise? Why hide Psyche under a hogshead?"

"Are you asking me those hard questions? For if you are," said Caper, "I will answer you thus: A fishwoman, passing along a street in Philadelphia one day, heard from an open window the silver-voiced Brignoli practising an aria, possibly from the Traviata: 'That voice,' quoth she, 'would be a fortune for a woman in shad time!'"

"'It is well to be off with the old love,
Before you are on with the new:'"

hummed James Caper, as he sauntered, one morning early, through the dewy grass of the Villa Borghese, with his uncle, Bill Browne, leisurely picking a little bouquet of violets—"dim, but sweeter than the lids of Juno's eyes, or Cytherea's breath"—and pleasantly thinking of the pretty face of his last love, the blonde Rose, who was at that moment smiling on somebody else in Naples.

"There is nothing keeps a man out of mischief so well as

the little portrait a pair of lovely eyes photograph on his heart; is there now, Uncle Bill?"

"No, Jim; you are 'bout right there. If you want to keep the devil out of your heart, you must keep an angel in it. If you can't find a permanent resident, why, you must take up with transient customers. First and last, I've had the pictures of half the pretty girls in St. Louis hanging up in my gallery. As one grows dim, I take up another, and that's the way I preserve my youth. If it hadn't been for business, I should have been a married man long ago; and my advice to you, Jim, is to stop off being a bachelor the instant you are home again."

"I think I shall, the instant I find one with the beauty of an Italian, the grace of a French girl, the truth and tenderness of a German, the health of an Englishwoman, and——"

"Draw it mild, my boy," broke in Uncle Bill; "here she comes!"

Caper and his uncle were standing, as the latter spoke, under the group of stone pines, from whose feet there was a lovely view of the Albanian snow-capped mountains, and they saw coming toward them two ladies. There was the freshness of the morning in their cheeks; and though one was older than the other, joy-bringing years had passed so kindly with her, that if Caper had not known she was the mother of the younger lady—they would have passed for sisters. When he first saw them, the latter was gathering a few violets. When she rose, he saw the face of all others he most longed to see.

He had first seen her the life of a gay party at Interlachen; then alone in Florence, with her mother for companion, patiently copying the Bella di Tiziano in the Pitti Palace; then in Venice, one sparkling morning, as he stepped from his gondola on the marble steps of a church, he met her again : this time he had rendered himself of assistance to the mother and daughter, in procuring admittance for them to the church, which was closed to the public for repairs, and could only be seen by an especial permit, which Caper fortunately had obtained. They were grateful for his attention; and when, a few days afterward, he met them in company with other of his American friends, and received a formal introduction, the acquaintance proved one of the most delightful he had made in Europe, rendering his stay in Venice marked by the rose-colored light of a new love, warming each scene that passed before his dreamy gaze. But other cities, other faces: memory slept, to awake again with renewed strength at the first flash of light from the eyes of Ida Buren, there, over the spring violets of the Villa Borghese.

The meeting between Mrs. Buren, her daughter, and Caper, was marked, on the part of the ladies, with that cordiality which the truly well bred show instinctively to those who merit it—to those who, brave and loyal, prove, by word and look, that theirs is the right to stand within the circle of true politeness and courtesy.

"And so," Mrs. Buren concluded her greeting, "we are here in Rome, picking violets with the dew on them, and waiting for the nightingales to sing before we leave for Naples."

"And forget," said Caper, "among the violets of Pæstum, the poor flowers of the Borghese? I protest against it, and beg to add this little bouquet to yours, that their united perfume may cause you to remember them."

"I accept them for you, mother," spoke Ida; "and that they may not be forgotten, I will make a sketch at once of that fountain under the ilex trees, and Mr. Caper, in classic costume, making floral offerings to Bacchus—of violets."

"And why not to Flora?"

"I have yet to learn that Flora has a shrine at—Monte Testaccio! where the Signore Caper, if report speaks true, often goes and worships."

"That shrine is abandoned hereafter. Where shall my new one be?"

"In the Piazza di Spagna, No. ——," said Mrs. Buren, smiling at Caper's mournful tone of voice.

"While the violets bloom, we shall be there. Good morning!"

The ladies continued their walk, and although, as they turned away, Ida dropped a tiny bunch of violets, hidden among two leaves, Caper, when he picked it up, did not return it to her, but kept it many a day as a souvenir of his fair countrywoman.

"They are," said Uncle Bill, slowly and solemnly, "two of the finest specimens of Englishwomen I ever saw, upon me word, be gad!"

"They are," said Caper, "two of the handsomest Americans I ever met."

"Americans?" asked Uncle Bill, emphatically.

"Americans!" answered Caper, triumphantly.

"Shut up your paint shop, James, my son; call in the auctioneer; stick up a bill, 'TO LET.' Let us return at once to the land of our birth. No such attractions exist in this turkey-trodden, maccaroni-eating, picture-peddling, stone-cutting, mass-singing land of donkeys. Let us go. Americans!"

"Yes, Americans—Bostonians."

"Farewell, seventy-five niggers; good-by, my speculations in Lewsianny cotton planting; depart from behind me, sugar crops on Bayou Fooshe! I am of those who want a Mrs. Browne, a duplicate of the elderly lady who has just departed, at any price. James, my son, this morning shalt thou breakfast with me at Nazzari's; and if thou hast not a bully old breakfast, it's because the dimes an't in me—and I know they are. Nothing short of cream de Boozy frappayed, paddy frog grass pie, fill it of beef, and myonhays of pullits, with all kinds of saucy sons and so forth, will do for us. We have been among angels—shall we not eat like the elect? Forward!"

During breakfast, Caper discoursed at length with his uncle of the two ladies they met in the villa.

Mrs. Buren, left a widow years since, with a large fortune, had educated her only child, Ida, systematically, solidly, and healthily. The child's mind, vinelike, clings for support to something already firm and established, that it may climb upward in a healthy, natural growth, avoiding the earth; so the daughter had found in her mother a guide toward the clear air where there is health and purity. Ida Buren, with clear brown eyes, high spirits, rosy cheeks, and full perfected form, at one glance revealed the attributes that Uncle Bill had claimed for her so quickly. With all the beauty of an Italian, she had her perceptions of color and harmony in the violets she gathered; the truth and tenderness of a German, to appreciate their sentiment; the health of an Englishwoman, to tramp through the dewy grass to pick them; the grace of a Frenchwoman, to accept them from Nature with a *merci, madame!*

Caper had now a lovely painting to hang up in his heart,

one in unison with the purity and beauty of the violets of the Villa Borghese.

There is lightness and brightness, music, laughter, merry jests, masks, bouquets, flying flowers, and *confetti* around you. You are in the Corso, no longer the sober street of a solemn old city, but the brilliant scene of a pageant, rivalling your dreams of fairy land, excelling them; for it is fresh, sparkling, real before your eyes. From windows and balconies wave in the wind all-colored tapestries, flutter red, white, and golden draperies; laugh out in festal garments gay revellers; fly through the golden sunlight showers of perfumed flowers; beam down on you glances from wild, loving eyes, sparkling with fun, gleaming with excitement, thrilling with witching life.

Hurrah for to-day! *Fiori, fiori, ecco fiori!* Baskets of flowers, bunches of flowers, bouquets of flowers, flowers natural and flowers artificial, flowers tied up and flowers loose. *Confetti, confetti, ecco confetti!* Sugarplums white, sugarplums blue, bullets and buckshot of limewater and flour. Whiz! down comes the Carnival shower: "*Bella donzella*, this bouquet for thee!" Up go the white camellias and blue violets; "down comes a rosebud for me." What wealth of loveliness and beauty in thousands of balconies and windows; what sheen of brilliance in the vivid colors of the varied costumes!

The Carnival has come!

Right and left fly flowers; and here and there dart in between wheels and under horses' legs, dirty, daring Roman boys, grasping the falling flowers, or *confetti*. From a balcony, some wealthy *forestiero* ("Ugh! how rich they are!" grumbles the coachman) scatters *baiocchi* broadcast, and down in the dirt and mud roll and tumble the little ragamuffins, who never have muffins, and always have rags—and "spang!" down comes a double handful of hard *confetti* on Caper's head, as he rides by in an open carriage. He bombards the windows with a double handful of white buckshot; but a woman in full Albano costume, crimson and white, aims directly at him a beautiful bouquet. Not to be outdone, Caper throws her a still larger one, which she catches and keeps—never throwing him the one she aimed! He is sold! But "whiz, whir!" right and left fly flowers and *confetti;* and—oh, joy unspeakable!—an Englishman's chimney-pot hat is knocked from his head by a strong bouquet; and we know

> "There is a noun in Hebrew means 'I am,'
> The English always use to govern d—n,"

and that he is using it severely, and don't see the fun, you know—of *throwing things.* Who cares? *Avanti!*

Caper had filled the carriage with loose flowers, small bouquets, a basket of *confetti*, legal and illegal size, for the Carnival-Edict strictly prohibited persons from throwing large-sized bouquets and *confetti;* consequently, everybody considered themselves compelled to *dis*obey the command. Rocjean, who was in the carriage with Caper, delighted the Romans with his ingenuity in attaching bouquets to the end of a long fish pole, and thus gently engineering them to ladies in windows or balconies. The crowd in the Corso grows larger and larger. The scene in this long street resembles a theatre in open air, with decorations and actors, assisted by a large supply of infantry and cavalry soldiers to keep order and attend to the scenes. The prosaic shops are no longer shops, but opera boxes, filled with actors and actresses instead of spectators, wearing all varieties of costume—the Italian ones predominant, gay, bright, and beautifully adapted to rich, peachlike complexions. Why call them olive complexions? for all the olives ever seen are of the color of a sick green pumpkin, or a too, too ripe purple plum; and who has ever yet seen a beautiful Italian maiden of either of these morbid colors?

The windows and balconies of the Corso are opera boxes. "Whiz!" The flying bouquets and white pills show plainly that the *prime donne* are making their positively first appearances for the season. Look at that French soldier in company with another, who is passing under a balcony, when a tiny bunch of flowers falls, or is thrown at him. He stoops to grasp it—too late, *mon brave;* a Roman boy is ahead of you; no use swearing; so he grasps his comrade by the arm, and points to the balcony, which is not more than six feet above his head.

"*Mon Dieu, qu'elle est gentille!*"

And there stands the beauty, a thorough soldier's girl; weighs her hundred and seventy pounds, has cheeks like new-cut beefsteaks, hair black as charcoal, eyes bright as fire, and an arm capable of cooking for a regiment. She is dressed in full Albanian costume, has the dew of the fields in her air, and oh! when she smiles, she shows such splendid teeth!—the *contadine* have them, and don't ruin them by continual eating! The soldier stops. "Oh Lord, she is neat!" He wants to return her flowery compliment with a similar one; but—*Tu bleu!*—one can't buy bouquets on four *sous* a day income—even in Rome: so he looks around for a waif, and spies on the pavement something green. He gallantly throws it up, and, with a smile and wave of the hand like a Chevalier Bayard on a bender, he bids adieu to the fair maiden. He threw up half a head of lettuce.

"*Ach mein Gott! wollen sie nur?*" and in return for a double handful of *confetti* flung into a carriage full of German artists ahead of him, "bang!" comes into Caper's vehicle a shower of lime pills and other stunners—not including the language—and he is in for it. A minute, and the whole Corso rains, hails, and pelts flowers and white pills. Nothing else is visible. Up there laugh down at them whole balconies, filled with delirious men and women, throwing on their devoted heads, Americans, French, German, rattling, tumbling, fistfuls of *confetti* and wild flowers. Even that half head of lettuce was among the things flying! English, French, Dutch, Spanish, Germans, Italians, Americans, and those wild northern bloods—all grit and game—the Russians, are down on them like a thousand of bricks. Hurrah! the carriages move on—they are safe. Hurrah for a new fight with fresh faces! *Avanti!*

Comes a carriage load of wild Russians. Ivan, the *moudjik*, fresh from the Nevskoï Prospekt, now drives for the first time in the Corso—*Dam na vodka, Sabakoutchelovek,* thinks he. Yes, my sweet son of a dog, thou shalt have *vodka* to drink after all this scrimmage is over. So he holds in his horses with one hand, crowds down his fur hat with the other, so that his eyes will be safe, and then bravely faces the stinging shower of *confetti* his lord and master draws down on him. Up on the back seat of this carriage, all life and fire, stands the

Russian prince, with headpiece of mail, and red surtout, a Carnival Circassian, "down on" the slow-plodding Italians, and throwing himself away with flowers and fun. Isn't he a picture? How his blue eyes gleam! how his long, wavy moustache curls with the play of features! how the flowers fly—how the rubles fly for them! Look at the other Russians—there are beards for you! beards grown where brandy freezes! but they are thawed out now. Look at these men! hear their wild northern tongue! how it rolls out the sounds that frighten Italians back to sleepy sonnets and voluptuous songs. Hurrah, my Russians! look fate in the face. *Your* road is—onward!

"Ah, yes; and really, my dear"—here a handful of white pills and limedust breaks the sentence—"really, my dear, hadn't we better"—"bang!" comes a tough bouquet, and hits milady on that bonnet—"better go to the hotel?"

"Indeed, now," milady continues, "they don't respect persons, these low Italians. They haven't the faintest idea of dignity."

These "low Italians" were more than probably fellow countrymen and women of the speaker; but they may have been "low" all the same in her social barometer; for they pitched and flung, hurled and threw all the missiles they could lay hands on into the carriage of their unmistakable compatriots, with hearty delight; since the gentleman, who was not gentle, sat upright as a church steeple, never moving a muscle, and looking angry and worried at being flung at; and the milady also sat *à la mode de* church steeple—throwing nothing but angry looks. They *went* to the hotel. Sorrow go with them!

Caper and Rocjean now began to throw desperately, for

they had a large supply of flowers and *confetti* on hand, which they were anxious to dispose of suddenly—since in ten minutes the horses would run, and then the carriages must leave the Corso. It was the last day of Carnival, and to-morrow—sackcloth and ashes. How the masks crowd around them! how the beautiful faces, unmasked, are smiling! Look at them well; stamp them on your heart; for many and many one shall we see never again. Another Carnival will bring them again, like song birds in summer; but a long, long winter will be between, and WE will be far, far away.

The Corso is cleared, the infantry half keeps the crowd within bounds, a charge of cavalry sweeps the street, and then come rattling, clattering, rushing on the barebacked horses, urged on by cries, shouts, yells, and frightened thus to top speed; while the Dutch metal tied to their sides increases their alarm—whir! they are past us, and—the bay horse is ahead.

Again the carriages are in the Corso. Here and there a few bouquets are thrown, floral farewells to the merry season. Then, as dusk comes on, and red and golden behind San Angelo flames the funeral pyre of the sun, and through the blue night twinkles the evening star, see down the Corso a faint light gleaming. Another and another light shines from balcony and window, flashes from rolling carriage, and flames out from along the dusky walls, till—*presto!*—you turn your head, and up the Corso, and down the Corso, there is one burst of trembling light, and ten thousand tapers are brightly gleaming, madly waving, brilliantly swaying to and fro.

Moccoli! ecco, moccoli!

Along roll carriages; high in air gleam tapers, upheld by those within; from every balcony and window shine out the swaying tapers. Hurrah! here, there, hand to hand, are contests to put out these shining lights, and SENZA MOCCOLI!— "Out with the tapers!"—rings forth in trumpet tones, in gay, laughing tones, in merry tones, the length of the whole glorious Corso.

Daring beauty, wild, lovely bacchante, with black, beaming eyes, tempt us not with that bright flame to destruction! Look at her, as she stands so proudly and erectly on the highest seat in the carriage, her arms thrown up, her wild eyes gleaming from under jet-black, dishevelled locks, while the night breeze flutters in wavy folds the drapery of her classic dress. *Senza moccoli!* she sends the challenge ringing down through fifteen centuries. He braves all; the carriage is climbed, the taper is within his reach.

"To-morrow I leave!"

She flings the burning taper away from her.

"Then take this kiss!"

"SENZA MOCCOLI!" black, witching eyes, farewell!

"Boom!" rings out the closing bell; fast fades the light. "Out with the tapers!"—the shout swells up, up, up, then slowly dies, as die an organ's tones—and Carnival is ended.

A handful of beautiful flowers, found among gray, crumbling ruins; a few notes of wild, stirring music, suddenly heard, then quickly dying away in the lone watches of the night: these are the hours of the Roman Carnival.

"Played is the comedy, deserted now the scene."

Miracles are no longer performed in Rome. As soon as the police are officially informed, they prevent their being worked, even in the Campagna. Official information, however, always travels much faster when the spurs of heretical incredulity are applied—otherwise it lags; and the performances of miracle-mongers insure crowded houses, sometimes for years.

Among Caper's artist friends was a certain Blaise Monet, French by nature, Parisian by birth, artist or writer according to circumstances. Circumstances—that is to say, two thousand francs left him by a deceased relation—created him a temporary artist in Rome.

"When the money is gone," said he, "I shall endow some barber with my goat's-hair brushes, and resume the stylus. The first have attractions—capillary—for me; the latter has the attraction-gravitation of francs—still more interesting—that is to say, more stylish."

Blaise Monet, with the May breezes, fled to a small town on top of a high mountain, in order to enjoy them until autumn. With the rains of October, he descended on Rome.

"How did you enjoy yourself up in that hawk's nest?" Caper asked him, when he first saw him after his return to the city.

"Like the king D'Yvétot. My house was a castle, my drink good wine, my food solid—the cheese a little too much so, and a little too much of it. No matter; the views made up for it. Gr-r-rand, magnificent, splendid; in fact, paradise for twenty *baiocchi* a day, all told."

"And as for affairs of the heart?"

"My friend, mourn with me. That hole was—so to speak in regard to that matter—a monastery, without doors, windows, or holes; and a wall around it so high, it shut out—hope! I wish you could have seen the camel who was my monastic jailer."

"That is, when you say camel, you mean jackass?"

"Precisely! Well, my friend, his name was Father Cipriano; though why they call a man father who has no legal children, I can't conceive, though probably many of his flock do. He prejudiced the minds of the maidens against me, and made an attempt to injure my reputation among the young men and elders—in vain. The man who could paint a scorpion on the wall so naturally as even to delude Father Ciprian into beating it for ten minutes with that bundle of sticks they call a broom; the man who could win three races on a barebacked horse, treat all hands to wine, and even bestow cigars on a few of the elders; win a *terno* at the Tombola, and give it back to the poor of the town; catch hold of the rope and help pull by the horns, all over town, the ox, thus preparatorily made tender before it was slaughtered: such a man could not have the ill will of the men.

"Believe me, I did all my possible to touch the hearts of the maidens. I serenaded them, learning fearful *rondinelle*, so as to be popular; I gathered flowers for them; I volunteered to help them pick chestnuts and cut firewood; I helped to make fireworks and fire balloons for the festivals; I drew their portraits in charcoal on a white wall, along the main street; and when they passed, with copper water-jars on their heads, filled with water from the fountain, they exclaimed:

"'*Ecco!* that is Elisa; that is Maricuccia; that is Francesca.'

"But I threw my little favors away. There was a black cloud over all, in a long black robe, called Padre Cipriano; and their hearts were untouched.

"I made one good friend, a widow lady, the Signora Margarita Baccio. She was about thirty-three years of age, and was mourning for a second husband—who did not come; the first one having departed for *Cielo* a few months past, as she told me. The widow having a small farm to hoe and dig, and about twelve miles to walk daily, I had but limited opportunities to study her character; but I believe, if I had, I should not have discovered much, since she had very little. She was deplorably ignorant, and excessively superstitious, but good natured and hopeful—looking out for husband No. 2. She it was who informed me that Padre Cipriano had set the faces of the maidens against me, and for this I determined to be revenged.

"A short time before I left the town, my oil colors were about used up. I had made nearly a hundred sketches, and not caring to send to Rome for more paints, I used my time making pencil sketches. Among the tubes of oil colors left, of course there was the vermilion, that will outlast, for a landscape painter, all others. I managed to paint a jackass's head for the landlord of the inn where I boarded, with my refuse colors. After all were gone, there still remained the vermilion. One day, out in the fields sketching an old tower, and watching the pretty little lizards darting in and out the old ruins, an idea struck me. The next day I commenced my plan.

"I caught about fifty lizards, and painted a small vermilion cross on the head of each one, using severe drying oil and turpentine, in order to insure their not being rubbed off.

"The next dark night, when Padre Cipriano was returning from an excursion, he saw an apparition: Phosphorus eyes, from the apothecary; a pair of horns, from the butcher; a tall form, made from reeds, held up by Blaise Monet, and covered with his long cloak, made in the Rue Cadet—strode before him, with these words:

"'I am the shade of Saint Inanimus, boiled to death by Roman legions, for the sake of my religion—in oil. My bones long since have mouldered in the dust, but, where they lie, the little lizards bear a red cross on their heads. Seek near the old tower by the old Roman road, here at the foot of this mountain, and over it erect a chapel, and cause prayers to be said for Saint Inanimus: I, who was boiled to death for the sake of my religion—in oil.'

"'Sh-sh-shade of S-s-saint Ann-on-a-muss, w-w-what k-kind of oi-oil was it?' gasped Padre Cipriano.

"The shade seemed to collect himself, as if about to bestow a kick on the padre, but changed his mind, as he screamed:

"'Hog oil. Go!'

"The priest departed in fear and trembling; and the next day the whole town rang with the news that an apparition had visited Padre Cipriano, and that a procession, for some reason, was to be made at once to the old tower. Accordingly, all the population that could, set forth at an early hour in the afternoon, the padre first informing them of all the circumstances attending the ghostly visitor, the red-headed cross lizards by no means omitted. Arrived at the tower, they were fortunate enough to find a red-cross lizard, then another, and another; and it being buzzed about that one of them was worth, I don't know how many gallons of holy water—the inhabitants, moreover, believing, if they had one, they could commit all kinds of sins free gratis, without confession, &c.,—there at once commenced, consequently, a most indecorous riot among those in the procession; taking advantage of which, the lizards made hurried journeys to other old ruins. The inhabitants of another small town, having heard of the *Miracolo delle lucertole*, came up in force to secure a few lizards for their households. Then commenced those exquisite battles seen nowhere else in such perfection as in southern Italy.

"His eyes starting out of his head, his hands and legs shaking with excitement, one man stands in front of another so 'hopping mad' that you would believe them both dancing the tarantella, if you did not hear them shout—such voices for an opera chorus!—

"'You say that to *me?* to ME? to ME!' Hands working.

"'I do; to *you!*'

"'To me, *me*, ME?' striking himself on his breast.

"'Yes, yes; I do, I do!'

"'What, to ME! ME! *I?*' both hands pointing toward his own body, as if to be sure of the identity of the person; and, that there might not be the possibility of any mistake, he again shouts, screams, yells, shrieks: 'To me? What, that to ME! to ME!' hands and arms working like a crab's.

"Then the entire population rush in, with 'Bravo, Johnny, bravo!' At last, after they have screamed themselves black in the face, and swung their arms and legs until they are ready to drop off, both combatants coolly walk off; and a couple of fresh hands rush in, assisted by the splendid Roman chorus, and begin:

"'What, ME? ME?' &c.

"But the battle of the lizards was conducted with more spirit than the general run of quarrels, for the people were fighting for remission of their sins, as it were—the possession of every sanctified red-headed lizard being so much money saved from the Church, so many years out of purgatory.

"The *gendarmeria* heard the row, and at once rushed down—four soldiers comprised the garrison—to dissipate the crowd. This they managed to do in a peaceable way. There happened to be a heretical spur in the town, in the shape of three German artists, and this incited the bishop of the province, who was at once informed of the miracle-working doings of Father Ciprian, to displace him.

"Thus, my dear friend, I was left to make love to the girls until I had to return to Rome—unfortunately only two weeks' time; for the newly-appointed priest had not the opportunity to set them against me.

"The moral of this long story is: That even vermilion can be worked up in a miraculous manner—if you put the powerful reflective faculty in motion; and doing so, you can have the satisfaction of knowing that by its means you can cause an invisible sign to be stuck up over even a country town in Italy: '*All Persons are Forbidden to Work Miracles Here!*'"

The government, aware of its foreign reputation for patronizing the *Belle Arti*, has an annual display of such paintings and sculpture as artists may see fit to send, and—the censor see fit to admit: for, in *this* exhibition, "nothing is shown that will shock the most fastidious taste"—and it can be found thus, in a building in the Piazza del Popolo.

Caper's painting for the display was rejected for some reason. It represented a sinister-looking brigand, stealing away with Two Keys in one hand and a split cap in the other, suddenly kicked over by a large-sized donkey, his mane and tail flying, head up, and an air of liberty about him generally, which probably shocked Antonelli's tool, the censor's, sense of the proprieties.

Rocjean consoled Caper with the reflection that his painting was refused admittance because the donkey had gradually grown to be emblematical of the state; in fact, was so popularly known to the *forestieri* as the Roman locomotive, with allusions to its steam whistle, &c., highly annoying to the chief authorities—and, therefore, its introduction in a painting was intolerable, and not to be endured.

The works of art included contributions from Americans, Italians, Belgians, Swiss, English, Hessians, French, Dutch, Danes, Bavarians, Spaniards, Norwegians, Prussians, Russians, Austrians, Finns, Esthonians, Lithuanians, Laplanders, and Samoyedes. There was little evidence of the handiwork of mature artists: they either withheld their productions from dislike of the managers, or through determination of giving their younger brethren a fair field and a clear show. A careful observer could see that these young artists had not profited to the fullest extent by the advantages held out to them through a residence in the Imperial City. There was a wine-yness, and a pretty-girl-yness, and tobacco-ness, about paintings and sculpture, that could have been picked up just as well in Copenhagen, or Madrid, or New York, as in Rome. Michael Angelo evidently had not "struck in" on their canvases, or Praxiteles struck out from their marbles. Theirs was an unrevealed religion to these neophytes.

The study of a piece of old Turkey carpet, or a camel's-hair shawl, or a butterfly's wing, or a bouquet of many flowers, would have taught the best artist in the exhibition more concerning color, than he would learn in ten years simply copying the best of the old painters; who had themselves studied directly from these things, and their like.

In sculpture, as in painting, the artists showed the same tame following other sculptors; the same fear of facing Nature, and studying her face to face. A pretty kind of statue of Modesty a man would make, who would take the legs of a satyr, the body of a Venus, the head of Bacchus, the arms of Eros, and thus construct her; yet scarcely a modern statue is made wherein some such incongruous models do not play their part. Go with a clear head—not one ringing with last night's debauch—and study the Dying Gladiator! That will be enough—something more than five tenths of you young Popolites can stand, if you catch but the faintest conception of the mind once moving the sculptor of such a statue. After you have earnestly thought over such a masterpiece, go back to your studio; break up your models for legs, arms, bodies, and heads; take the scalpel in hand, and study *anatomy* as if your heart was in it. Have the living model nude before you at all times. Close your studio door to all "orders," be they ever so tempting. If a fastidious world will have you make "nude statues dressed in stockinet," tell it to get behind you! After long years of earnest study and labor, carve a hand, a foot. If, when you have finished it, one living soul says, with truth, "Blood, bones, and muscles seem under the marble!" believe that you are not far off from exceeding great reward.

In the Popolo exhibition for 1858 was a marble statuette of Daphnis and Chloe, by Luigi Guglielmi, of Rome.

Chloe had a low-necked dress on.

The Roman censor disapproved of this. In a city claiming to be the "HOME OF ART"—THEY PINNED A PIECE OF FOOLSCAP PAPER AROUND THE NECK OF CHLOE.

Rome is the cradle of Art: if so, the sooner the world changes its nurse, the better for the babe!

CHAPTER X.

THERE are three quiet old places on the Continent that Caper always remembers with solemn pleasure—Breda in Holland, Segni in Italy, Neufchâtel in Switzerland. He reposed in Breda, rested in Segni, was severely tranquil in Neufchâtel. The real charm of travelling is best appreciated when one is able to pause in one's headlong career in some such place, and meditate over it. Caper paused for many months at Segni.

SEGNI, or Signia, a Latium city of the Volscians, was, after its colonization by the Romans, always faithful to the Republic. Strabo, Pliny, Plautus, Martial, Juvenal, Silius Italicus, Dionysius Halicarnassus, and Livy, all make mention, in one way or another, of this city. Little is known of its history, from the fact that it was burned to the ground by the order of the Duke of Alva, viceroy of Naples, on the 14th of August, 1557; and in the fire all records of the city were destroyed. Its polygonal or Cyclopean walls, of Pelasgic origin, still remain in many parts as perfect as they ever were: consisting of gigantic blocks of hewn limestone, they are fitted one into another with admirable precision. No mortar was used in laying them; and there they stand, these well-named Cyclopean walls—for some of the stones are twelve feet long by five feet wide—firmly as if centuries on centuries had not sent a myriad of storms to try their strength. There are several gates in these walls, noted among which is one called the Saracen's Gate. It is known in architecture from its indicating, by its form, one of the first attempts toward the pointed arch.

In walking through the town, you find here and there bits of Middle-Age architecture, which have escaped ruin; here a door, there a window, of graceful design, built around with the rough masonwork for which Segni is noted in later days; but the greater number of the houses are constructed in the rudest manner, indicating the poverty and ignorance of the majority of the inhabitants. It is, however, a decent poverty; for, to the credit of the town be it spoken, there was not, when Caper was there, a professional beggar, excepting the friars, in or around it.

Taking the first street—if a rough road winding around the top of the mountain, and but four or five feet wide, may be called so—Caper saw at the doors of the houses, standing chatting to each other, many old women, their white hair flying in every direction, who, as they talked, knitted stockings, or, with distaff in hand, twirled the spindle, making flax into thread for spinning, or wool into woof and web for weaving. Hearing a shuttle, he looked in at an open door, and found a young girl busily weaving a heavy blue cloth at a queer old loom. Not far from her, an elderly woman was weaving flax thread into coarse, heavy linen goods. Passing along, he heard the whir of millstones, and, entering a house, saw a girl working one of the handmills of the country. On a stand, where there was a stone basin, the girl turned in the wheat; another stone, fitting exactly in the basin, was attached to the ceiling by a long pole; catching hold of this, she gave the stone a rotary motion, grinding the wheat very fairly.

Suddenly Caper saw in the back part of the room a woman holding what seemed a large, red-headed caterpillar, without any fuzz on it. She was evidently nourishing it in the way represented in that famous painting, "The Roman Daughter," thus proving that it was a baby. Its resemblance to the caterpillar arose from the way it was swathed. Around all the Segnian infants they wind a strip of knit or woven cloth, about eight feet long and four inches wide, fairly mummifying them; then, to crown the work, they put on their little bullet heads a scarlet cap with brilliant flowers and ribbons, making the poor babies resemble anything but Christian productions. In a neighboring town they hang their babies up in a wicker basket, resembling the birch-bark contrivances for our Indian pappooses.

Continuing his walk, our artist next came to where they were building a house; and its future occupant, who was a man of some enterprise and action, told Caper, with a long face, that he almost despaired of seeing it completed. The harvest came, and almost every workman went off to the wheat fields, leaving the house unfinished until they were ready to recommence work on it, well knowing that there were no other ones in the town able to do their labor. However, those who mixed mortar, carried tiles, and stone, and plaster, were hard at work. These laborers were girls of from twelve to sixteen years old; and one or two of them, spite of dirt and hard labor, were really handsome, with bright, intelligent countenances. They earned one *paul* (ten cents) each a day, and seemed contented and happy, joking with each other, and laughing heartily nearly all the time. Probably our Chippewa Indians would think twice before they set the young women of their tribe to hod-carrying as a livelihood; but then the Chippewas are savages. The hods carried by these girls on their heads were flat, wooden trays, square at each end. Once poised on the head, they balanced themselves, and were carried around without a fall. This carrying on the head, by the women, from an eight-gallon barrel of wine down to a sickle or pocket handkerchief, helps to give them their straight forms and fine carriage of head, neck, and shoulders.

Napoleon the First, in breaking down most of the feudal customs of the Papal States, should be regarded by the poor inhabitants as one of their greatest benefactors. Still, many a remnant of the middle ages remains firmly marked in the habits of the country people. Even now the inhabitants of the Campagna live, not in isolated houses, but in small towns built around the once protecting castle or powerful monastery, where, in times past, they fled, when attacked in the fields by the followers of some house inimical to the one under whose protection they lived. Follow the entire Campagna, from Rome to Naples, by way of Frosinone, and you will see the ruins of watch towers, built to warn the workmen in the fields of the approaching enemy. Thus, in Segni, although the fields cultured by the inhabitants lay miles away at the foot of the mountain, yet every day seven eighths of the five thousand inhabitants walked from four to six miles or more down the mountains to the scene of their daily labors, returning the same distance at sunset. Often and often Caper saw the mother, unable to leave the infant at home, carry it in a basket on her head to the far-away fields, bringing it back at night with the additional burden of corn shelled or wheat garnered in the field. Trotting along gayly at her side, you may be sure, was the ever-present black pig, with a long string wound around his body, by which he is attached to some tree or stone as soon as he reaches the fields, and thus prevented from rooting where he should not root. The day's labor of his mistress finished, she unties him, wraps the string around his body, and he follows her up to the town with the docility of a well-trained dog.

It is the women, too, who daily walk four or five miles up the mountain for their supply of firewood. Arriving at the forest of the commune, they collect split wood and fagots, tying them into round bundles, a yard long, and two or three feet in diameter, and return to Segni, carrying this small woodpile all the way on their heads. It is the women, too, who bring water from the fountains for their household use, in copper vessels (*conche*) holding from two to three gallons. These are placed on the head, and carried, self-balancing, sometimes for long distances. At a fair held at Frosinone, Caper once saw several women, each one carrying on her head two of these *conche*, filled with water, one balanced on the other; and this for half a mile up a steep road, from the fountain at the foot of the mountain, to the town above.

The women, too, do their fair share of harvesting. They cut the wheat with sickles; then, after it is cut, separate the grains from the stalk by rubbing a handful of stalks with a small piece of wood in which a series of iron rings are placed, making a rude rasp; collecting the grains, they then carry them from the fields, sifting them at their leisure in a large round sieve, suspended from a triangle of long poles; then, on a breezy day, you may see them standing over a large cloth, holding a double handful of wheat high above their heads, and letting it fall: the wind blows away the chaff, and the clean grain falls on the outspread cloth.

In the autumn, when the men are employed in the vintage, comes the chestnut season; and then the women, who are not busy in the vineyard, and who regard it as a frolic, go for miles up in the mountains, collecting the nuts, large as our horse chestnuts. They form no small part of the winter stock of food for the mountaineers, while the refuse nuts are used to fatten the pet pig. We can have but small conception of the primeval look these chestnut woods wear, the trees growing to an enormous size, many a one being ten to twelve feet in diameter. The weather is glorious during this season: clear, bright, and buoyantly refreshing blow the autumn winds; and as Caper, day after day, wandered among the old trees, now helping an old woman to fill a sack with the brown nuts, now clubbing the chestnuts from the trees for a young girl, he, too, voted chestnut gathering a rare good time. Far off, and now near, the girls were singing their quaint wild songs. Thus heard, the *rondinella* sounds well. It is of the woods and deserts; strange, barbaric, oriental, bacchantic, what you please, save dawdling drawing-room and piano-ic.

To resume the walk around the town: Caper, after leaving the man who was employing the sylphide hod-carriers, called in at the shop where cigars were sold, and outside of which was a tin sign, on which was painted the Papal coat-of-arms, and the usual words, indicating that the government monopolies, salt and tobacco, were for sale. Having bought some cigars, he entered into conversation with the man who kept the store. He learned, what he already knew, that everything in the town was done by hand—weaving, spinning, threshing, grinding wheat and corn, &c.

"Do you know," said Caper, "that in some countries all these labors are done by steam?"

It is dangerous to tell great truths; and after our artist had spoken, he saw, by the expression of the man's face, that he had placed himself in danger; but suddenly the cigar-seller's face was illuminated with intelligence, as he exclaimed:

"Oh! you mean that infernal thing that goes *boo-hoo-hoo?* I saw it when I was in Rome, last week. It's going to drag cars to Civita Vecchia on the iron road."

"That's it," answered Caper, greatly relieved.

"*Benissimo!* we never had anything of the kind; and, what is more, WE DON'T WANT ONE!"

Caper walked out, determined to write to New York, and beg some of the good people there to save a few missionaries from death among the Feejees, and send them to Segni, where there was a wide field open for the dissemination of knowledge.

Passing along, he next came to the small square in front of the church, where, once every week, a market was held. Here he found a man who had just arrived with fresh fish from Terracina—the Terracina of the opera of "Fra Diavolo." Among the small fish, sardines, &c., which were brought to town that day, in time for Friday's dinner, when every one kept *vigilia*, was one large fish, which our artist determined to buy, and present to his landlord at the inn. He asked its price.

"That fish," said the fishman, "is for the dinner of the Illustrissimo and Reverendissimo Monsignore the Bishop; and if you were to turn every scale in its body into *baioccho, and give them all to me,* you couldn't have it."

Caper was sorely tempted to turn the scales in his own favor, for he knew, if he were to pay well, he could bear off the fish triumphantly, spite of the seller's declaration; but a thought of the sore affliction he would bring into the mind of the fat old gentleman in purple, with a gold chain around his neck, who rejoiced in the name of bishop, deterred him from his heretical proceeding, and he walked away in deep meditation.

The patron saint of Segni is San Bruno; and, to do him honor, every other male baby born in the town is called Bruno; so our artist, in his walks around town, heard this name howled, cried, screamed, shrieked, called, and appealed to, on an average once in five minutes, through the hours when the male inhabitants were about and awake. This similarity in names was by no means accompanied by similarity in appearance; for there were more light-haired and blue-eyed men by this name in the place than any one, having the popular idea of what an Italian looks like, would believe could be found in a town of the same size in America. Trying to account for the Norse look of many of the Segnians, and the Oriental look of many others, Caper climbed up to the top of the mountain above the town, and, seating himself in the shadow of the old Cyclopean wall, looked down the mountain side to the broad valley below him.

As all roads lead to Rome (soliloquized he), it's no wonder that those two famous old ways down there in the valley, the Via Trajana and the Via Latina, should have once been passed over by white-haired, blue-eyed Goths, and, seeing the old town perched up here, they should have climbed up, having **strong legs**. Once here, they put all the men to the sword, made love to the girls, plundered all that was plunderable; drank up all the liquor, Sambuca, Rosoglio, "Rhum di Giamaica," and Acqua viva, they could put their paws on; then, having a call further on, left the girls, small babes, and other *impedimenta* (baggage!), rushing on to Rome to settle accounts with their bankers there, like hon-o-rable men. So you find many flaxen-haired, sky-eyed people up here, and they are rough and bold and independent.

Years and years after them, clambering over the mountains from the seacoast, came the Saracens—oh, you were the boys! —and they, being a refined and elegantly educated circle, compared with the Goths, of course did the same amount of slaughtering and love making, only more refinedly and elegantly; cutting off heads instead of knocking them in; and with the gold spoons and other instruments that they found in the church, instead of making sword hilts and helmets, they at once worked them into graceful, crescent-shaped earrings, and curious rings, chains, and brooches, giving them to the girls, and winning their hearts in the old-fashioned style. The girls, for their part, declared to each other that when these odious Moors went away, they would give all the earrings and brooches back to the Church. But they forgot to; which accounts for their wearing them, or those of similar pattern, to this day.

The gentle Saracens, moreover, wishing to introduce their own school of music, taught the girls to sing; proof of which is the horrible songs the *contadini* still have, resembling in no wise pious Christian hymns, but rather a cross between a growl to Odin and a yell to Allah! A growl to Odin, for the girls could not forget the Goths, albeit they only knew them through reports of their foremothers.

Then the Saracens turned their attention to crockery ware, pots, pans, and water jars; forming like fruits and flowers the yielding clay, and establishing models that are every hour to be seen around one in this old nest. Clothes, too, they thought, should be made as they saw "fit;" and, accordingly, head-dresses and dresses, under garments, &c., *à la Saracenesca*, were all the rage; and as the colors were in no wise sombre or melancholy to behold, the girls took kindly to them, and, slightly modified, wear them still. When you see the *pane*—the white cloth worn on the women's heads—remember, it was once an Oriental *yashmak*, falling around and concealing the face of the Italian lady love of a Saracen; but when the Saracens departed, they rolled up the veil, and disclosed to delighted Christians the features of Rita or Maria, who figured for a time as Zoe or Fatima.

With their religion, the Saracens were not so successful—they could not make it popular; so they waived this point, contented with having set the fashions and introduced their own style of music, crockery, and jewelry.

Thus reflecting, Caper stopped short, regarded his watch, found it was near dinner time—the pastoral hour of noonday—and then turned to walk down to the inn. On his way he passed a store having French calicoes in the window, and mourned in his heart to think how short a time it would be before these became popular, and the homemade picturesque dresses of the female Segnians would be discarded. The time, too, was fast coming—with the railroad from Rome to Naples—when travellers will overrun these mountain towns, and the price of board shoot up from forty cents to a dollar or two. Then the inhabitants will learn geography and become mercenary, and will learn arithmetic and blaspheme (in their way) at *forestieri Inglese*, *Americani*, *Francese*, or *Tedeschi*, and cheat them. Then the peace of the Volscians will have departed, never, oh! never more to return.

Then the women will wear—bonnets! and cheap French goods; will no longer look like moving woodyards, bringing fagots on their heads down mountain sides; no longer bear aloft the graceful *conche* filled with sweet water from the fountain, for hydraulic rams will do their business; no longer lead the sportive pig to pastures new, but pen him up, and feed him when the neighbors are not looking on! These days will sorely try the men. Now they labor in the fields in shirts and drawers, never thinking of putting on their pantaloons until they return to the very gates of the town, where, at sunset, you may see them, ten or twelve deep, thus employed before entering the city; but in the future they will have to observe *les convenances*, and make their toilette in the fields. This they will do with great grumbling, returning homeward, and they will sing *rondinelle* bearing severely on the *forestieri*, who have ruined the good old pod-augur days when they made *vendetta* without trouble. Thus reflecting, the donkeys they ride, while their wives walk and carry a load, will receive many virulent punches intended for other objects.

"Signor Giacomo, dinner is served," said the landlord, as Caper entered the old inn.

Cool wine, roast lamb, wild pigeons, crisp salad, with a broiled partridge; great bunches of luscious grapes, figs freshly picked, *and* maccaroni à la Milanese. Such was our artist's dinner that day. Patriarchally simple of a necessity; but then, what can you expect in a town where the British lion has never yet growled for a bushel of raw beef when he is fed, or swore at the landlord for not having a pint of hay boiled in hot water (tea?) for breakfast, when he is nervous?

Do not believe, in spite of all you hear about the benighted Papal States, that the people spend their holidays groaning and begging to depart from this vale of tears. On the contrary, the ignorant wretches believe in enjoying every moment of life; and, to judge by the Segnians, who are by no means dyspeptical, they do so with all their might. They know, if they fall sick, good Doctor Matteucci attends them carefully and well, without any charge, for he receives a salary from the commune. They know, if they have good health and do their work, they will be rewarded every now and then with a holiday, in which religion is so tempered with lottery tickets, wine drinking, fireworks, horse races, and trading, that, shorn lambs as they are, paying to the Church three cents for every twenty-five pounds of corn they may grind, and as large a portion of their crops for the rent of the lands they till, they still have jolly good times at the fairs and festivals in their own and neighboring towns.

Every town has its patron saint, and it is in honor of his day that they hold one grand festival each year. To accommodate temporal affairs, a fair is also held on the same day, so that the country people of the neighborhood may purchase not only the necessaries, but the simple luxuries they need or long for.

Besides the one principal festival and fair in Segni to San Bruno, already described, they had three minor celebrations of minor saints—substitutes, as Rocjean declared, for Pomona, Bacchus, and Ceres. Certainly, the saints' days fell very curiously about the same time their predecessors were worshipped.

It is, however, of five festivals and fairs held in five neighboring towns, that the present chapter treats; so let the drums beat while our three artists proceed to enjoy, on paper, the days they celebrated.

One evening, the *vetturino*, Francesco, came to the trio and told them that on the next day but one, Sunday, there would be a fair and *festa* at Frosinone, a town about twenty-three miles from Segni, and that if they wished to go, he had three seats to hire in his *vettura*. Having heard that the costumes to be seen there were highly picturesque, and anxious to study the habits of the people in holiday guise, our artists determined to go. At daybreak on the appointed morning, having breakfasted, and filled their flasks with wine, they started with a guide to walk down to Casa Bianca, a small *osteria*, distant, as the guide assured them, about two miles; three miles, as Francesco swore to; four miles, as Gaetano, the landlord, declared; and six miles, as Caper and Rocjean were ready to affirm to. Down the mountain road they scrambled, only losing their patience when they found they had to wade a small marsh, where their tempers and polished boots were sorely tried. Once over, they reached Casa Bianca, and found the *vettura* there, having arrived an hour before from Rome, thirty odd (and peculiar) miles distant; and now, with the same horses, they had to make twenty-three miles more before ten A. M., according to agreement. Rocjean and Caper sat outside the carriage, while Dexter sat inside, and conversed with two other passengers, cheerful and good-natured people, who did all in their power to make everybody around them contented and jolly.

The road went through the fertile Sacco valley; right and left rich pasture grounds, or wheat and corn fields; the mountains on either side rising in grandeur in the early sunlight, their tops wreathed with veils of rising mist. They soon passed Castelaccio (the termination *accio* is one, according to Don Boschi, of vilification; consequently, the name may be translated, Bigbad Castle). This castle belongs to Prince Torlonia, *à propos* of which prince it is rather singular that all his money cannot buy good Latin; for any one may read at Frascati, staring you in the face as it does, as you wind up the villa, engraved on a large marble tablet, an inscription touching

TORLONIA ET UXSOR EJUS, ETC.

UXSOR may be Latin, but it is the kind that is paid for, and not the spontaneous gift of classic Italy.

The carriage next passed through Ferentino, *Ferentinum* of the Volscians, where it stopped for a time to let Rocjean see the stone called *La Fata*, whereon is inscribed the noble generosity of Quintilius Priscus, who gave *crustula* and *mulsum* (cakes and mead) to the old people; *sportulæ* (cold victuals?) to the decurions, and *nucum sparsiones* (a sprinkling of nuts) for the small children.

After which antiquarian research, and a drink of wine at the *Hotel des Etrangères*, the trio called loudly on Francesco to drive on; for the name of the inn suggested similar signboards, Hotel d'Angleterre, Hotel Vittoria, Hotel des Isles Brittaniques, at all of which one or other of our travellers had been savagely fleeced.

The carriage at last arrived at the tavern, at the foot of the mountain on which Frosinone stands, and our artists found that the ascent must be made on foot. This, in the face of the broiling sun, was equal to two hot baths at least. However, they determined to take it easily, and accordingly tarried for a while by an old bridge crossing a small stream, running bright and clear, where cattle were drinking; then they stopped at the neighboring fountain, where the girls were filling copper water-jars, and dusty *contadini* were washing themselves in order to present a clean face at the fair; and listened with pleasure to the hearty laughter and holiday jests bandied about with profusion. Thus, in refreshed spirits, they commenced the ascent.

On the brow of the mountain, in front rank of the houses of the city, arose the walls of what they thought at first glance was a very large factory; they subsequently learned it was a male-factory, or prison. This, with the governor's palace and other lofty buildings, gives Frosinone a stately air, only lost on entering the place and finding the streets narrow, steep, and not particularly clean. On entering the street leading to the main gate of entrance, their ears were saluted by the squealing and grunting of many hogs collected together in small droves, on both sides the way, for sale or barter. Here stood a bronzed peasant, dressed only in shirt and drawers, with boots up to his knees; a steeple-crowned straw hat, with a large carnation pink in it, shading his closely shaved face, on which no hair was seen save two long curls pendent in front of his ears, while the back part of his head was shaved nearly as smooth as his face. This man held in his arms a small pig in a violent state of squeals. Mixed up among the pigs were many women dressed in lively-colored costumes, looking graceful and pretty, and gaining added effect from the dark tones of the old gray houses around them. Advancing upward, at times at angles of forty-five degrees and more, through narrow streets crowded with picturesque houses (if they did threaten to tumble down), they at last reached the Piazza. Here the squeeze commenced: crockery, garlic, hardware, clothing, rosaries and pictures of the saints, flowers; while donkeys, gensdarmes, jackasses, and shovel hats, strangers, and pretty girls, were all pressing with might and main—they did not seem to know where—probably to the nearest wineshops, which were driving a brisk trade.

Reaching an inn, our artists ordered dinner, and amused themselves, while it was being prepared, looking out of the window at the crowds in the street beneath. On the opposite side of the way were two open windows, evidently "behind the scenes" of the main church, since many of the principal actors in the ceremonies were here attiring themselves in curious robes prior to their appearing in public. A tallow-faced looking youth, with no hair on the extreme crown of his head, while swinging a long wax candle around, struck a fat old gentleman, with a black silk gown and white lace bertha over it, in the back; whereupon, I regret to write it, the fat old gentleman struck the tallow-faced youth the severest kind of a blow below the belt, entirely contrary to the rules of the P. R. Dexter, having watched the performance, at its conclusion shouted for very joy; whereupon the stout man, raising his eyes, saw in the opposite windows the three *forestieri;* and I do assure you that such a look of malevolence as crossed his face for a moment, contained all the Borgias ever knew of poisons and assassinations. Luckily, the artists did not have to go to confession to that man.

Dinner finished, Rocjean proposed a walk. They first went to the old church, but found its interior ruined with whitewash and tawdry decorations. The music, however, was excellent, but the crowd of worshippers intense; so they repaired to the cattle market, in the piazza in front of the prison. They had been there but a short time, before the procession in honor of the patron saint of Frosinone, whose full-length seated effigy was carried by bearers, passed them. Along with other emblems borne by priests or laymen, was a cross, apparently of solid wood, the upright piece fully twelve feet long, and as large round at the base as your thigh; the transverse piece of the cross was proportionately large. This was borne with ease by a moderate-sized man. Caper was at a loss to account for the facility with which the bearer handled pieces of timber as large as small joists of a house; so he asked a good-natured looking citizen standing near him, if that wooden cross was not very heavy?

"Eh! that heavy? Why, it's not wood; it's made of stove pipes!"

The citizen also told Caper that the seated effigy of the patron saint had had a hard time of it some years ago, for the country around Frosinone suffering from a long drought, the inhabitants had in vain prayed, begged, and supplicated the aforementioned saint to send them rain; but he remained obdurate, until at last, seeing him so stubborn, they seized him, in spite of the priests, carried him down to the bridge, neck and heels, and threatened him, by all his brother and sister saints, to put him to bed—bed of the stream (it was nearly dry)— unless he speedily gave them a good supply of rain. In a couple of days, sure enough, the rain came down, and in such torrents, that there was a grand rush of the country people from the vicinity, begging the saint to hold up. Since that time he has behaved very decently, and just now is in high favor.

There were some fine cattle at the fair; and Dexter, noticing a peculiar and becoming head-dress to several of the long-horned oxen, made of the skin of some animal, ornamented with bright-colored strips of woollen with tassels at the end, tried to purchase a pair, but found the owners generally unwilling to sell them. However, one man at last agreed to sell a pair made of wolfskin, with bright red, yellow, and green strips and tassels, for a fair price, and Dexter at once bought them—as a study, and also as an ornament for his studio.

The Tombola in the Piazza Tosti drew together a large crowd; and then it was that Rocjean was in his element, Caper delighted, and Dexter rejoiced in the study of costumes and motives for painting. The straw hats worn here looked more picturesque than the black felt conical hats of the other end of the valley, but the "soaplocks" of the men were villanous. The women were brilliant in holiday attire, among their dresses showing that half-modern Greek, half Neapolitan style, uniting the classic with the middle age. The *ciociare*—as those who wear *ciocie*, or sandals, are called—were there in full force. One of these men, with whom Rocjean had a long conversation, told our artist that the price paid for enough leather for a pair was forty cents. Each sandal was made of a square piece of sole leather, about twelve inches long by five inches wide, and is attached to the foot by strings crossing from one side to the other, and bending the leather into the rough resemblance of a shoe. The leather is sold by weight, and the *ciociara* declared that sandals were far better than shoes.

11*

"But, when it rains, your feet are wet," suggested Rocjean.

"*Seguro*" (certainly), answered *ciociara*.

"And when it snows, they are wet; and when it is muddy, they won't keep the mud out; and when it's dusty, where is the dust?"

"Down there, in the Campagna!" answered the man. "But you seem to forget that we wrap cloths over our feet and legs, as high as the knee, and tie them all on with strings; or else our women knit brown woollen leggings, which cover our feet and legs. Well, good or bad, they are better for *us* (*noi altri*) than shoes."

Fireworks and a ball at the Governor's palace closed that saint's day; and the next afternoon our artists left the town, to return to Segni; but as, toward midnight, they began to ascend the long, steep road leading to the town, they were overtaken by a thunder storm, which for grandeur equalled anything that Caper at least, had ever seen. The lightning was nearly incessant, at one flash revealing the valley below them, and distant mountain peaks after peaks trembling in white light, then all black as black could be; patches of road in front of the old carriage, silver one second, sable another; while the thunder cracked and roared, echoing and reëchoing from rock to rock, ringing away up the wild gorge around which the road wound. The rain fell in torrents, and pebbles and stones loosened from the mountain sides came falling around them. Francesco, the driver, on foot, urged the tired horses onward with blows and the most powerful language he could bring to bear. He accused the off-horse of being a pickpocket and an *arciprete*, and a robber of a small family, of which Francesco assured him he knew he was the father. Then the mare Filomena came in for her share of vilifications, being called a *"giovinastra* (naughty girl), a *vecchierellaccia* (vile old hag), a ———" Here the rain, pebbles, lightning, and thunder interrupted the driver, and Rocjean told him to take breath and a pull at his flask, which was filled with *Sambuca*. Thus refreshed, although soaked to the skin, Francesco livened up, and from despondency passed to hope, then to joy, finally landing the old carriage near the gate of Segni, in time for the artists to see far below them the clouds rolling rapidly away, and hear the thunder grumbling far off, over some other town, some other benighted travellers.

VALMONTONE was the next town visited, and the festival in honor of its patron saint, Luigi Gonzago, was a decided success; the singing in the church operatically excellent; a good-sized tombola; a funny dinner in the back room of a grocery store, one half of the floor of which was covered with shelled corn, while the other half was occupied by the united legs of two tables, a dozen chairs, four dogs, one cat, six male and three female country people. There was a lamb roasted whole, a small barrel of wine, plenty of bread, find-your-own-knives-and-be-happy dinner. Coming out of this small den, and passing a fine large house, opposite the grand palace of the Prince of Valmontone, behold an Italian acquaintance of Caper's standing in a balcony with a very handsome woman. Another moment, and Caper was invited in, and passed from poverty to wealth in the twinkling of an eye. Rooms full of guests, tables covered with damask linen, silver, flowers, crystal glasses, delicate food (too late!), good wine (just in time!), charming ladies.

"*Condessa*, permit me to present Signor' Cahpeer, Americano."

A rich, full, musical voice, lovely eyes, a brilliant toilette—is it any wonder the heart of our artist beat *con animo*, when the beautiful woman welcomed him to Valmontone, and hoped it would not be his last visit. Other introductions, other glasses of sparkling wine; then off for the street, excitement, music, coffee, and a cigar; pretty girls with tender eyes; the prince's stables, with hawks nailed to the doors, and blood horses in their stalls; *contadini*, cowbells, jackasses; ride home on horseback by moonlight; head swimming, love coming in, fun coming out. Exit festival the second.

GAVIGNANO was the scene of the third festival. It is a small town, lying at the foot of Segni. Caper went there on horseback, and, after a regular breakneck ride down the mountain, the path winding round like a string on an apple, arrived there in time to escape a pouring rain, and find himself in a large hall with three beautiful sisters, the Roses of Montelanico, numerous *contadini* friends, and the wine bottles going round in a very lively and exhilarating manner. The rain ceasing, Caper walked out to see the town, when his arm was suddenly seized, and, turning round, who should it be but Pepe the rash, Pepe the personification of Figaro—a character impossible for northern people to place outside of a madhouse, yet daily to be found in southern Europe. Rash, headstrong, full of deviltry, splendid appetite, and not much conscience; volatile, mocking, irrepressible.

Pepe seized Caper by the arm with a loud laugh, and, only saying, "*Evviva*, Signor' Giacomo, come along!" without giving him breathing time, rushed him up narrow streets, down dirty alleys, through a crowd of mules, mud, and mankind, until they both caught a glimpse of a small church, with green garlands over the door. Hauling Caper inside, he dragged him through a long aisle crowded with kneeling worshippers, smashed him down on a bench in front of the main altar, tearing half a yard of crimson damask, and nearly upsetting the priest officiating; and then, while Caper (red in the face, and totally unfit to hear the fine chorus of voices, among which Mustafa's, the soprano, came ringing out) was composing himself to listen, Pepe grabbed him, with a

"Music's over; *andiamo* (let's go). Did you hear Mustafa? *Bella voce*, tra-la-leeeee? Mustafa's a *contadino;* I know his pa and ma; they changed him when only five years old. Thought he was a Turk, didn't you? He sings in the Sistine chapel. Pretty man—fat; positively not a sign of a beard."

Struggling to escape, Caper was rushed out of church, and into a *caffè* to have a tumblerful of boiling coffee poured down his throat, and again be expressed up hill at a breakneck rate, catching sights of tumbledown old houses, mud, water, flowers, peasants, costumes, donkeys, until he was landed in the Gran' Piazza. Whew!

"Must see the hall where the concert is to-night. Beautiful girl, *bellisima, pfisp!* (imitating kiss) girl from Rome; sings three pieces, Ernani, Norma, *pfisp!* Come along!"

Smack, bang! into the hall, where the silence and presence of a select few, including Monsignore and the Governatore, in council assembled, commanded silence. Pepe wouldn't hear of it anywheres, so again they were in the open air. The band was playing good music in the square; the tombola was about to commence, and *contadini* were busy with pencils and tickets, ready to win the eighty *scudi* put up.

Tombola commenced, and Pepe at once supervised all the tickets within reach. Bravo, twenty-seven! you've got it, Tonio; scratch it, my lamb.—You haven't, Santi, *poverino mio.*—It's *non c'é,* Angeluccio.—Ah, Bruno, always lucky.— Fifty-four, *Santa Maria !* who would have thought it?—*Caro* Bernardo, *only* one more number to win the *terno !* "

Sómebody won the tombola at last, and Pepe told Caper he should wait for the fireworks and the concert. " Beautiful girl, ah ! *bella,* sings three pieces." Here he burst out with that song,

> " *Ninella mia di zucchero,*
> *Prende 'sto core, ed abbraccialo :* "

not waiting for the end of which, Caper interrupted him by saying that he should not wait for the evening, as he intended returning to Segni at once.

" Will you ? " asked Pepe. " Oh, *bravo !* good idea. Concert room will be crowded to suffocation; get hot, perspire, catch cold. Fireworks nothing. I'll go with you; great fools to wait. Here is a wineshop ; let us refresh ! "

In they went, and finished a quart, after which Pepe proposed visiting another wineshop, where they had some frascati, good and sweet. So he hurried Caper along so fast through mud and narrow streets, all the way down hill, that his feet could not begin to hold on the slippery stones, and both went ahead on the plan of not being able to stop. At last they reached a landing place, where the wine was sold. Hastening in, they nearly fell over a tall, splendid-looking girl, who was standing in the hall.

" *Iddio !* it's my *cara* Giulia, lovely as ever. Come with

us, and finish a bottle. This is our friend Giacomo, Americano
—brave youth, *allegro !* "

"It pleases me well to make the acquaintance of the Signor. I have often seen him in Segni———"

"And *now* you'll fall in love with him,

"' *E tu non pienž a mi,*'"

sang Pepe. "This comes of my headlong hurry introducing pretty girls to interesting strangers. Ah, *bella* Giulia!"

"*Zitto!* Pepe, and pour me out a glass of wine."

Pepe poured out the wine, one glass after another. Suddenly springing from his seat, he said, "Wait here a minute; I see Gaetano. Will be back again *prestissimo!*"

He went, and Caper and Giulia were left seated, talking merrily over the wine. There were stars shining when Giulia bid good night to Caper, yet Pepe did not return. He had seized some new idea—may-be the pretty Roman who sang at the concert. Then Caper saddled his horse, and rode out into the night—glad that he had met black-eyed Giulia.

The night-rides up the mountain! Here's romance, real and beautiful. Are you not treading an old Roman road, over which the legions have marched to victory, war chariots rattled? Up the mountains, on the old road once leading over the mountains to Terracina, the *Tarracina* of the Romans, who made it one of their naval stations; up that road you go, trusting solely to your horse, one slip of whose foot would send you into eternity *via* a ravine some hundred feet sheer down. Here, bright light from a *casina* where the *contadini* are loading mules with grapes to be pressed in the city up there near the stars! High above you, nothing but a wall of black rock, up, up so high! Stars gleaming down, the comet tailing from side to side of the ravine, while the path in the ragged, jagged, storm-gullied rock is so dark you see nothing. Your horse stops, his hind feet slip—no! he clings, his hoofs are planted firm. Up he goes, and there, in the hands of Providence, you are tossed and pitched, as he winds up and plunges down. The merry ringing, jingling bells of mules ahead, and the voices of their drivers: turn a corner, and the bright light of torches flashes in your eyes. Look again and earnestly at the beautiful scene: mules, drivers, black rocks, olive trees above, all flamboyant in the ruddy light, appearing and disappearing; a weird, wild scene. Up, up, long is the way; past the fountain where the stars are flashing in the splashing waters; past gardens; past the mountain path at last. *Ecco*, the inn of Gaetano.

ANAGNI held its festival in honor of San Magno (*Prottetore della Città*) on the 19th day of August. Gaetano, the landlord, invited Caper to attend it, putting his famous white horse at the disposal of the artist, accompanying him on a small bay beast that was extremely fond of showing his heels to the surrounding objects. Leaving Segni about ten o'clock in the morning, they had hardly reached a bridle path down the mountain, nothing more, in fact, than a gully, when they were joined by a cavalcade of four other Segnians. One of them, the "funny fellow" of the party, was mounted on a very meek-looking donkey, and enlivened the hot ride across the valley of the Sacco by spasmodic attempts to lead the cavalcade, and come in ahead of the others. He had a lively time as they approached the city, and a joke with every foot passenger on the way; but Gaetano, whose reserve was one of his strong points, and who was anxious to enter Anagni under favorable auspices, gave the word to Caper, and in a few minutes they left cavalcade and donkey rider far behind.

Anagni, the ancient *Anagnia,* was the capital of the Hernici. The favorite residence, in the middle ages, of several of the popes, it still shows in its buildings marks of the wealth it once enjoyed. Having stabled their horses with a friend of Gaetano's, who insisted on their finishing the best part of a *bottiglia* of red wine with him, the artist, under the landlord's guidance, set out to see the town. They climbed up street to the cathedral, a fine old pile, trembling with music, and filled with worshippers, paintings of saints *in extremis,* flowers, wax candles, votary offerings, and heat; then coming out, and feeling wolfish, looked round for a place where they could find dinner! Here it was! a scene that would have cheered Teniers: a very large room, its walls brown with smoke; long wooden tables, destitute of cloth, but crowded with country people eating, drinking, talking, enjoying themselves to the utmost extent. Forks were invisible, but every man had his own knife, and Caper, similarly provided, whipped out his long pocket weapon and commenced an attack on roast lamb and bread, as if time were indeed precious. Wine was provided at Fair price; and, with fruit, he managed to cry at last, "Hold, enough!"

Gaetano, having a message for a young priest in the seminary there, asked Caper how he would like to see the interior of the building, and the way the *prete* lived? Caper assenting, they entered a fine large establishment, with broad walls and high ceilings, and mounting to the second story, and knocking at the door of a chamber, they were admitted by a tall, thin, sallow young man, about eighteen years old, evidently the worse for want of exercise, and none the stronger minded for his narrow course of education and instruction.

Gaetano introduced Caper to the young priest, and the artist, who, a moment before entering the room, was as lively as the Infant Bacchus, at once became melancholy as the Infant Samuel, and a feeling of such pity seized him, that, endeavoring not to show it, he turned it to a sentiment of interest in the young priest and his surroundings, admiring the beautiful view from the window, and, turning inward to a poor wreath of paper flowers hanging over a holy-water fount attached to the wall, praised their resemblance to natural flowers. (Was that untruth unforgiven?)

"I made them," said the young priest; "but they are nothing to the ones I have made for our church in Montelanico. I will show those to you." Opening a large paper box, he showed Caper wreaths and festoons of paper flowers. "I have spent weeks on weeks over them," he continued, "and they will decorate the church at the next *festa*. I spend all my leisure hours making artificial flowers."

In answer to a question from Caper, if the dress he then wore was the usual one worn by the seminarists on important occasions, the young priest answered him that it was not, and at once produced the full dress, putting on the upper garment, a species of cassock, in order to show him how it looked. He next called his attention to a curious old work, full of engravings illustrating the different costumes of the different orders of priests, and was in full course to describe them all, when Gaetano told him that he was sorry, but that he had to go, as he had some matters to attend to at the fair. So Caper bid the young priest good-by, saying he regretted that he had not time to further study the ecclesiastical costumes. A feeling of relief seized him when he was once more in the open air—thoughts of gunning, fishing, boating, horse riding, foot racing, fighting, anything, so long as it was not the making paper flowers by that poor, pale-faced boy—it was terrible!

There are several resident families in Anagni having titles. These are known as the *stelle d'Anagni* (stars of Anagni), and number, among the ladies, many beautiful faces, if those pointed out to him were the true stars. But it was while smoking a cigar over a cup of coffee, that he saw enter the café, without exception one of the loveliest and most attractive women he met in Italy. The word *simpatica*, so often used by Italians, expressing, as it does, so much in so short a space, exactly applied to the charming woman who passed him, as she entered the room where he was seated. She was accompanied by several gentlemen, one of whom, on whose arm she leaned, having the most character of all the others in his face, and the finest-looking man in figure and carriage, Caper selected as her husband; and he was right.

Gaetano, having finished his business, soon entered the café in company with a dashing, handsome-looking man, in half-ecclesiastical costume; for though he wore a shovel hat and long-tailed black frock coat, yet his other clothes, though black, had the air of being made by an *à la mode* tailor. His manner was cordial, frank, hearty. He proposed a walk around the town, to see what was going on among the *villani*. Caper calling his attention to the lady mentioned above, the ecclesiastic, making his excuses for his sudden leave, at once hurried over to salute her, and was evidently very cordially received. He returned in a few minutes to Caper.

"It is the *Principessa* ————, and she insists on having an introduction to the American. She is making the *villegiatura* among these mountain towns for a frolic. She will be in Segni, with her husband, the Signor ————, and it will be pleasant for you to know them while there."

"Introduce me, by all means. She is the most beautiful woman I have seen in Italy."

The introduction was made, and our artist surpassed himself in conversing intelligibly, much to the delight of the fair Italian and her friends, who declared they were prepared to converse with him solely by signs. Promising that when they came to Segni he should not fail to call upon them, and give them a long account of the savage life he lived among his Indian brethren in America, he laughingly bid them good day.

The dashing priest now went with Caper and Gaetano through the crowded streets, pointing out objects of interest, architectural and human; past booths where all kinds of merchandise was exposed for sale, out to see the ancient massive walls of travertine, where divers stunning objects were carved, inscriptions, &c. Then they found a wineshop, where it was cool and tolerably quiet, and smoked and drank until sunset, having much sport conversing with the amiable *villane*, who were as comfortably tipsy as their circumstances would permit. At sunset, the Piazza Grande was brilliant with hangings, crimson and gold, and colored tapestry hung from the windows of the surrounding houses. Here the tombola was held, and here the crowd was excited as usual. The lucky ones bearing off the prizes were in such rapturous state of bliss—"one might have stuck pins into them without their feeling it."

About sunset, Gaetano and Caper saddled their horses, and left the city, striking over the valley to Segni, passing on the road country people mounted on donkeys, or travelling along on foot, nine tenths of whom were vigorously canvassing—the life of Saint Magno?—no, indeed, but the chances of the lottery!

There was to have been the next day, at Anagni, a curious chase of buffaloes, in accordance with some passage in the life of San Magno, as the people said; but, according to Rocjean, more probably some neglected ceremony of the ancient heathens, which the party in power, finding they could not abolish, gracefully tacked on to the back of the protector of the city. These kind of things are done to an alarming extent around Rome; and the Sieur de Rocjean, when he lost his calendar containing the dates of all the festivals, said it was of no importance—he had an excellent Lempriere!

The fifth festival—if you have patience to read about it—was held at GENAZZANO, and was decidedly the most celebrated one of the season. It came off on the 8th of September, and for costumes, picturesqueness, and general effect, might have been called, to copy from piano literature, *Le Songe d'un Artiste*.

The town itself looks as if it had just been kicked out of a theatre. Round towers at entrance gate, streets narrow, and all up hill, the tiles on the houses running down to see what is going on in the gutter, quaint old houses, gray with time, with latticed windows, queer old doors, a grand old castle in ruins. It is one of the scenes you long so much to see before you come abroad, and which you so seldom find along the Grande Route. Spend a summer in the mountain towns of Italy! among the Volscian mountains or hills—and have your eyes opened.

As Caper entered the gate, the first objects meeting his sight were: A procession of genuine pilgrims, dressed precisely as you see them in Robert le Diable, or Linda di Chamouni, or on the stage generally—long gray robes down to their feet, cocked hats with cockle shells, long wands; some barefoot, some with sandals: on they passed, singing religious songs. Then came the peasantry, all in perfect theatrical harmony, costumes rigidly correct *à la Sonnambula*. German artists dressed in Sunday clothes *à la Der Freyschutz*. A café with festoons of lemon peel hung from window to window—they are not up to this idea in *Fra Diavolo*. Pretty girls in latticed windows, with red bodices, white sleeves, flowers in their hair —*legitimate Italian drama*. Crockery ware in piles—*low comedy*. A man with a table, Sambuca and Acqua-vita bottles on it, and wee glasses, one cent a drink—*melodrama*. Fresh oranges and figs, pumpkin seed and pine cones; a house with mushrooms strung on thread, hanging from window to window —this was not for festival display, but is the common way of the country. Notices of the *festa*, containing programme of the day, including amusements, ecclesiastical and secular, hung up alongside the stands where they were selling lottery tickets —*tragedy*. Fountains, with groups of peasantry drinking, or watering horses and donkeys—*pantomime*. Priests, in crow-black raiment, and canal-boat or shovel hats—*mystery*. Strangers from Rome, in the negro-minstrel style of costume, if young men; or in the rotund-paunch and black-raiment dress, if elderly men; or in the *chiffonée* style, if Roman women attempting the last Parisian fashion—*farce*.

Here are the booths with rosaries, crucifixes, Virgin Mary's, holy-water holders, medals of Pio Nono, or jewelry; gold crescent ear-rings, *spadine* (long silver hair-pins); silver hearts, legs, arms, for votive offerings, and crosses without number.

Caper entered the church. It was filled, and stifling with heat, and frankincense, and *contadini*, and wax lights burning before the shrine, on which the sun shone. There were beautiful faces among the *pajine* (people in fine raiment), showing what can be made from the *contadine* (people in coarse clothes) by not overworking them.

Once more our artist was in the pure air, and, walking up the main street, came to a house with a beautifully carved stone window, half Byzantine, half Gothic, while a house on the opposite side of the street boasted of two other windows finely carved. While looking at them, Caper was hailed by name, and a stout, fresh-colored English artist, named Wardor, whom he had known in Rome, came over and welcomed him to Genazzano. Wardor, it turned out, was spending the summer there, as he had done the year before; consequently, there was not a nook or corner in the old town he did not know; and if he had not been so lazy, he could have filled his sketch book with a hundred picturesque studies. But no; with the keenest appreciation of every bit of color, every graceful pose of a human figure, every beautiful face, every fine effect of light or shadow—he made no sign. *His* legitimate function was friendly guide to the stranger, and in this office he carried Caper all over the old castle, out to the long shady walk on the esplanade behind it, pointed out beautiful views over the valley; finally showing Caper his studio, which, as it was a large room, and his *padrona* could impose on his good nature, was fairly glittering with copper pans, hung on the walls when not in use in the kitchen. On an easel was a painting, to be called The King of the Campagna; all that was apparent was the head and horns of the king. Wardor had thus actually spent three months painting on a space not so large as your fist, while the canvas was at least three feet by two feet and a half. But the king, a buffalo, would be a regal figure, for the head was life itself.

Caper proposed finishing a bottle of wine with Wardor, in honor of the day; so the latter piloted him up street and then down a flight of steps to a quiet wineshop, where, sitting on a shady terrace, they could calmly enjoy the lovely landscape spread below them, and look over the town, over the valley, to far-away Segni, high up in the Volscians. The landlord's wife, a buxom, comely woman, in full holiday costume, brought them a flask of cool wine and glasses, presenting them at the same time with a couple of very large sweet apples, the largest of which was thirteen inches in circumference by actual measurement. So you see they have apples as well as oranges in Italy; only, apples are practical, so they are generally omitted in the poetical descriptions of the blue-skyed land.

Caper and Wardor dined together in a very crowded inn, where the maccaroni must have been cooked by the ton, to judge of the sized dish the two artists were presented with—and which they finished! Chickens, lamb chops, salad, and two flasks of wine at last satisfied them. When they left the table, Wardor proposed their calling on a Roman family, who were spending the summer in the town. They found the house they occupied crowded with guests, who, having finished dinner, were busily employed dancing to the music of two guitars and a flute; that is, the younger part of them, while the elders applauded vociferously, entering into the amusement with a reckless spirit of fun and good nature, which people who have to keep shady nine tenths of the year for fear of their rulers, are very apt to indulge in the remaining tenth.

Elisa, the daughter of the Roman family, received Caper with hearty welcome, chiding him for having been all summer at Segni, and yet not coming near them, and entreating him to come to Genazzano and make them a long visit. She introduced him at once to her affianced husband, a handsome young doctor of the town, a man of sterling ability and sound common sense, who very soon made Caper at home, insisted on his dancing the *Tarantella* and *Saltarella Napolitana* with a lively, lithe young lady, who cut our artist's heart to fiddlestrings before they had danced five minutes together a polka—for, let the truth be told, Caper never could dance the Tarantella.

Wardor, in the mean time, had been led off in triumph to a side table, and was making a very hearty second dinner; he not having force of mind enough to do like Caper, and refuse a good offer! Caper had to drink a few tumblers (not wine glasses) of wine, and found it beneficial in dancing. It may be as well to repeat here, in order to calm all apprehensions of our artist being a hard drinker, that all these wines around Rome, with few exceptions, are little stronger than mild sweet cider, and that satiety will generally arrive before inebriety. Ask any sober and rigorously correct traveller, who has ever been there, if this is not so. If he speaks from experience, he will say:

"Certainly!" "Of course!" "To be sure!" And again, "Why not?"

It is not asserted here that the Romans of the city or surrounding country never get tipsy; but that it is only occasionally they have change enough to do so; consequently, a beautiful state of sobriety is observed by those travellers who—never observe anything.

The moon was shining over the old gate towers of Genazzano, when Caper mounted his horse, and, in company with two Segnians, rode forth from the fifth *festa*, and over the hills through Cavi, and over the valley past Valmontone, and then up the steep road to his summer home; wondering if, in faraway America, they were dreaming of a man who was going through a course of weekly Fourth-of-Julys, and how long it would be before the world came to an end if such a state of things existed in any country where people had liberty to study geography, and were ruled by politicians instead of priests?

"May I ask your candid opinion of the great moral effect of so many holidays on an uneducated population?" inquired Caper, one day, of Rocjean, while speaking of the festivals of the Papal States.

"Certainly you may! My opinion is, that the head of the state, carrying out the gigantic policy of his predecessors, believes, 'That that government governs best that gives the greatest amount of fiddling to the greatest amount of its children.'"

"But," objected Caper, "I don't see where the fiddling comes in."

"In the churches!" sententiously remarked the Sieur de Rocjean.

"Oh," quoth Caper, "I was thinking of festivals."

Reader, do you think likewise when you are with the Romans.

CHAPTER XI.

CAPER returned to Rome one morning in November, and at once went to the Café Greco to meet his old friends. He found Rocjean there in conversation with a young American artist who had lately arrived in Rome, and was taking his first breakfast at the Greco. The letter of introduction brought by him to Rocjean mentioned his name as Raphael Steele; that he came to Rome to study Art; and that, as his means were limited, any information that Rocjean could give him regarding his making his money go as far as possible, would greatly oblige, &c., &c.

Nothing gave Rocjean more pleasure than the imparting to newly-arrived artists the information he possessed as to where and how to head off swindlers, and enable strangers to lead the pure, simple, and cheap lives of the Romans. He was that morning in full tide of initiating Raphael Steele into all the mystery of saving pence, in order to spend pounds.

"In the first place," said Rocjean, "your breakfast this morning will cost you at least twenty-five *baiocchi* (same as our American cents, as I suppose you know), while I shall have precisely the same, and it will not cost me ten cents. You ordered coffee, and, accordingly, I see that you have the 'Strangers' Coffee Pot,' silver plated; milk in a separate jug, and sugar in a bowl. Now, when the waiter brings me my coffee, he will bring it already mixed in a tumbler. I shall pay two cents and a half; you will pay twelve cents."

"Yes," said Steele; "but how will the waiter know whether you want little milk or much; sugar or no sugar, &c.?"

"If you like your coffee well milked, you will order *caffe latta*; if less milk, *ombra di latta* (a shade of milk); if still less, *schizzo di latta* (a mere sketch of milk); if without milk, *caffe nero*; without milk, and extra strong, *caffe nero forte*. If your taste leads you to coffee with cream and butter in it, you order a *mezza crema*. As for bread, these rolls, crisp and long, are called *simoline*; those over on that table, sweetened, and light like buns, with seeds of pine cones or raisins in them, are called *maritozze*; white bread in small loaves, *pane di birra*; toast, *pane brusciato*. As for eggs, we have them slightly boiled, *uove da bere*, or *à la coqua* (bastard French for *à la coque*), or *al integama*, dropped in a crockery or tin pan in hot butter; then there are omelettes called *fritatte*, and so on. The advantage of having eggs *al integama*" (I have never seen this word printed, so I guess at it), "is, that you need not order butter for breakfast, but you dip your bread in the dish, Roman fashion, and—save your coppers—to buy wine. During Lent, really good Catholics do not drink milk with their coffee—it would be criminal. They can, however, substitute brandy for milk—and a number do.

"As for dinner, we will visit in succession sundry restaurants: the Lepre, the Falcone, the Tre Ladroni (Three Thieves!), the Gabioni, and Quattro Nazioni. I would advise you to flee from the other more expensive eating houses, or they will fleece you; from the other cheaper ones, lest they flea—but this is no joking matter. Bear it in mind, that bread and maccaroni are not dear, and that a sixpence worth of these makes a big breach in the strongest appetite. Then, you can wind up the siege by sending in a wild boar or beef steak, with figs, pastry, and wine, never forgetting a salad; the sum total for which will be twenty or thirty cents. Never eat more; it is unwholesome, and leaves you more money for tobacco and wine.

"As for clothes, I am happy to say that, with care, fifty dollars a year will enable you to appear like a *milordo*. To prove to you that clothing is not dear, I may cite a dress coat made for me by Francesco Paoletti, Via di Torre Argentina, No. 59, at a cost of eight dollars, and which graced the Embassy ball the other night. My hands, the same night, were clothed with white kid (?) gloves, at an expense of fifteen cents a pair; you can buy them of those three severely correct ladies near the Caffe Nuovo. The bouquet I presented to the elderly lady I escorted to the same ball cost fifteen cents; while the *legno*, or carriage, was hired to take me to the ball, and return, for thirty-seven and a half cents more; the half cent (*mezzo baioccho*) was part of a premium, or *buona mano*, to the driver. I smoked a cigar coming home, price one and a half cents. These little economies, so shocking to you Americans, come very natural to me. If I cannot drink green seal Johannisberg, which I really like, I am very happy with a mug of beer, a glass of sweet wine, or sugar and water."

"Can you tell me," asked Steele, "where I can find a good room, with a good light, that will answer for bedroom and studio? I suppose I ought to find one for four or five dollars a week."

"My dear sir," said Rocjean, impressively, "you shall find two rooms for five dollars a month, instead of week. You shall be treated kindly, and shall see pretty faces every day, and take their portraits, and learn to speak Roman-Italian, and eat *broccoli*, raw chick-peas, roast chestnuts, and buffalo cheese; squashes stuffed with veal, raw ham, and pumpkin and pine-cone seeds; stewed cocks'-combs and giblets; *pollenta*, and maccaroni *à la Napolitano:* have your room sprinkled with holy water once a year, and drink Accetosa water of warm spring mornings; go with your landlady and her pretty daughters to Ponte Molle, and see them paddle in wine like ducks. In fact, you shall cut the Frank quarter, and live among 'them old Turks'—I should say, leave the English quarter, and dwell amid the Romans. But, even in this Eden, look out for the snake that lurks on the stairs, in the shape of an entry lamp at ninety cents a month. Put your foot on its head the instant you see it in your first bill; don't have it at any price; crush it out. If you don't pay for it, nobody else will, and it's a great deal pleasanter to have dark entries, when you want them, than light ones. Suppose the Countess Badobadi wishes to have her portrait taken, unbeknown to the grim count, can she come pattering up stairs in the light? If there is to be any light, you are the one to make it, with a piece of waxed cord and a Lucifer;—Lucifer makes light of a good many things round Rome. Be sure that there is some kind of a place for a stovepipe, something in the shape of a chimney, in your rooms; for, as to burning charcoal in an iron pot on legs, it not only gives your studio the air of being occupied on shares by a roast-chestnut woman, but it gives you the headache. As for the Roman fashion of saving in wood to spend in wool, and wearing in winter the thickest under and over clothes to be purchased, though sensible, it requires time to follow. If you have a wood fire, unless you have proved your landlady's honesty, you had better make a bargain with her to find you in firewood at so much per week. If you buy your own, of your own accord, you will find discord; it goes somewhere so fast. A scientific lady once proved to me that, as the wood was cut green, and there was consequently a great deal of steam in it when it was burned, therefore it was bound to go fast! I accounted for her logic from the fact that her husband swept out the College *De Propaganda Fide*—and had my next cord of wood piled under my bed.

"It need not cost you much for lights, for, by going every night to the Life class, or Costume class, or Capranica Theatre, or café, and spending about ten cents, you will have fire and lights as cheap, nearly, as you would have them in your own rooms; besides, the amusement—and instruction.

"As for models, four or five of you can club together, and have one for all; thereby paying a shilling for what singly would cost you half a dollar: and the club plan is much the most animated and spirited. Besides, the model will act as teacher of Italian, without the trouble of splitting your head about grammar; and, at no extra expense, you will thus learn the genuine Roman tongue, free from all the conventionalities that make it high-toned and respectable. By such little kindnesses as permitting your male models to pick up all the cigar stumps on the studio floor, and not noticing the female model when she takes a private pull at your wine bottle, when your back is turned, you will win their admiration and respect; besides, they stand better when they have these rewards in perspective.

"In choosing your bootmaker, go into the by-ways; you can buy cheaper there, on that account. When I first came to Rome, I priced a pair of shoes in the Corso; their price was eight dollars. I priced a pair in the Condotti; seven dollars. In despair, I gave it up, and was going home through a small alley—the Via Carozze—when I saw a humble shoeshop with one pair of excellently-finished shoes in the window. I went in. There sat the semblance of a first tenor of an opera company, on his lap a shoe, in his hand a knife. In some doubt, I asked him:

"'Are you master of this household?' (*Siete padrone?*) I expected to see him rise, and sing:

"'Yes, I am, oh! yes, I am, oh! the maestró
Of this shop, oh!'

Instead of which, with flashing eyes, he sprang to his feet, brandished his knife with an air of animation impossible for Brignoli ever to hope to equal, and exclaimed:

"'*Signor! Io son' artiste.*' (Sir! I am an artist.)

"'So am I,' said I, proud of my profession.

"'I am an artist—in leather,' he continued; 'but' (here he knit his brows, and shook the shoe held in his left hand) 'but I am poor—yes, poor. Had I a shop in that broad street, the Corso, or Condotti, I should charge as they charge, and should soon be rich; but as it is——'

"'I'm glad you are not,' interrupted I; 'for I want to buy a pair of shoes cheap; and as we are both in the same business, that is, we are both artists—in poverty, I expect you will charge me trade price.'

"A smile stole over the face of the leather artist, as he

said: 'Signor, I will deal justly by you, for you are not afraid to joke.'

"He made me an excellent pair of shoes for four dollars—for he was a just man; and, some day when he is first tenor, he will be adorable, for he was graceful, and had the voice of a nightingale, *not* in the body of a—pump."

"About visiting galleries of paintings," asked Steele; "how much ought I to give the doorkeepers?"

"Give them ten cents the first time you visit them," said Caper.

"After that, give them a nod," added Rocjean; "and bear it in mind, that Rome is the home of Art; consequently, as an artist, you must make yourself at home here. The truth is, these janitors would make fortunes, if it were not for the commissionaires, who make them disgorge half that they receive from the strangers they bring into their clutches. I remember one May morning, when the dull season had begun, entering a palace, and finding a commissionaire there in earnest talk with the janitor. The janitor afterward told me that this man had just given him three dollars as a present, in order to keep friends with him, and induce him to give the commissionaire one half the proceeds of the next winter's harvest the rich strangers he would bring to the palace should leave with the said janitor. It seems to me, if Titian, Vandyke, Raphael and Company could only have foreseen that their works were to minister to these extortionists, they never would have worked.

"There is one matter you should always bear in mind here, and that is, you must always bargain for what you buy. It is an understood thing among all Romans, that they rarely, if ever, pay the first price asked. Time is not valuable with them, and they accordingly devote a great deal of it to a purchase, no matter how small. Besides, I believe they like the excitement of cheapening an article; it makes buying a lottery, and the Romans have a passion for this pastime. The English have endeavored to introduce the one-price system—the Fixed Price arrangement—and, accordingly, some of the shops where they deal have the sign exposed: *Prézzo Fisso*——"

"Which I pronounce Precious Fizz, oh!" interrupted Caper.

"You are nearly right; but the sign draws the English and French; as for you Americans, you prefer paying without cheapening, taking your revenge in denouncing the Roman shopkeepers as swindlers. They let you talk, and—pocket your money.

"I only remember one instance, since I have been in Rome, where a man would not abate one cent from the first price asked; and, you may believe it or not, I paid him it. It was thus: I had a room once in the Via Babuino, its windows facing the street. For several nights, at a very late hour, I was woke up by a man howling under my window. He would sit down there, on the edge of a large stone basin full of water falling from a fountain, probably to cool himself off after extra drinking, and there he would do what he probably thought was singing; but more ear-stunning howling you cannot fancy. The third night of this *serenáta* I jumped out of bed, and, throwing open the window, asked him if he had lost any friends lately. He said he hadn't. 'Well, then, where does *she* live?'

"'Ah, Signor, I'm past that; I'm married, and have got

the rheumatism,' he answered. 'I'll tell you what I'm doing it for: I'm doing it for a living. I'm chorus singer at the Apollo Theatre, and I'm practising for the new opera of Aroldi, by Maestro Verdi.'

"This accounted for the howling.

"'*Benissimo!* now won't you go somewhere else, and practise, for I can't sleep a wink while you—sing,' I said to him.

"'Signor, I would do so with pleasure, but I have no place else to go. They have driven me away from home, from the Piazza Spagna, from a dozen other places. It wasn't so when I practised Donizetti, or Bellini, or Rossini's music; but this Verdi makes me utter such a bull-bellowing' (*mugghiaménto di toro*), 'that the neighbors won't suffer it.'

"'I pity you, poor man,' I remarked.

"'So you ought to,' he answered. 'It's worse than crying "Broc-co-li!"—and that nearly tore my throat to rags, when I used to sell it. But if they go on giving Verdi's operas, I'm going back to "*Broc-co-o-o-li!*"—here he gave an actual cry, as if he had hold of a real handbarrow full, and was anxious to dispose of it at once.

"'Come,' said I, 'I want to go to bed; and, what is more, to sleep. What do you charge to go away?'

"'*Eccellenza!*'

"'What is it?'

"'Do you want to see a poor man driven to hard work?'

"'Very much, indeed, if you are that poor man, and, by hard work daytimes, would sleep at night, instead of howling. But why do you ask?'

"'For a cause. You see, if I don't practise, I can't sing

at the Apollo; and if I don't sing, I can't gain two *pauls* every night, and something extra when I go errands for the first bass; so, if I go away from here without practising, I may lose two *pauls;* but I am willing to lose them—if your excellency will do me the pleasure to find them again for me.'

"I found them, and threw them down to him wapped up in a piece of white paper, for it was a very dark night, and he would not otherwise have seen them.

"When he had picked them up, he remarked: 'You see, I am a man of my word; I *am* going: but—I have the pleasure of being sure, that when I have finished sawing away on Verdi, and am again " pirooting " and flourishing on Donizetti, you will pay me for coming, instead of going. *Addio dunque a—Donizetti!*'"

"You had a lucky escape," spoke Steele; "and now, if you are ready, I would like to see some of the rooms to rent, you offered to show me."

"I'm ready," answered Rocjean; "but, Caper, what do you think of the Trastevere for Steele? Do you think he would like it over there?"

"I think it would be a little too Roman for a stranger to begin with. Suppose you try the houses round the Capitoline Hill, to commence; that is far enough away from the foreigners' quarters to insure low prices, and it's a good airy position to study the Roman *Chi va al cinque piáno va a buon mercato e sano;* or, To the fifth story go; you'll 'live high' and 'low!'"

So Steele, that day, took his first lesson on the Cheap Side of Roman life.

Rocjean was painting away very busily, one day, when he heard a knock at his studio door.

"*Entrate!*" shouted he, and in came a round-paunched, jolly little man, a Roman artist, named Pancia, an old acquaintance of Rocjean's, and one he was always glad of seeing, for he was a newspaper on legs—an object common in all countries, but only valuable in Rome, where there are no newspapers, to speak of. In addition to all the news of the day, he told good stories, made good jokes, and was without malice.

"*Ah caro mio*," said he, as soon as he opened the door; "I mounted those stairs of yours without stopping but once."

"And why once?"

"This confounded asthma, and such a view from your entry window!—a lovely maiden, lovelier than Bella Sparaghélla!"

"Who *is* Sparaghélla? *I* know all the models in Rome," half soliloquized Rocjean, "but don't remember her."

"She wasn't a model," laughed Pancia, "for anybody to copy, except in cunning, and by that she outwitted the *sbirri* (constables), not long since, oh! so bravely."

"Come, take a cigar, and tell me the story, while I finish up this foreground of rocks and trees."

"Well, Sparaghélla is for Rome what a Traviata is for Paris—enough said. Now, it happens that there is a famous preacher named Fra Volpe. You don't attend our Church, so you probably have never seen him."

"But I've often heard of him."

"And you shall hear of him again; he is the hero of my story. One Sunday in Carnival, Sparaghélla, quietly dressed, went to hear him preach. At the first sight of him, her heart beat quickly; for he is a handsome man, of commanding presence, with an eye like an eagle, and a voice that would have made his fortune as first baritone in an opera company. He has talent, and mental vigor to make it tell, and at one glance you see that he is *molto simpatico*. So Sparaghélla thought; and when, in impressive silence, he arose, and, with full, measured voice, commenced:

'*La Chiesa é* L'OPERA *di Dio*'—

Sparaghélla wished she had brought her lorgnette, that she might bring that noble face still closer to hers.

"Fra Volpe is human; and, as time and again he saw Bella Sparaghélla attending his preaching, and gazing at him with admiration in her eyes, he came at last to look for her impatiently, and grow uneasy when she was absent. At last it was rumored that Fra Volpe was the lover of la Bella Sparaghélla.

"You have lived long enough in Rome to know that not entire love and peace exist among the brethren of our Church; and Fra Volpe had enemies high in power. They hired *sbirri* to follow his every step. Night and day there were two shadows wherever he went. At last, one stormy night, Volpe was run to ground—the fox was earthed; and at once half a dozen beagles in the shape of *sbirri* were on his tracks.

"'Lovely Sparaghélla,' said Fra Volpe, imprinting, or rather engraving a kiss on her dear little mouth, "how long will this dream continue? Shall we not be too rudely awakened? Will it be the fate of Fra Volpe to fall from the high position he now holds, and be numbered among the ignoble shepherds?'

"'What do you say? You don't think of going round in sandals, and a long blue cloak, and stick, with big dogs, following sheep, I hope? Never! I'd a great deal rather you would be a shoemaker; and then, oh! then you could make me *such* gaiter boots.' Here the fair girl stuck out the prettiest, cunningest little black slipper, with a foot in it, that treads the Corso.

"'But hark!' said she, suddenly; 'what noise is that?'

"''Tis the wind, oh! love,' answered Fra Volpe, starting to his feet.

"'No, not the window, but the front door. Excuse me, love, while I shade the light, and then look out in the street.'

"'Oh! Volpe, Volpe!' she suddenly exclaimed, in tremulous whispers, 'we are undone; the *sb-b-birri* are at the door!'

"'*Di*——!' exclaimed Fra Volpe. Whether he intended to end this exclamation with an *o*, or an *avolo*, will never be known. For what was his astonishment, at seeing la Bella Sparaghélla tear a red rose from her hair, pull out the stiletto that held its silken coil confined, and let the full length of her magnificent black tresses fall dishevelled around her shoulders, where they hung, nearly touching the ground; then, throwing herself in agony at his feet, Fra Volpe saw the great tears streaming from her lovely eyes, as she hastily whispered:

"'I am a penitent. You have come here to teach me repentance.—The door is unlocked. *Tace!*'

"They heard the front door opened—the rush of men up the stairs.

"'Daughter,' rolled out the resonant voice of Fra Volpe, 'thou hast sinned, indeed, but——' (Here the door flew open, and in came, pell mell, the *sbirri*.) 'Though thy sins were as scarlet, shall they be white as wool.' (The *sbirri* looked like sheep, as they saw the tableau before them, and were awestruck with the words so grandly rolled out.) 'For thee, our Mother Church still opens her arms; for thee, and not only thee, but for those who have fallen lower and lower in the sink of sin; for murderers' (one *sbirri* groaned), 'for thieves and robbers' (here all the *sbirri* groaned in concert), 'for those who bear false witness against their neighbors, who would cast from his high seat the pure, the noble, and the incorruptible man, and in vain endeavor to lower him to their own bestial level; the pure man, of whom one of them might say, *Ou ouk eimi ikanos, kupsas lusai ton imanta toon upodematoon autou!*' (The Greek did their business. Down on their knees fell the *sbirri*, and fairly trembled, when Fra Volpe, with all the power of his voice, his fine figure drawn to its utmost height, raised his hand, with outstretched finger, as if calling down the thunderbolts of Jove, and spoke :) 'But, full of mercy as our Church can be, she, too, can punish, and call down on these, the wicked ones of earth, a curse that shall wither every nerve and sinew, dry up the blood, blast brain and bone, and leave them drivelling madmen to their last dread day of life; and, even then, torment them after death, for ages and for ages yet to come. Why do I hesitate this instant to call down this awful and tremendous punishment?'

"The *sbirri* gave one fearful shriek in chorus, and sprang for the door, as if an instant only was between them and an awful fate. An instant more, and up the Corso darted the whole pack, never drawing breath until they reached Cardinal ———'s door. And when they entered the palace with their report, it was with pale faces and trembling limbs they told the most awful lies to the **secretary** of his *Eminenza Reverendissima*. They assured him that Fra Volpe was the most innocent man in the States of the Church; that he had never been near the Sparaghélla; that he had never seen her; never even heard of her; that they had made a grievous error, and mistaken a young *milordo Americano* for Fra Volpe, and that they had run the wrong fox to earth—upon their words of honor!

TOLKOUTCHJI was born in St. Petersburg, in a large house on the Dvortsovaïa Nabéréjenaïa. Before he was five years old, his *sloujanka* caught him scratching a caricature of an *ischvostchik* on the copper *samovar*. [N. B. If the above sentence is not understood by many readers, it's their fault! It is not more affected than using French phrases, or Italian; and as the writer pleads guilty to the last crime all through these sketches, Russian can't stop him. As he has a hard subject to write about, second thoughts lead him to make the road easy, so he will begin again.]

TOLKOUTCHJI was a Russian artist. When quite young, he displayed a talent for design, by scratching the copper teapot, and furniture, with an old nail; and the scratches were declared by the nursery maid to be capital portraits of hack drivers and old houses of her acquaintance. At a more advanced age, the Russian Government gave him an annual allowance of roubles, and sent him to Rome to perfect himself as a painter, by the study of the old masters—and Art generally.

He invited Rocjean, one night, to call around to his rooms, in the Via Sistina. Rocjean went there, unfortunately, precisely five minutes too late to find him in his rooms, but exactly in time to find him lying on his back—in the entry of the house, where he had fallen in a duel with the Count de Cognac, a bitter enemy of his. Rocjean took him carefully by the hind legs, and drew him into his studio; then, lighting the three-wicked *lucerna*, or Roman brass lamp, he looked around for the weapons used in the late duel. He found them on top of a table covered with red satin damask, with a gold fringe, and at once made proof of their temper. They were fourth proof, and he ran himself through with about half a tumblerful; when, looking around, he saw Tolkoutchji glaring at him with an expression of "brandy, or your life!" so he poured him out a glassful, not before he had growled, "*Dateme*—ik! *una* —ki! *bichierr'*—off! *di quella*—fsky!" or, to be rational, "Give me*ik* a*ki* glass*off* that*sky*" (not whiskey).

It is unnecessary to continue the dialogue in drunken Italian, with Russian terminations; suffice it, that, before long, Rocjean, having helped Gospodin Tolkoutchji to his feet, had the pleasure of seeing that the brandy he had swallowed seemed instantly to run down into his legs, leaving his Russian head calm, cool, and collected. Giving himself a shake, as if to insure a complete precipitation of all the brandy to the extremities, he addressed Rocjean in French, the grammar and pronunciation of which were remarkably correct; and, thanking him for calling, begged that he would be seated; offered him a pipe of Turki-krepi tobacco, or, if he preferred, stronger Mahorka, regretting that he could not offer him Latakiah, as Abbas Pacha had neglected sending him his usual annual present of this delightful tobacco.

Conversation turning upon Art, Tolkoutchji gave his visitor a very interesting account of the art of boar hunting; describing, with animation and force, a late hunt he had shared with six of his countrymen in the Pontine Marshes. They had been rewarded by killing five full-grown ones, and had enjoyed themselves grandly. The Russian had painted a boar hunt from sketches made during the time he was in the marshes, and, at Rocjean's request, showed it to him. Even by lamp-light its effect was startling; the boar, coming down a narrow path, head foremost, seemed springing from the canvas, the foreshortening of the animal being admirably handled. Behind him, on fire with the ardor of the chase, came the Russians, on horseback. There was vitality in every touch of the brush—the vitality of reality. You knew that it could paint lifelike little children, could give them wings, and curly hair, and send them flying through the clouds; but, they would not be angels.

The Russian, after Rocjean had asked it as a favor, showed him half a dozen other paintings. They were either figure, or animal and figure pieces; and, whether taken from sacred or profane history, or real life, were all filled with the same actuality. There was the subject, Danae and the Golden Shower. Danae was none other than Giacinta the model, in a state of wardrobe that would soon render the dressmakers' trade of no earthly use, and only leave the shoemaker employed—while the coins were unmistakably roubles; and the head of Jupiter in the clouds, bore a very close resemblance to that of Gospodin Tolkoutchji while engaged in one of his numerous fierce duels with the Count de Cognac, before mentioned.

The Maiden and the Monkey was another work evidently not intended for the Popolo exhibition; while a Samson and Delilah was finished with a truth to nature and boldness that astonished even Rocjean. In this painting, the services of the tailor, as well as dressmaker, were overlooked, and only the sandalmaker found employment. A drunken Moudjik falling from a droschky, actually staggered you with its truth to life; it seemed to have been painted in brandy, with a decanter for a brush.

Our Russian informed Rocjean that his paintings were all finished with a view to their effect by lamplight, as well as by daylight; for, destined, as they were, to be hung up in private palaces or houses, their chance of being seen only when balls, late dinner parties, or evening reunions were given, was of sufficient consequence to the artist to be borne in mind in their execution. Speaking of the fine effect given many scenes by the aid of lamp or torchlight, Rocjean bitterly regretted having missed seeing an illumination of the forum and Colosseum the previous winter, saying, however, he hoped to be more successful the present season.

"I will tell you one thing," said Tolkoutchji, impressively; "the first thousand or two roubles I win at lansquenet, shall light them up. Bear this promise in mind; and, when you receive my card, with 'Colosseum to-night' on it, go out, and take as many Americans with you as you can find. But let us drink to Good Luck; it's my guardian angel."

While they were drinking, there was a knock at the studio door, and in came a portly, good-looking man, who showed that he had either intelligence, or so very much wealth that he could afford to appear plain in his dress, natural in his manners, and independent in his habits.

Tolkoutchji greeted him warmly, and at once introduced to Rocjean the great Russian banker, Sevnpersentsky, who had that day arrived in Rome from Madrid, on his way to St. Petersburg.

"I inquired of Torlonia, to-day, at dinner," said the banker to his countryman, "if you were still in Rome; and he told me you were, and were in your old quarters; so I came here this evening. I see that you have been busy the last year. Let me look at that wild boar hunt." The artist held the light to the painting.

"Lifelike—admirably painted. You have improved in coloring since last year. Now show me every finished picture in your studio." Thus speaking, the banker lit a cigar, seated himself in an armchair, and carefully examined each work as it was placed in turn on the easel. When he had looked at the last one, he asked Tolkoutchji for a pen and ink.

"For what amount shall I fill up a draft on Torlonia for all of them?" inquired the banker, waving his hand toward the pictures.

"Five thousand dollars," said the artist.

The banker's pen flew over the paper. There was Sevnpersentsky, with a flourish, at the bottom of it, and the affair was finished.

Our Russian banker then accepted an invitation to put a glass of brandy under his waistcoat; told Tolkoutchji and Rocjean that his carriage was waiting at the door to take them to his box at the opera, and he would give them ten minutes to get ready to go with him. At the expiration of the time, off they rolled to the Apollo, to hear that dear mountain of flesh, Chiaramonte, sing as sweetly as she could in Aroldi.

After the opera, broken in two, Roman fashion, by a ballet, in which the principal female dancer wore about enough drapery to make a good-sized handkerchief, Sevnpersentsky gave the two artists a supper, at which the Moet Champagne flowed as if running in a vinumduct (can't say aqueduct), direct from those cellars of Moet's, in Epernay, where you remember you noticed a black-marble slab, on which, engraved in letters of gold, is the name "Napoleon," commemorating a visit made there by that great man, The Little Corporal.

Two days after this, Rocjean received Tolkoutchji's card, with "Colosseum to-night" written on it, and at once apprized all his American friends of the expected illumination. They went that night, and found the forum and the Colosseum lit with torches; none of those red and bluelight exhibitions, giving a sixpenny theatrical look to the scene, but the clear light of burning wood or oil. There were thousands of lights, and Rocjean came to the conclusion that lansquenet must have nearly ruined some one to enable Tolkoutchji to have won enough to pay for the illumination. It is impossible to describe the wildness and startling effect of the ruins in the forum, marked in blazing light on a dead black background, or the curious optical delusions caused by the eye being unaccustomed to these effects of light and darkness. The interior of the Colosseum was startlingly grand and impressive. Crowds of strangers, who had heard of the intended illumination, were continually entering the arena, moving here and there, gazing in rapture, and, for the most part, in silence, on the strangely brilliant scene, revealed to them in a manner so unusual, and with effects so wild, so impressive, and so wonderful.

Report said that a noble Roman prince had caused the illumination to be made in honor of the beautiful Contessa Falamore, *con licenza*. Others whispered 'that Cardinal Fadanaro had done it for political purposes, *con permissione*. Again, it was rumored that General Goyon had paid for it, in order to keep in with the Romans, and not be put outside the walls, *con animo*. That it was the result of a *scomméssa* (bet) between one *milordo Inglese* and another *milordo* ditto. (Rocjean overheard a young Roman, who looked like a head waiter, but who was a shopkeeper, state this to his friend, who was in the same plight.) A hundred other rumors as to its giver were circulated, and to this day no one in Rome, save Rocjean and Tolkoutchji, knows the truth of the matter—that it was really given, *con amore*, to please little Petipa of the Opera Comique, who found herself in Rome that winter, under the protection of a Russian artist incognito; and who declared she never would go back to Paris until the Colosseum was illuminated; and she saw it. After which performance, Tolkoutchji saw her off to Civita Vecchia, on her way to—Paris, he hoped. She had commenced to "make conversation;" the police office refused to give her a new *Carta di Soggiorno;* he was heartily tired of her, and anxious to devote himself entirely to Art, and to perfecting himself not only in oil, but also in water (brandy and water?) colors.

Chapin, the sculptor, once asked Rocjean:

"Don't *you* think, now, that that Rooshan Tallcodgi is a noble in disguise?"

"None of my business," answered Rocjean, "as to his nobility; but I will say, that I've seen him drunk as a lord, dressed like a count, generous as a prince, and happy as a king. So much for Tolkoutchji!"

CHAPTER XII.

The front windows of the inn of Gaetano, at Segni, commanded a fine view of the mountains which rose before them, shutting in the distant Mediterranean Sea. The street was clear of houses immediately in front of the inn, and was bounded by a wall about fifteen feet in height, above an esplanade, also bounded by another wall overlooking the main road leading up to the town gate. On the latter wall, at sunset, the men, who had been busy through the day in the fields, or at mechanical work in the town, congregated. Here, straddled out, with legs and arms in every direction, they watched those who were returning form the country—especially the women, with whom they talked and chatted as they passed along.

Caper and Rocjean were seated, one evening toward sundown, at one of the front windows of the inn, carefully observing the means used by a blacksmith, in the street below, to shoe a refractory mule. With assistance, the animal was thrown on his back, and, his legs being tied, he was kept quiet as a lamb until the shoes were fastened. Watching the process was an elderly *contadino*, who, even after all the excitement of the shoeing was over, and the mule, blacksmith, and assembled crowd departed, remained in earnest conversation with another old man.

"Yes," said the elderly *contadino*, "Bruno shall marry Rosa, for he is young and strong, and can do as hard work as any man in Segni. And the sooner they are married, the better for them."

Our two artists overheard every word of this conversation. Rocjean at once commenced philosophizing:

"Don't you notice, in what that old man has just said, the keynote of all society?"

"Not a note," replied Caper, watching the landscape with half-shut eyes.

"More is the pity. Now, see here: if one of those Roman shopkeepers in the Condotti were asked to whom he would like to marry his daughter, what would he say?"

"Is it a conundrum? For, if it is, you know I am a poor hand at those bellows. You look cross—so it's serious. I think the shopkeeper would like his daughter to marry a shrewd, active young shopkeeper, with coral shirt studs, who bade fair to make a fortune."

"Exactly," remarked Rocjean. "Now, if the Orsini had a daughter to marry, to whom would he like to marry her?"

"Let me see; the Orsini is reported to have about twenty thousand dollars a year. Well, he would prefer a Corsini, for that prince has about one hundred thousand dollars net revenue."

"From all of which I infer," continued Rocjean, "that humanity, even in marrying its daughters, wants to go FORWARD, by muscle, brains, or wealth and titles. After a while, muscle gets brains, brains gain wealth and titles; and as long as wealth and titles hold on to the brains, so long they keep at the top of the social pyramid."

"Otherwise?"

"They slide down the opposite side to which they came up."

"Good! but I don't see where Progress comes in, if all humanity is to go on *ad infinitum* climbing up, only to slide down again."

"There it is!" replied Rocjean, with warmth. "Those who slide down, carry with them all the pure airs and fine views they had when they were on the apex, and bring such glowing accounts to poor muscle at the base, that it puts renewed energy into it; and, by a wise provision of Providence, the top of the pyramid is higher every generation. Some day it will reach heaven!"

"H'm!" spoke Caper; "don't you think you've mistaken your calling? Don't you think, instead of painter, you ought to have been preacher?"

"I'll answer that, suddenly: the best of preachers are painters; and the best of painters were preachers. The best preachers of the present day, using the word in its broad sense —inculcators of anything with earnestness—are those who use such strong, plain language, that every man may understand them. They paint, on the mind of the most uninstructed hearer, plain pictures in primitive colors. Painters were preachers when they were inculcators of anything with earnestness; when, instead of confining themselves to works that would sell, they gave freedom to the pencil, and aided mankind to ennoble, and not debase, the poorest of their fellow men."

Rocjean, during his discourse, had retired from the window, and was energetically sawing the air with his right arm, to help along his elocution; while Caper was just as industriously noting the men and women returning from the fields and vineyards.

Certainly, Segni had more than her portion of muscular catholicity, and it was a constant source of pleasure for our artists to notice the completion of figure attained by nine-tenths of the female inhabitants. The men run to bone and muscle, and were not as erect in their carriage as the women, who owed their straight forms and stately figures, to a degree, to their continually carrying so much weight on their heads. The only fat persons in the town were those who led sedentary lives, and there were not, at the most, half a dozen of these bulky weights.

Among them was a widow rejoicing in the name of Mariuccia, the mother of several mature sons and daughters, who, either out of respect to their deceased father's will, or wishes, were anxious that their mother should continue her widowhood for an indefinite period. An obstacle to this arose in the shape of about five feet two inches of humanity, called Nuto, which is the abbreviation for Benvenuto, and which name was given him because he was born on that saint's day—the twenty-second of March. This "obstacle" was by no means a master of the triangular hoe with which most of the field cultivation is performed; neither did he swing an axe with commendable vigor; and any one ignorant of arithmetic might count all the live stock—in the shape of mules or hogs—he owned. The prospect was, that widow Mariuccia, in taking this man for her husband, might say, I take him to help me to eat, but not to help me to meat—a wide difference in a mountain country, and one her children disliked. She was going a non-progressive road.

Caper and Rocjean, while at the window, noticing heavy banks of black clouds rising over the mountains, foretelling a thundergust, omitted their usual sunset walk. When supper was served, and while they were at table, several flashes of lightning, with distant roaring, heralded the approaching storm, and the two artists were expecting to hear, every moment, a grand crash announcing its being overhead, when—they heard it under foot.

"New kind of thunder, that—eh, Rocjean?"

"Yes—flashy. Too much tin pan and fishhorn about it to be natural. I should like to know what it's all about. *Filomena!*"

At this call, there came running into the dining room a tall, strongly built young woman, who acted as waiter at table during meals, and maid-of-all-work at other times. She had large blue eyes, very light hair, and, I'll bet a *scudo*, could curry a horse, tend corn, cut wheat, or chop wood, with the best man of her weight for ten miles around. A little more attention to her toilet would have materially enhanced her value as a housemaid; for, pretty as a light blue bodice, laced with silken cord may be, when it *is* laced, it is otherwise when loose, and the blue ribbons over the shoulders are not half tied. Then, too, her coral necklace hung on askew, and the gathered folds of white linen over bosom and shoulder were—neglected. The silver dagger in the hair, sticking up in the air like a conductor to a lightning rod, and a generally draggled air to the entire person, suggested to Caper the idea of his great oil painting, The Shiftless Beauty, which afterward obtained admittance to the annual Exposition of Beaux Arts, in the large glass hothouse in the Champs Elysées, and was registered in the catalogue of the exhibition:

CAPER (JACQUES), *à New York (Amerique); et à Paris, Hotel des Princes*, 97 *Rue de Richelieu, Chambre N.* 136.
3617—Poney irlandais trottant (effet de pluie).

The directors were of it very much *fâché* (Irish, fashed) that Monsieur Capre should be of the printer a victim; that an error so grave—calling a Dame Italian, a Poney Irish—actually of them made to stand up (*dresser*) the hairs on the head. But what will you? At present the catalogues are all printed—the error cannot be corrected; but—to him they made their compliments of the tableau! They were of it, to speak frankly, very content, charmed, ravished, enchanted; they for it—the tableau—felt the most great satisfaction, infinite joy, great pleasure; they of it, him felicitated with all their heart. CHOUETTE.

"Coming, in a minute!"—Let us return to Filomena. When she entered the dining room, Rocjean asked her what was all the noise about?

"'*M beh!*" (Mountain Italian for *Ah, bene!* Ah, well!) "*s'nor*', it's a *Scam-pa-nacci-a-ta!*" Here, either owing to the construction of the word, or an obstruction in her head, Filomena sneezed; whereupon Caper exclaimed at once:

"*Salùte!*" (Health!) In Northern Italy you say, *Felicità!* (Happiness!) when any one sneezes; and the sneezer responds, both north and south, as the waiter girl did:

"Thanks!"

"And now, Filomena, tell me, what is a Scamper-gnash-a-tater?"

"Who kn——"

"Don't say, Who knows? but think a moment before you speak," interrupted Caper, "and tell us what is the cause of this infernal noise."

"*'M beh! s'nori*, it's the widow Mariuccia."

"What! is that her voice?"

"*Ma ché*, I mean, the noise is made because she has thrown herself away on Nuto."

"Why, she weighs two hundred and fifty pounds. I expect she has crushed him to pieces. Poor fellow! Awful groans, ain't they, Rocjean?"

"*Oh! s'nor'*, why can't you understand me?" cried Filomena, wildly. "I mean to say she's married him, and all the rowdies in town are serenading them. Now, don't you understand?"

"Certainly—perfectly. It's a band of Callithumpians making a charivari," quoth Caper.

Filomena heard these fearful words, crossed herself, and fled to the kitchen, there to reiterate her belief to the landlady, that the entire race of *forestieri* were crazy.

The noise growing louder and louder, our two artists determined, as the thunder storm had passed away without visiting Segni, to sally out and see the performance. Entering the main alley, popularly called street, they found themselves in the midst of a large number of men and boys armed with ox horns, pieces of sheet iron, old fiddles—in fact, anything that would make a noise—the crowd working the instruments with hearty good will. In a few minutes they all straggled off in a body up the main alley, past the church and postoffice, until they came near the bishop's palace, when they halted, and began the most infernal serenade to be heard. It was not long before a window in the bishop's house, alias palace, was opened, and, as far as could be seen from a light inside, a tall priest stepped out, and begged the crowd, in rather commanding terms, to clear out and go to bed, and not be disturbing His Reverendissimo with such *sventuratissimo schiamazzo* (wretched noise).

"It's not for his Reverendissimo, but for that wicked Mariuccia, who's going to starve her infants to feed Nuto," shouted one of the Callithumpians. The noise grew worse and worse; the Army of the Church then in the town (seven gensdarmes) began to yawn, and two on guard in the prison twirled their moustaches, and prepared to think how many *baiocchi* they would gain in case they were to sack the town.

Our two artists had lately discovered a very comely widow, named Berta, who kept a select *caffè*, where only the priests and soldiers had entrance; but their *baiocchi* and politeness gained them admittance, and the two strangers were always welcomed heartily. As it was very near the bishop's house, Caper and Rocjean went in there to take coffee and smoke a cigar, knowing that the serenade was of that kind that thick walls only added to its charmingness, by mellowing the discords.

"*Prosst!*" said the comely widow, as they entered.

"*Viva!*" answered the artists.—It may be well to explain here, that the salutation of *prosst*, so common around Rome, is an abbreviation of the three Latin words, *pro sit te*—May it be (well) for thee. The landlord uses it when you sit down to dinner, often accompanying it with the expression, A good appetite.

"An awful night—for music, *padrona mia*," said Caper to the widow Berta.

"Yes, indeed; it rains howls and yells, and blows big horns. Verily, it is hard for the poor Mariuccia; they will not let her sleep a wink to-night, *poverina!*" (poor little thing!)

"*Poveraccia!*" (poor big thing!) "you mean," said a man in the corner.

"Ha, Bruno, you are jealous of Nuto. Wouldn't you like to have such a bridal march played when you are married?" asked the widow.

"Perhaps, if I had"—(here the man held his two hands, palms turned out, by the sides of his head)—"like Nuto, I might."

They kept up the noise for an hour, the excitement growing greater every moment, and finally culminating in a shower of stones, and the precipitate retreat of the serenaders on hearing that the gensdarmes were coming with loaded guns.

They kept up the racket for three nights, defying the authorities to stop them. The authorities knew better. "Slaves will dance, so let them have Saturday night, and be hanged to them;" but as for learning geography, that they shall not do. The idea of making prisoners walk a treadmill that turns a hand organ, is peculiarly delicate and apposite, since, according to Petrarch, it is to Pope Vitalian, once an inhabitant of this town, that we are indebted for the invention of organs; and it was during his residence in Segni that the first one ever known was manufactured there.

Where this Scampanacciata would have ended—for bad blood was brewing—it is hard to tell, had not the authorities been miraculously protected by a saint, whose birthday came along just in time to distract the attention of the *popolaccio*, and call them away from secular affairs. The saint had, in his honor, a torchlight procession, and illumination of many of the houses with paper lanterns and little earthen lamps, as antique in shape as those used two thousand years ago. The procession was very picturesque. The night was dark, and the lights, winding up the steep streets, illuminating those houses not otherwise lighted, and reddening here the old prison, there the piazza and church, or colonaded Communal Palace; the chorus of voices singing, or shouting, *Evviva Maria!* when a halt was commanded; the young women dressed in white, with wreaths of flowers around their heads; Capuchin friars with brown robes, ruddy cheeks, and long, flowing beards; banners, crucifixes. Why, it completely extinguished the Scampanacciata; and the Gonfaloniere reasserted his clerically-civil sway over the three nights turbulent city of Segni.

With September came quail shooting, and Caper, who was then alone in Segni, Dexter and Rocjean having left, weeks before, for other parts, learning from his landlord, Gaetano, that he, too, was desirous of giving these birds a few shots, the two joined forces, and opened the campaign.

The quail of southern Europe is a migratory bird. Arriving from Africa in May, they are, after their long flight, in miserable condition; but in the autumn, prior to their return to winter quarters, they are fat, finding plenty of food in the stubble of the wheat fields.

One afternoon, mounting their horses, with guns slung over the left shoulder, Caper and Gaetano rode down the mountains to the plains, where they found wide fields of wheat-stubble to work over, and where they heard there were plenty of birds in fine condition. They had previously made appointment with two men, who were to meet them by an old ruined monastery, and have with them two or three good quail dogs. The ruin reached, they looked in vain for men or dogs, but not a hat or tail was to be seen. Putting up their horses in a corner of the old ruin, and loading their guns, they started off. With slow steps they walked around a small piece of woods belonging to Prince Borghese, hoping to find the men with whom they expected to hunt, the other side of it; but no, they were not in sight.

Caper, unable to start a single quail without a dog, saw, some distance off, a flock of wild pigeons, and, in hopes of bagging a few, crossed a small stream, and was cautiously creeping toward them, when, long before he was within decent rifle shot, they took wing. Retracing his steps, he mounted a bank with caves in its sides—black, pokerish holes in the *pozzolána*; and, as he reached the top of the bank, he saw Gaetano in conversation with a shepherd, in goatskin overalls, long staff, conical black hat, gold earrings, curls over his ears, and his hair cut short behind; sandals on his feet, a pink waistcoat, with blue sash around his waist; while his jacket hung on his shoulder blade, which answered for a nail. The two were moving slowly over a piece of stubble, while a lean, wiry, hungry-looking, straight-haired cur dog was running around in front of them, as if looking for a lost beef bone. As Caper came up, the shepherd was shouting to the dog: "*Tr-r-r-o! tr-r-ro!*

Toca! Qua! qua!" (Find! catch! here!) and, as our artist stood laughing at the scene, "Whirr-irr!" up sprang a quail, only to tumble down again; and, whirr! another, Gaetano stopping both with his double barrel. They got up and killed a half dozen quails within ten minutes, the dog working like a high-pressure engine with a full head of steam on; being rewarded, as each bird fell, with its trail; for, in this warm climate, you must draw your birds as you bag them, or else you will draw—out nothing but carrion when you have knocked off gunning. What with a late start and the time lost in hunting for the men who were to meet them, and didn't, it was growing late, and so our two gunners had to stop shooting, particularly as the shepherd had to be going hutward, his large flock of goats having preceded him, and had to take his watchdog with him. Caper offered to buy him, but the shepherd charged too high a figure, guaranteeing that he would *catch* snipe, woodcock, quails, hares, and rats! And it was this catching part of his education that made the half dozen quails shot over him such captivating amusement. Bang! went the gun, down fell the bird, at it pitched the cur, devouring it at two bites, unless you could choke him off; the shepherd yelling, Gaetano shouting, and anathematizing the dog, as they hurried up to grab the quail. How their black eyes gleamed, and how excited they were! It beat cock fighting. Imagine the manner that dog would be broken by a thorough sportsman, for mouthing birds in that manner!—Across the back? Yes, sir.

By good fortune, Francesco, the *vetturino*, learning from Caper that five dollars would be paid for a good dog, at once determined to make his fortune; and the next time he came from Rome there was a full-blood pointer passenger, worth at least fifty *scudi*, for Segni! He promised to take him again to the city after the gunning season was over, and return him to his owner; but it was Caper's private opinion that the owner had very little to do with that dog's country excursion. He was well broken, and Gaetano and Caper knocked quails and red-legged partridges over him in a manner highly soothing to their nerves, when, by accident, these were unstrung by any allusion to their first day's quail-shooting with a rat dog.

The wild pigeons were quite numerous, but hard to shoot. The few killed by Caper he found excellent eating, while, artistically, he made more than one oil sketch of these beautifully plumaged birds. The feathers under their fore wing, and on the breast, were like our own; but on the back and wings their plumage was brown and mottled, like a woodcock; while their legs and feet were bright red.

Among the smaller birds, the far-famed Fig Peckers (*Beccafichi*) offered many a morning's good sport, and many a good relish for dinner. But the funniest shooting that Caper found in the Campagna, was with an owl. Gaetano had long promised to give our artist an insight into this novel mode of gunning; and, after sundry huntings in old houses, one of the boys of the town succeeded in catching one of these pets of Minerva, and carried it to the landlord, who, next morning, invited our artist to assist at

LA CACCIA DELLA CIVETTA.

While the east was glowing like the wattles of a turkey cock making a free exhibition of himself, and before the sun had climbed high enough to shine, Gaetano and Caper were walking down a mountain path, brushing the dew from path-side bushes, and feeling that delightful sense of full-blooded life a fresh morning in October owes healthy men. They stopped near a lodge in a vineyard, and Gaetano cut one of the long canes that are grown for the purpose of training grape vines on, which canes are the same as our fishpole canes of Southern growth. Thus equipped, they went on. They soon overtook a funny-looking, bright-eyed little man, who had over his shoulders some fish nets, with which he was going down to a small stream in the plains, where he expected to make a good haul of fish. The majority of these fish being minnows, they are cooked and eaten whole. The fisherman was very talkative, and very enthusiastic as to the number of wild pigeons about in the valley. "Thousands of 'em, thousands. Last year, Bruno and I caught, one night, in a little over an hour, eighty-five of 'em!"

"How was that?"

"Oh! Bruno, he carried the light, and rang the bell, and I had a net at the end of a long pole, and covered them, so!" (Here he showed the way he cast the net.)

In fact, they "fire hunted" the pigeons, as negroes in Louisiana "fire" woodcock and snipe.

In a short time they passed the ruins of some old Roman tombs near the Via Trajana, and the fisherman told them that many of the country people had found coins and lamps near these ruins. "A woman, while hoeing, turned up a small urn —a very dear little one (*una criatura*)—full of silver coins, which she sold to a priest who collected such sort of goods (*roba*). He actually gave her *good* money for it, piece for piece—for he was a very just man!"

They reached the plain, or rather rolling prairie, leaving

the fisherman by his field of labor—a small mud-puddle—and pushed on, in the early sunlight, for a point that Gaetano showed Caper. Small birds in flocks went twittering by, larks were rising and singing, country people turning up the rich earth with triangular hoes. They saw the young wheat, two inches high, greening the fields, the great furrows worn in the dark-red soil by heavy rains, until, at last, they came to a place well suited for their purpose. Gaetano now planted an iron-shod stake in the ground, undid a hunting basket, and displayed a small live owl, working its eyes as if it wanted to roll them out of its head. It ruffled its feathers, stretched its neck, jumped up on the side of the basket, and evidently enjoyed the fresh air. Gaetano next brought out what looked like a bright-red, round pincushion, with a wooden bottom, in the centre of which was a hole. In this hole one end of the cane was thrust. The owl, with a string made fast from the cane to one of his legs, was placed on the red cushion, which served as a roost; and the cane, being elevated, was slipped over one end of the iron-shod stake; the bird of Minerva was thus elevated twelve feet, or so, in the air. Hardly was the owl placed, before a couple of small birds pitched at him, circling round and round his head.

"Don't fire!" said Gaetano; "they're nothing but *cardelli* (linnets?); the larks (*lodole*) will be here shortly. You take a stand over there, with your back to the sun. I'll stay here." Then, with a bird whistle, he commenced calling. Suddenly, up whirled a couple of larks, and, as they darted over the owl, Gaetano knocked over one, and Caper shot the other as it poised. But the day, which held out such fine promises at sunrise to pay good weather, became overcast in an hour. After bagging eleven larks, they changed their ground to where they saw some men with a spring-net (*roccolo*), who were after the same game. Hardly had they placed their owl a second time, and killed a few more birds, before there came over the plain, mounted on a stout black horse with flowing tail and jingling harness, Signor Candido; and he hailed them afar off, to know what sport. Then he dismounted, tied his horse to some bushes, and came on the ground with a gun and an iron-shod stake—another owl, thought Caper. "*Nonne, s'nore,*" (which is mountain tongue for No, sir!)

Candido planted the stake, and then took from his pocket a triangular piece of wood, painted red, with round pieces of looking glass the size of a dollar let in on its sides. From another pocket he brought out a piece of mechanism, consisting of a long string round a steel spring; this he fitted on the stake. He then wound up the string, and placed the piece of triangular wood over the spring and cord, on an iron spindle, which, being pulled by the spring, gave a rotary motion to the triangular piece of wood, making the looking glass flash in the sunlight, which had again burst forth, the clouds scattering before a stiff southeasterly wind. The owl proved more attractive than the looking glass, though but few birds were on the wing, owing to the wind. So, during a truce, our gunners took out food and flasks, making a hearty dinner, interrupted, now and then, by having to pick up their guns to fire at a chance lark darting owlward.

After dinner, they pulled up stake, pulled down owl, and walked off to the vineyards, to take a few shots at whatever might fly up, killing a few thrush, and, by bad luck, missing a shot at a fine large hare that bounded down the rocks at tip-top speed. So they worked their way up through the vineyards to the olive groves, getting a shot now and then, and having the hardest climbing—or digging one's toes into loose stones, and then slipping back, for it was too steep to bring the heels to bear among the olive trees—that Caper ever tried. But the walk put a wire edge on our artist's appetite, and, after a bird supper, with a bottle of wine, then coffee and a cigar, he slept the sound sleep awarded to the owl-hunter in the Volscians.

The Game Laws, as known in England, are unknown or ignored in the Papal States; and the Roman game market, which has been declared by competent authority to be one of the best in Europe, owes its excellence more to the skill of pot hunters than to the ability of true sportsmen. Fire hunting, traps, nets, are all used to kill game; and that game is abundant, any one who has lived in the Campagna during the proper season can readily bear witness, not to mention those who, in the autumn and winter months, have visited the Roman game market around the Pantheon. It is true that, with the game birds, one cannot help noticing there is enumerated many of the feathered tribe who are by no means game; and it is necessary to go back in one's ideas a few generations, to reconcile one's palate to eating nightingales and other songsters, before they can come under this heading.

There were two places near Segni where small birds were caught during the month of October, in great numbers, in what were called

BRESCIANE;

and as Caper never saw anything similarly arranged in the United States, it may be well to describe one.

The *bresciana*, belonging to the Allegrini family, was an

enclosed space, planted on three sides with double rows of small trees, leaving a long alley in the middle open, and about fifty feet long by twenty feet wide. The trees were allowed to grow about ten feet high, and the branches were trained and trimmed so as to form a flat surface on the sides facing the interior. Silk nets, with pockets, were then stretched from these trees, on three sides, from their tops to the ground. On the end of the enclosure not occupied by trees or nets, was a small house, in which the trapper sat looking out through a window in the house. Singing birds in cages were hung under the trees, and decoy birds, with clipped wings, were allowed to run about in the open space of the interior of the *bresciana*, where plenty of bird seed was scattered. Several large trees were left to attain their natural growth in the immediate vicinity, serving as roosts. The wild birds flying over or settling on the roosts, attracted by the singing birds, and the sight of the decoy birds feeding on the seeds, alighted in the open space of the *bresciana*, and, when the netter thought there were enough, he pulled a rope which was suspended from one end to the other of the enclosure, thus raising it three or four feet from the ground, causing sundry bunches of rags attached to it to flutter, and a bell to ring, whereupon the frightened birds flew right and left in a direct line, and were caught in the pockets of the extended nets. A bushel or two of small flyers were caught sometimes in this trap in a day, and, for those who relish tom-tits, yellow birds, wrens, and sparrows, they undoubtedly might afford a very game repast.

The Pontine Marshes, a day's journey from Segni, offer, in winter, good wild-boar hunting. More than one wolf, too, was killed in the mountains immediately around the town, while

Caper lived there. In fact, a shepherd boy, of whom our artist once asked the question why he kept so many savage dogs to guard his flock, told him he had them to keep off wolves and Christians.

What local meaning Christians (*Cristiani*) may have among Segnians, Caper never discovered; but it is evident, from this answer, that, among these good Catholics, they are regarded as little better than heathens.

"Segni," said an army chaplain once to Caper, "is air and Cyclopean walls. When you have said that, you have said everything."

The protector of the city of Segni, and of the above-mentioned air and walls, was Saint Bruno. In his honor a great many of the inhabitants were named, and, yearly, a grand festival was given especially to him, when a life-size plated-silver bust was shown to the populace as a real portrait of their saintly protector. They had great faith in that bust, not the less so that they believed it solid silver. It should be borne in mind that Saint Bruno was no relation to Giordano Bruno, who was burned alive at the stake in Rome, February 17, 1680; and who, when the flames lapped round him, stinging their way to his brave heart, turned his face away in disgust from a monk who held up for his admiration a crucifix. No! the Saint Bruno who protected Segni was another sort of human being. The citizens pointed out to you, far away on a mountain top, a lonely ruin where their saint fasted and preyed on himself, until cakes and ale were vain to tempt him, and he passed away from their allurements. For this self-denial he was calendared Protector of Segni. He had a curious protectorate—one where the admirers of a high tariff would have found an elysium; where the advocates of free trade would have stumbled over an *inferno*. The inhabitants were as nearly independent of the rest of the world as men could be; they wove their own cloths, made their own clothes, raised their own food, got up their own fights, and dug their own graves. If they were well, they worked hard for the priestly gentlemen in black who held communion with Saint Bruno; and if they were unwell, the gentlemen in black found a physician for them gratis, in order to cure them, and set them to work as quickly as possible—for the honor of their patron saint —and the pockets of his officers.

In the midst of the vintage—it was one Sunday morning— the weather suddenly changed, and a heavy rain storm commenced. One of Caper's friends, named Giovanni looked, that morning, gloomier than the weather.

"Well, Giovanni, what is the matter?"

"By all the saints, our bishop is a beast. Here have I barrels full of grapes, all picked, down there in the vineyard, and they will be spoiled unless I can bring them up this morning, and put them in the press; and yet the bishop refuses to let me bring up a grape: while he has just sent half a dozen of his own men down to bring up his own! *Per tutti i santi!* I shall have to pay five *scudi* if I break the Sabbath; but" (here Giovanni raised his arm and his voice) "I'm going to break it; and I'd break a hundred more, and pay for the pieces, before I'll be swindled by the old brute. If his men work, why can't mine?"

So you see that, even in Arcadia—I should say Segni— where tariffs are unknown, the rights of man begin to assert themselves, and the Giovanni of to-day dares question the bishop's right to unjustly treat him.

Every load of wood entering the city, whether it comes on mule, horse, or donkey back, pays one stick tribute as it enters the gate: it drops it there, and, once a day, a sturdy blacksmith gathers it up. It is his, for he has paid the public school, to whom this perquisite belongs, eighteen dollars a year for it, agreeing, moreover, to keep up fires in the schoolhouse, when wanted. Giovanni tells me he makes money by the bargain.

There is a dainty little tax on everything. I met, one morning, my friend Bruno carrying a cock and two hens to a house where dwelt two of the nobility of Segni—two old maids, who scarcely ever stirred from the house, and lived in stately dignity upon some little money they inherited. Bruno stopped, as I passed him, to ask me about a horse he had promised to hire for me. I praised the hens.

"Yes," said he; "poor things! I am carrying them to the Signora Antonia, in payment for two roosters she caponized for me yesterday."

"*What?*"

"Certainly; the Signora Antonia makes all the capons for the commune; no one is so skilful as herself. On this account she eats chickens every week."

"Well!"

There are very few chimneys in the town, consequently the smoked interiors of the houses are rich in color, and very picturesque, looked at artistically.

There is very little immorality; for the gentlemen on guard, with shovel hats and black clothes, pay strict attention to this matter. If a young unmarried girl is unfortunate, they at once find out the name of the author of this misfortune, and, *presto!* there is a wedding; for the author knows that San Bruno's hands that pat, may turn into claws that will tear and rend; so he submits.

There is very little robbery—for there is nothing to steal.

A few miles from Segni, at the foot of the mountain, lies the picturesque old town of Montelanico. Passing through its main street, on the morning of a festival held there, Caper saw two men in angry dispute. One had kicked an old hen belonging to another. That evening, as he left the town at an early hour, and was slowly riding up the mountain path to Segni, he heard a single gun fired, and, knowing that they were to have fireworks in Montelanico that night, he turned round, thinking the report might be that of a rocket. All that could be seen was a faint cloud of blue smoke passing away from a tree by the roadside far below him. Four days afterward, he learned that the man who had kicked the old hen had been shot dead that very night; the report of the gun heard was his death knell. His murderer was carried to Velletri.

A Frenchman, who passed some weeks at Segni, with his family, learning that there was to be a fair and festival at Velletri, went there. When he returned, his face was long, and his look despondent. Caper asked him if he were unwell.

"Ugh! that supper at Velletri was positively atrocious. I remember nothing half so horrible, except the scene in the Borgia, when the fair Lucrèce appears, and tells the gentlemen they are all poisoned. Figure to yourself that we arrived on a rainy night at Velletri, and went to a dirty tavern. We found a dirty dining room, with a dirty supper set out before a dozen dirty cutthroat-looking blackguards. But we were hungry; we began to eat, when, suddenly, I heard a priest in angry dispute with an officer of gensdarmes.

"'I tell you,' said the priest, 'it is infamous to bring these men here. I shall report it to the bishop.'

"'Report, and be hanged!' said the officer. 'What if they are condemned to death; haven't the poor fellows a right to a little amusement while they live? They have eight days' leave of absence from prison to recruit themselves; and you, *you* grumble about it!'

"The fact was, that eight of the men then at table with us were murderers, and several of them murderers of the most horrible description. It was raining like a second deluge, but we left that tavern at once, and—I never want to eat again in Velletri."

You see, that Saint Bruno has many curious things under and around his protectorate. Superficial let our examinations be; we must not dig too deep; we would disclose dirt and superstition, ignorance and prejudice enough to make angels weep; and yet, there is a contentment apparent among the Segnians, that we do not find anywhere else, save among savages and the uneducated peasants of the rest of Europe, who, like these their brothers, have never yet had intelligibly explained to them that they had souls, and were immortal; that they were made in the image of God, and that the keys of heaven were in every man's hands—not hung up in the Vatican.

VALETE

ET

PLAVDITE.

www.ingramcontent.com/pod-product-compliance
Lightning Source LLC
Chambersburg PA
CBHW022051230426
43672CB00008B/1136